A HIDDEN HISTORY OF F

The publisher gratefully acknowledges the generous support of the Ahmanson Foundation Humanities Endowment Fund of the University of California Press Foundation.

This work was supported by a grant from the Academy Film Scholars Program of the Academy of Motion Pictures Arts and Sciences.

A Hidden History of Film Style

Cinematographers, Directors, and the Collaborative Process

CHRISTOPHER BEACH

UNIVERSITY OF CALIFORNIA PRESS

University of California Press, one of the most distinguished university presses in the United States, enriches lives around the world by advancing scholarship in the humanities, social sciences, and natural sciences. Its activities are supported by the UC Press Foundation and by philanthropic contributions from individuals and institutions. For more information, visit www.ucpress.edu.

University of California Press
Oakland, California

Library of Congress Cataloging-in-Publication Data

Beach, Christopher, author.
A hidden history of film style : cinematographers, directors, and the collaborative process / Christopher Beach.
pages cm.
Includes bibliographical references and index.
ISBN 978-0-520-28434-0 (cloth)
ISBN 978-0-520-28435-7 (pbk. : alk. paper)
ISBN 978-0-520-95992-7 (ebook)
1. Motion picture producers and directors—United States. 2. Cinematographers—United States. 3. Motion pictures—Production and direction—United States. 4. Cinematography—Special effects. I. Title.
PN1993.5.U6B34 2015
791.4302'3—dc23

2014039744

Manufactured in the United States of America

24 23 22 21 20 19 18 17 16 15
10 9 8 7 6 5 4 3 2 1

In keeping with a commitment to support environmentally responsible and sustainable printing practices, UC Press has printed this book on Natures Natural, a fiber that contains 30% post-consumer waste and meets the minimum requirements of ANSI/NISO Z39.48–1992 (R 1997) (*Permanence of Paper*).

Contents

List of Illustrations vii
Acknowledgments xi

Introduction 1

1. Pioneers in Babylon: D. W. Griffith and Billy Bitzer 19
2. Rebel with a Camera: Gregg Toland, William Wyler, and the Development of Deep-Focus Technique 55
3. Peering into Corners: Billy Wilder, John Seitz, and the Visual Style of Film Noir 86
4. The Color of Suspense: Alfred Hitchcock and Robert Burks 115
5. What Rule Are You Breaking? Collaborating in the New Hollywood 140
6. Cinematography, Craft, and Collaboration in the Digital Age 163

Notes 179
Works Cited 213
Index 225

Illustrations

1. An elegantly composed use of deep space by cinematographer Billy Bitzer. (*A Corner in Wheat*, Biograph, 1909) 32
2. Bitzer's use of rack focus in an innovative shot. (*The Musketeers of Pig Alley*, Biograph, 1912) 34
3. Multiple planes of visual focus combined with natural lighting. (*The House of Darkness*, Biograph, 1913) 36
4. A highly effective visual staging of history: Lincoln's assassination. (*The Birth of a Nation*, D.W. Griffith/Epoch, 1915) 41
5. A striking use of the close-up for dramatic effect. (*The Birth of a Nation*, D.W. Griffith/Epoch, 1915) 42
6. Harsh side-lighting creates a documentary-like effect in the execution scene from the "Modern story." (*Intolerance*, Triangle/Wark, 1916) 43
7. Expressive lighting of the Mighty Man of Valor in the "Babylonian story." (*Intolerance*, Triangle/Wark, 1916) 48
8. Gregg Toland's masterful use of chiaroscuro lighting to create tonal anxiety. (*Wuthering Heights*, Goldwyn, 1939) 69
9. The technique of deep focus allows the viewer to look through a window from the perspective of Cathy and Heathcliff. (*Wuthering Heights*, Goldwyn, 1939) 70
10. Low-key lighting with localized sources of light to create atmosphere. (*Wuthering Heights*, Goldwyn, 1939) 71

11. Toland's extreme use of deep focus, with Herbert Marshall in the foreground and Bette Davis in the background. (*The Little Foxes,* Goldwyn, 1941) 75

12. A complicated shot using deep focus technique to move from interior foreground to exterior background. (*The Little Foxes,* Goldwyn, 1941) 75

13. The famous double-mirror shaving scene. (*The Little Foxes,* Goldwyn, 1941) 77

14. Visual narrative: Bette Davis remains in focus and brightly lit, while the figure of Herbert Marshall is reduced to a dark blur in the background. (*The Little Foxes,* Goldwyn, 1941) 78

15. Depth of focus turns an ordinary domestic scene into an artistic composition. (*The Best Years of Our Lives,* Goldwyn, 1946) 82

16. The real action in the phone booth is juxtaposed against the much more visible foreground action at the piano. (*The Best Years of Our Lives,* Goldwyn, 1946) 83

17. A signature shot by John F. Seitz, lit only by streetlights, a car's headlights, and construction flares. (*Double Indemnity,* Paramount, 1944) 101

18. The essence of noir cinematography: light from the venetian blinds casts a distinctive wall pattern, while the glamour lighting of Barbara Stanwyck creates the ultimate femme fatale. (*Double Indemnity,* Paramount, 1944) 102

19. Expressive lighting as visual storytelling: Barbara Stanwyck lit only by a practical lamp, with Fred MacMurray in complete darkness. (*Double Indemnity,* Paramount, 1944) 104

20. Wilder and Seitz use disturbingly off-center compositions to emphasize the disoriented state of alcoholic writer Don Birnam (Ray Milland). (*The Lost Weekend,* Paramount, 1945) 106

21. Objects placed in the foreground increase the feeling of depth. (*The Lost Weekend,* Paramount, 1945) 107

22. Technical virtuosity: an extreme close-up of Birnam's eye. (*The Lost Weekend,* Paramount, 1945) 108

23. Deep-focus composition, with the aging star Norma Desmond (Gloria Swanson) in the foreground and her servant Max (Erich von Stroheim) in the far background. (*Sunset Boulevard,* Paramount, 1950) 111

24. Gloria Swanson is dramatically lit from behind by the film projector as she watches herself on screen. (*Sunset Boulevard,* Paramount, 1950) 112

25. Stylistic innovation to express character: Norma Desmond moves in for her close-up, breaking through the conventional wall separating actor and camera. (*Sunset Boulevard,* Paramount, 1950) 113

26. Hitchcock noir: the murder scene as reflected in the victim's eyeglasses. (*Strangers on a Train,* Warner Bros., 1951) 118

27. The camera eye as voyeur: Lars Thorwald (Raymond Burr) is in perfect focus as he is observed from across the courtyard. (*Rear Window,* Paramount, 1954) 123

28. The iconic kiss, captured by Robert Burks in extreme close-up: Grace Kelly and James Stewart. (*Rear Window,* Paramount, 1954) 126

29. Burks uses shallow focus to capture Kim Novak in a stunning profile shot. (*Vertigo,* Paramount, 1958) 129

30. A haunting image of an avian apocalypse, combining cinematography and special effects. (*The Birds,* Universal, 1963) 133

31. Visual stylization: Mark Rutland (Sean Connery) runs toward the camera, as the long corridor of the ship increases the feeling of depth. (*Marnie,* Universal, 1964) 135

32. Strong compositional framing and multidirectional lighting give a surreal tone to this shot from the ending of *Marnie.* (*Marnie,* Universal, 1964) 137

33. A luminous shot of Mrs. Miller (Julie Christie): Vilmos Zsigmond flashed the film to create the slightly faded look of an antique photograph. (*McCabe and Mrs. Miller,* Warner Bros., 1971) 146

34. A resonant image: Jim Garrison (Kevin Costner) and "X" (Donald Sutherland) with the "paranoid space" of the nation's capital behind them. (*JFK,* Warner Bros., 1991) 154

35. The look of authentic combat footage: Steven Spielberg and Janusz Kaminski re-create the Normandy landing. (*Saving Private Ryan,* DreamWorks/Paramount, 1998) 157

Acknowledgments

I would like to thank Dartmouth College for offering me appointments as Visiting Scholar for the academic years 2010–11, 2012–13, and 2013–14. The use of the Dartmouth College Library and its Jones Media Center has been instrumental to my research as well as the production of images for this book. I have also made significant use of the Margaret Herrick Library of the Academy of Motion Pictures Arts and Sciences. Particular thanks go to special collections librarian Barbara Hall for her help in finding archival materials that have added depth to my research.

Several people have given generously of their time and energy in helping me to complete this book and clarify its ideas. Kathryn Ragsdale read several chapters of the book at an early stage. Patrick Keating read the entire manuscript and provided comments that were both supportive and uniquely well-informed. John Bailey offered valuable insights from the perspective of a professional cinematographer.

I am extremely grateful for the support of the Academy of Motion Pictures Arts and Sciences. As a recipient of the Academy Film Scholars award in 2013, I received financial support that allowed me to complete the book, as well as a much-appreciated vote of confidence in the project.

Finally, the most profound thanks go to my wife, Carrie Noland, whose support on all levels has made this book possible.

Introduction

Though it has become fashionable in recent years to proclaim the death of auteurism as a mode of filmic analysis, the auteur theory has remained a dominant paradigm in film studies for the past half century. If many academic film scholars now see the concept of "individual creative genius" as outdated, auteurism remains central to published film scholarship, to the teaching of film and media, and to popular writing on film. C. Paul Sellors has identified an "entrenched auteurism" in film studies, or "a strong propensity to consider a film's director as its author," even among well-informed scholars.[1] Not only do books and articles on individual directors continue to be published in large numbers, but directors are treated—both in the popular media and in the vast majority of academic film scholarship—as if they were unquestionably the creators of the films to which their names are attached. Most discussions of film mention the work of collaborators such as screenwriters, cinematographers, production designers, and editors only in passing, if at all, while directors continue to be given credit for everything from camera moves to shot selection to lighting.[2]

In this book, I seek to complicate this notion of the director as author by foregrounding the role of the cinematographer in the production of the cinematic image. The book's central argument is that the cinema represents an interactive collaboration between technology and art, a creative encounter in which the director and the cinematographer personify these two different forces. As a general paradigm, the cinematographer is responsible for discovering, inventing, introducing, and improving new visual technologies that the director can then apply in the creation of cinematic art. However, the functions of the cinematographer and director are by no means mutually exclusive, nor are they rigidly fixed. The work of the cinematographer inevitably involves aesthetically motivated decisions, decisions based not only on a technical understanding of film stocks, lighting, and lenses but also on an aesthetic understanding of composition, light and shadow, and texture and color. In the creation of cinema, technological and aesthetic elements build upon and mediate each other through the process of collaboration. Unlike still photography, an art form in which one individual is responsible for adapting technology to the creation of art, cinema is the result of a complex set of interactions between two individuals, each of whom contributes to the actualization of an imagined universe.

Thomas Schatz has noted that "the closer we look at Hollywood's relations of power and the hierarchy of authority, . . . the less sense it makes to assess filmmaking or film style in terms of the individual director—or any individual, for that matter."[3] I agree: no one person involved in the production of a film can claim a privileged status as its author. In fact, the history of American filmmaking is full of cases in which the film's producer, screenwriter, cinematographer, actors, production designer, editor, or special effects supervisor can take as much credit for the creation of a film as its director. During the studio era, for example, studios often hired a more experienced cinematographer to work with a less experienced director. The veteran cinematographer James Wong Howe was hired to work with directors such as Daniel Mann and Joshua Logan, overseeing many aspects of the production while teaching these new directors the techniques of filmmaking. In making *Citizen Kane,* the novice director Orson Welles relied heavily on the experience and talents of cinematographer Gregg Toland, who designed and executed much of the visual plan of the film. More recently, Woody Allen developed significantly as a visual director as a result of his multifilm collaboration with Gordon Willis.

The failure of most film scholars to look beyond the creative impact of the director represents an unwillingness to examine more closely the circumstances behind the production of films. It is certainly easier—at least on a formal level—to analyze films in terms of the work of individual directors; their corpus can be dissected and explained in terms of a unifying style, vision, career trajectory, or set of thematic or theoretical concerns. This focus on the director avoids having to examine the complex patterns of interaction among the large number of artists and technicians who collaborate on any given film. Peter Wollen has gone as far as arguing that if someone other than director plays a decisive role in the making of a film, the film becomes "inaccessible to criticism":

> What the auteur theory does is to take a group of films—the work of one director—and analyze their structure. . . . Of course, it is possible to approach films by studying some other feature; by an effort of critical

> ascesis we could see films, as Von Sternberg sometimes urged, as abstract light-show or as histrionic feasts. Sometimes these separate texts—those of the cameraman or the actors—may force themselves into prominence so that the film becomes an indecipherable palimpsest. This does not mean, of course, that it ceases to exist or to sway us or to please us or to intrigue us; it simply means it is inaccessible to criticism. We can merely record our momentary and subjective impressions.[4]

While I agree with Wollen's point that approaching film as a collaborative enterprise makes critical access and theorization more complex, I find his conclusion radically misguided. Does it in some way limit our understanding or appreciation of *The Little Foxes* (William Wyler, 1941) to be aware of the intersecting roles played by producer Samuel Goldwyn, writer Lillian Hellman, cinematographer Gregg Toland, art director Stephen Goosson, and actors Bette Davis and Herbert Marshall? Does *Blade Runner* (Ridley Scott, 1982) become less cogent as an example of filmmaking when we consider the production design of Lawrence Paull, the cinematography of Jordan Cronenweth, the special effects of Douglas Trumbull, the music of Vangelis, and the acting performances of Harrison Ford, Rutger Hauer, and Sean Young? On the contrary, a more detailed knowledge of the contributions of these various collaborators is essential to any thorough analysis of the filmic text. Rather than creating an "indecipherable palimpsest," the reading of elements such as actors' performances and cinematographers' visual interventions produces a more richly layered understanding of a film.

If the field of film studies is to move beyond the de facto auteurist bias that has dominated it for the past half century, film scholars will need to adopt a model in which the intersecting career paths of producers, directors, writers, cinematographers, editors, and art directors yield new insights into the filmmaking process. Such a model will allow a more accurate description of how films are made, and it will enable us to understand developments in film history that are not apparent from a study of directors as auteurs. One prominent example is the development of deep-focus cinematography during the 1930s and early 1940s. The development of deep-focus techniques was driven far more by cinematographers' experiments with lenses, film stocks, and lighting than by directors' desire to achieve greater depth of focus. Only after Gregg Toland and other cinematographers had brought deep focus to some degree of perfection did directors begin to realize what it allowed them to accomplish in terms of staging and composition.

Though the director—or during the studio era, the producer or studio production head—may have the final say about the visual style of the film, it is other film workers such as the cinematographer, production designer, art director, set decorator, costume designer, makeup artists, matte painters, and special effects coordinators who produce the detailed, fine-grained particulars of the film's "look." Factors that earlier generations of filmmakers did not consider—such as the film's budget, the studio's house style, the tastes of audiences, the variety of lighting technologies, and the quality and speed of film stocks—all affect stylistic vocabularies.

Although cinematography is a crucially important aspect of filmmaking, it has received relatively little attention from film scholars and historians. There are, I believe, several critical and historical reasons for this neglect. First, simply less information is available on the careers of cinematographers than of actors or directors. There are virtually no biographies of cinematographers, and there are only a few books devoted to analyzing their work.[5] The researcher needs to do a good deal of sleuthing and archival work to piece together a satisfactory account of a cinematographer's career.

A second challenge to the historian of cinematography is the sometimes daunting technical complexity of the subject. The analysis of a film's cinematography, including the many decisions the cinematographer made in the course of shooting the film, requires at least a rudimentary understanding of lighting and camerawork techniques. People who have a thorough knowledge of the intricacies of lighting, cameras, film stocks, and lenses are usually working cinematographers, not academic scholars, and there is regrettably little interaction between the two communities. As a result, film scholars have few opportunities to gain a better understanding of the subject they are attempting to analyze and discuss.

The third challenge to scholars seeking to work on cinematography is that studies of technology and its impact on film style have rarely been at the forefront of film scholarship. Richard Dyer observes that "studies based upon the science and techniques of film, its physics and chemistry, the practices and possibilities of the camera and the other apparatuses of filmmaking [have not] very often been seen as indispensable to the study of film."[6] Two notable exceptions that are devoted to the role of film technology in the production of cinematic style are Barry Salt's *Film Style and Technology: History and Analysis* (currently in its third edition) and David Bordwell, Janet Staiger, and Kristin Thompson's now-canonical *The Classical Hollywood Cinema: Film Style and Mode of Production to 1960*. However, such histories of filmic technology, as Paul Ramaeker suggests, tend to focus more on "epochal shifts in film production and exhibition [such as] the coming of sound, of color, of widescreen, [and] of CGI" and less on the development of particular technologies or the use of innovative techniques.[7]

I would argue further that most of the work that has been done on technology and style takes a fundamentally director-as-auteur approach. Salt's work, for example, despite its laudable specificity concerning the development and use of film technologies, focuses primarily on the impact of directors on film style rather than on the influence of other film workers such as cinematographers and editors. His statistical analysis of such features as average shot length, scale of shot, and amount of camera movement to establish "the existence of an individual style in the work of a director" constitutes an interesting and valuable project.[8] Unfortunately, however, it ignores the impact that other members of the production team often have on film style. Editors, for example, have an impact on average shot length, and cinematographers are often involved in decisions regarding framing and camera movement. It is to be hoped that the next generation of film critics will build on Salt's foundational work by incorporating a greater awareness of the contributions of film workers other than the director to the styles of Hollywood, post-Hollywood, and independent filmmaking.

Finally, discussion of specifically *visual* technologies is even rarer than that of sound technologies, which has undergone something of a boom in recent years.[9] With the exception of Patrick Keating's excellent study of Hollywood lighting, little scholarly work has been done on cinematography from either an aesthetic or a technological perspective.[10] More scholarly and critical work on the historical, technical, and aesthetic dimensions of cinematography, and on its place within the larger context of filmmaking, is badly needed. A diachronic study of cinematography such as the one I present here can lead to important insights not simply about how films were made from a technical standpoint but also about working relationships between film workers occupying different spaces within the pre-Hollywood, Hollywood, and post-Hollywood systems of production.

• • •

Nearly every discussion of cinematography asserts that the work of the cinematographer allows the director to engage in more effective forms of storytelling. This notion is to some degree accurate, but it is a rather limited view of the cinematographer's role and thus tends to perpetuate the idea of the director as visionary auteur and the cinematographer as a technical craft-worker who simply carries out the director's wishes. There is, in fact, evidence that from the earliest days of cinema directors and cinematographers have worked together as creative partners. Charles Musser notes that Edwin S. Porter and other filmmakers of the pre-Griffith era "worked as part of a collaborative partnership" that involved cameramen, actors, scenic designers, and others.[11] Porter's collaborators included George S. Fleming, G.M. Anderson, Wallace McCutcheon, J. Searle Dawley, and Hugh Ford, and these collaborative efforts were "creative teams . . . modeled after standard business partnerships."[12]

By the time motion pictures entered their second decade—around 1907—the craft of the cinematographer was becoming more specialized, and a new relationship was developing between the cameraman—now responsible for the lighting and the operation of the camera—and the director, who now dealt with the staging of scenes and the performance of the actors. Cinematographers were expected to do more than simply produce an image that was clear and legible. Most film commentators of the period from 1907 to 1913 shared a belief that cinema's unique aesthetic was predicated on both "reproductive realism and believability," according to Charlie Keil in his exploration of silent cinema.[13] In other words, cinematographers were now tasked not only with reproducing the physical world with a flexibility and precision that gave the filmic medium a "visual advantage" over the theater but also with achieving a sense of "believability" or "authenticity" in the images they presented.

After the shift from a "cinema of attractions" to a narratively based cinema, the public expected cinematographers to avoid obvious artificiality—such as the makeup on actors' faces or the phoniness of cheap or badly decorated sets—whenever possible. Further, with the greater sophistication of filmmaking techniques during this period came a sense that film photography should contribute to a film's visual style. This final requirement of cinematography—that it be an important component, perhaps the *most* important component, of a film's visual style—has divided commentators almost from the beginnings of the cinema. A discussion of cinematography inevitably raises the pesky but very pertinent question: To what extent is cinematography simply the "handmaiden" of cinema, as some early critics expressed it, and to what extent is it an integral part of the filmmaking process, as central to the production of a successful motion picture as a good script, skilled actors, or a competent director?

As early as 1909, film writers were raising the question of whether film photography was merely a means to an end or a crucial part of a greater aesthetic whole. The critic David S. Hulfish, writing in the trade journal *Nickelodeon,* articulated one side of the debate by maintaining that photography should be seen "as merely the means for placing before the audience the thoughts of the author of the picture . . . the art of the picture being developed fully in the scenes themselves before the motion picture camera is called upon to record them."[14] This rather extreme position is essentially that of filmmakers such as Alfred Hitchcock, who would later argue that cinematography is essentially a means of recording on celluloid the images that the director has already imagined.

On the other hand, some of Hulfish's contemporaries showed greater appreciation for the pictorial or cinematographic qualities of the film medium. Writing in *Moving Picture World,* one unidentified critic who seems to have had an unusually good grasp of filmmaking technique encouraged film companies to give their films "their own pictorial individuality" rather than conforming to a single stylistic norm:

> One [film]maker might go for delicate grays; one might go for razor-edge definition [with] fine focusing and a well stopped-down lens; others again might diffuse the lens slightly. . . . There is, in fact, a wide field open for individuality of expression in the photographic end of moving picture making.[15]

What this early critic is espousing is essentially a model of stylistic differentiation, in which it is possible to discuss the moving picture as a picture, apart from considerations such as the scenario and the quality of the acting. This approach signals the growing awareness of critics and audiences that visual style is an important component of films, and that each filmmaker is capable of creating a distinctive visual style, one based in large part on the photographic qualities that are emphasized. By the early 1910s, we see this kind of stylistic differentiation throughout the industry. As Keil notes, critics began to pay attention to "distinctive qualities of pictoriality" in motion pictures after filmmakers—taking advantage of an increasing array of artificial lighting technologies—started to use artificial lighting to highlight sets and separate actors from backgrounds, while also experimenting with atmospheric forms of lighting to support characterization and enhance storylines.[16] Directors—working collaboratively with their cameramen—sought increasingly to create a recognizable style that would help distinguish their productions from those of other filmmakers.

One of the first director-cinematographer collaborations in which we can clearly see this process of conscious aesthetic differentiation at work is that of D.W. Griffith and G.W. "Billy" Bitzer. Other such partnerships soon followed, such as the collaboration of Cecil B. DeMille and his cameraman Alvin Wyckoff—which produced some of the most strikingly lit films of the 1910s and early 1920s—and that of Rex Ingram and cinematographer John F. Seitz, who collaborated on a dozen visually innovative films in the early 1920s. The tendency of certain directors to work with one cinematographer over a number of films indicates not simply the desire for a stable working environment but the belief that a long-term collaboration would result in a productive meeting of minds, a symbiotic artistic partnership that could bring out the best in both individuals.[17]

• • •

The narrative traced by the chapters of this book begins at a crucial moment in the history of American film, one that can be located in the years between 1908 and 1913. During this period the multireel "feature" film began to replace the one-reel short, resulting in a greater premium on production values and the techniques needed to achieve them. In the following half-decade, from 1913 to 1918, there would be a sea-change in American film production as filmmakers scrambled to make feature films from five to eight reels in length. In 1913, fifty-six feature-length films were produced in the United States; in 1914, the number increased sixfold, to 350 features. The production of short films decreased correspondingly as it became clear that audiences generally preferred longer films and that profit margins on feature-length films were far better than on one-reelers. By 1918, when over 800 features were released in the United States, the era of one- and two-reel shorts was virtually over. Studios that had bet heavily on short-film production, such as Biograph, Kalem, Lubin, Edison, Essanay, and Selig, were forced to close their doors, leaving the field open for a handful of more forward-looking studios—Metro, Lasky–Famous Pictures, Fox, and Universal among them—that would constitute the core of the Hollywood system of the 1920s and 1930s.

It was during this same period that, Griffith and other film directors began to assert their authority in a field that had previously been dominated by cameramen. Though the cinematographer continued to play a major role in the movies directed by Griffith and other filmmakers of the silent era, the director began to assume much greater decision-making authority, and the aesthetic input of the cinematographer was consequently diminished. Both David Bordwell and Patrick Keating have noted that the role of cinematographers during the studio era was fraught with contradictions imposed by their professional association—the American Society of Cinematographers (ASC), founded in 1919—and by the studios for which they worked. *The Classical Hollywood Cinema* describes how the ASC articulated a "contradictory task" for its members:

> The ASC encouraged its members to think of themselves as creative people, comparable to the screenwriter or director. Implicitly, then, each cinematographer's work was to have something distinctive about it. . . . But at the same time, the ethos of the craft held that the cinematographer's work must go unnoticed by the layman.[18]

On the one hand, cinematographers were expected to be artists with creative responsibilities comparable to those of the director and to exhibit "individual innovations and virtuosity." On the other hand, as Keating puts it, cinematographers "usually subordinated their aesthetic aspirations to their professional obligations," especially in the period after 1930.[19] In the 1920s, there were still a number of competing visions of how the cinematographer should contribute to the style of motion pictures, ranging from a more "classical" approach (the cinematographer should sacrifice extreme displays of artistry to unobtrusive storytelling) to a "non-classical" approach (the cinematographer should add an element of beauty or pictorial elegance for its own sake, even if it is noticeable to the viewer). But by the beginning of the sound era, the discourse surrounding American cinematography had begun to grow more homogeneous, coalescing around the more conservative aesthetic that came to define classical Hollywood style. Although a handful of elite cinematographers were able to achieve relatively greater autonomy within the studio system (Gregg Toland, Lee Garmes, and James Wong Howe, for example) and occasionally even to engage in displays of pictorial spectacle, the average studio cinematographer of the 1930s was not afforded a great deal of latitude in the development of a personal style. Instead, we see a gradual capitulation to the ideal of a cinematographic style that was virtually invisible apart from its function within the narrative structure of the film. In the words of ASC president John Arnold, the goal was "to so perfectly suit the cinematography to the story that the former is imperceptible and the latter is subtly heightened."[20] The model for cinematographers throughout the studio era was one of unobtrusive artistry: they were expected to light and shoot their films in the most effective way they could without distracting the audience with the quality of their lighting or camerawork.

If cinematographers of the 1930s were reluctant to comment negatively on their situation—perhaps out of fear of losing their secure and relatively well-paying jobs during the Great Depression—cinematographers in the early 1940s began to complain about their restricted and regimented function within the studio system. A 1942 editorial in *American Cinematographer* expressed the frustration of many Hollywood cameramen over the tight controls of the studios, which insisted that "all photography on the lot conform to rigid, if perhaps unwritten, regulations dictated by the personal preferences of someone in authority."[21] The studios' ostensible purpose may have been quality control, but the result was in many cases a uniformity of house style, in which the stylistic mandates of the studio counted for more than the particular vision of the director and cinematographer.

Most Hollywood cinematographers of the studio era were willing to accept this somewhat contradictory situation, and relatively few claimed—at least publicly—to have their own style of lighting or camerawork. With the exception of the few cinematographers who worked for independent producers or smaller studios—such as Gregg Toland at the Goldwyn Studio and Joseph Walker at Columbia—Hollywood cinematographers belonged to a team of contract cameramen working for a particular studio. In 1931, Paramount had forty-eight cameramen on its payroll, with a roster of A-list cinematographers that included Lee Garmes, Victor Milner, Karl Struss, Charles B. Lang, George Folsey, and Harry Fischbeck. Cinematographers were routinely assigned by the studio to work on particular films, and most were contractually obligated to work on whatever film they were assigned to shoot. Only in rare cases, such as that of Walker at Columbia, did the contract allow the right of refusal.

In order to differentiate their productions from those of their competitors, each of the major studios adopted a stylistic trademark, and both directors and cinematographers were strongly encouraged to maintain the appropriate look. Paramount's films had a slightly softer style created by the use of heavy diffusion, while MGM, which had the strictest internal controls of any studio, was known for films with a high-key, sharp-edged polish. Warner Brothers' look, on the other hand, tended to be low-key, with source lighting and a more frequent use of shadows.[22]

Studios frequently put pressure on their cinematographers to stay within the parameters of the prevailing house style. The long-time head of MGM's camera department, John Arnold, was infamous for his interference in the work of the studio's cinematographers. Nicknamed "The Policeman," Arnold was a strict company man who displayed little tolerance for cinematographers who attempted to deviate in any way from the studio's glamorous visual style. Cinematographer John Alton felt that Arnold was jealous of his success and that Arnold had tried on several occasions to undermine him or get him fired from films.[23] James Wong Howe, another cinematographer with a strong personal vision, was fired from the 1936 MGM film *Whipsaw* because he refused to conform to a house style he considered overly "frothy."[24]

Less frequently, producers and production heads interfered directly in the cinematography of their films. David O. Selznick, for example, was infamous for making decisions about artistic and technical matters usually left in the hands of the director. Selznick replaced cinematographer Harry Stradling with Gregg Toland on *Intermezzo,* and he replaced Lee Garmes with Ernest Haller on *Gone with the Wind.*[25] Selznick was known to come onto the set to check setup and lighting before approving a take.[26] In the case of many Hollywood films of the studio era, such behavior by producers made the possibility of creative collaboration between directors and cinematographers more remote.

After World War II, as studios were forced by antitrust laws to divest themselves of the theater chains that had provided much of their income and guaranteed a ready market for their products, their power began to wane. Eventually, all the major studios were bought by larger corporations, further contributing to the breakdown of the studio system as it had previously existed. By the late 1960s, two factors led to a dramatic shift in the demographics of Hollywood cinematographers. First, death and old age began to erode the ranks of active cameramen and directors of photography, and they began to be replaced by the members of a younger generation. Second, the restrictive union regulations that prevented all but a handful of cinematographers from entering the profession in the 1940s and 1950s were finally lifted, allowing for a greater influx of younger cameramen.

Though a few members of the old guard—including James Wong Howe, Robert Surtees, and Burnett Guffey—continued to work in Hollywood throughout the 1960s and in some cases even into the 1970s, they were gradually replaced by a generation of much younger cinematographers, many of whom had gotten their training in television production. Directors of photography such as John Alonzo, Bill Butler, Michael Chapman, Jordan Cronenweth, William Fraker, Conrad Hall, Laszlo Kovacs, Owen Roizman, Haskell Wexler, Gordon Willis, and Vilmos Zsigmond—all born between 1921 and 1936—represented the first significant new generation of cinematographers to enter the industry in several decades. No longer subject to the constraints of studio photographic departments, these DPs were freer to engage in experimentation with different techniques of lighting and camerawork. Their collaborations with directors such as Robert Altman, Hal Ashby, Francis Ford Coppola, William Friedkin, Paul Mazursky, Mike Nichols, Alan Pakula, Bob Rafelson, Martin Scorsese, and Steven Spielberg produced films in which cinematography played an increasingly important role.

• • •

The chapters of this book describe an arc that takes us through various stages in both the role of cinematographers and their relationship with directors. The five stages I delineate here are not intended to be historically exclusive; however, they roughly follow a progression from the early silent era to the studio era and finally to the post-Hollywood era. An exploration of American cinema history whose focus is the collaborative work of directors and cinematographers raises questions about the development of visual style in American cinema, about changes in collaborative practices over time, and about the intersection of cinematographic and directorial techniques. Does the arc from silent film collaborations to those of the late twentieth century represent a movement toward increasing visual self-consciousness? Or, to put it another way, does it suggest a movement toward the foregrounding of visual style as an end in itself? If so, is this greater stylistic self-consciousness an artifact of trends in cinematography? Or is it instead a sign of active collaboration between directors and their cinematographers? Do changing styles of filmmaking create distinct approaches to collaboration, or are they engendered by them?

My first chapter—on the collaboration of D.W. Griffith and G.W. "Billy" Bitzer—documents the first of these five stages: one in which the cinematographer and the director were engaged in an exploratory process by which certain technical problems were solved through both conscious experimentation and accidental discoveries. The primary focus in the early years of Bitzer's collaboration with Griffith was on making the most effective use of the relatively crude technologies of lighting, film stock, cameras, and lenses that were available to them, while overcoming the inherent limitations of those technologies. In the period from 1908 to 1924—during which Griffith and Bitzer made nearly five hundred films—their collaboration evolved toward a far greater sophistication both in the technical aspects of filmmaking and in the ability to use visual technologies for powerful aesthetic effects.

The second stage in the development of cinematography corresponds to the classical studio era, in which the primary goal of studio cinematographers was to make the technology disappear as a legible part of the filmmaking process: in effect, to render the work of the cinematographer nearly invisible. Despite technological advances that might, under other circumstances, have allowed for the development of more strikingly original stylistic vocabularies, directors and cinematographers did not generally foreground visual style in their productions of the 1930s.[27] Most cinematographers of the period either relied on conventional high-key lighting, or they engaged in a procedure that Patrick Keating calls "selective emphasis," reserving dramatic lighting effects for key moments in the film, while shooting most scenes in a relatively unimaginative high-key style.[28] Keating lists selective emphasis as one of four strategies adopted by cinematographers of the studio era to achieve greater expressive and artistic freedom in spite of tight studio controls. The other three strategies are sacrifice (for example, sacrificing realism for the sake of glamour), compromise (for example, following the convention of lighting the female star differently from the male star, even if it resulted in a lack of stylistic continuity), and the gradual shift (using a number of stylistic conventions in a film, but keeping each subtle enough that it would not draw attention to the artifice of the cinematography).

The relatively conservative style of both lighting and camerawork that predominated in the 1930s was in stark contrast to that of the late silent era, when films like *Sunrise* (1927)—directed by F.W. Murnau and photographed by Karl Struss and Charles Rosher—achieved a number of spectacular camera effects—including complicated dolly shots—along with innovative lighting and trick effects. The less adventurous lighting and camerawork of Hollywood films of the early 1930s was the result of several factors: technical limitations imposed by the late-1920s shift to sound production (which required cameras to be placed in immovable soundproof booths), the generally tighter controls on cinematography resulting from the hierarchical and highly centralized structure of the studios, and the studios' emphasis on glamour lighting as the highest priority for cinematographers.[29]

The change in cinematographic practices between the late silent era and the first decade of the sound era is apparent in the discourse used by cinematographers themselves. Karl Struss, for example, substantially changed his assessment of the ideal cinematographer between his 1928 essay "Dramatic Cinematography" and his 1934 essay "Photographic Modernism and the Cinematographer." In the 1928 piece, written at the end of the silent era, Struss advocated a pictorially expressive camera that "seems to live with the characters and follows them around for expressive realism."[30] By 1934, however, Struss had pulled back considerably from this view, proposing instead an extremely passive role for the cinematographer. Rejecting cinematography that called attention to its own artistry—including that of the "sensational German and Russian silent films of the early part of the last decade"—Struss championed an "idealized realism" in which cinematography would "always remain the vehicle for the story, and . . . never call attention to itself at the expense of either story or players."[31] Struss's own style as a cinematographer changed as well during the period, becoming more "invisible" and shunning the "unusual camera angles, dramatic lighting schemes, and 'unrealistic' diffusion effects" that had marked his films of the 1920s."[32] We can see a similar retrenchment in the style of other Hollywood cinematographers such as John Seitz and William Daniels, though a few directors of photography, such as Joseph August, Lee Garmes, and James Wong Howe, continued to use more adventurous methods in the early 1930s.

The first significant advance in sound-era cinematography, I would argue, was the development of deep-focus cinematography during the late 1930s and early 1940s. Though American cinematographers began to use deep-focus techniques as early as the 1920s (and in some cases even earlier), it was not until Gregg Toland and other cinematographers began experimenting with techniques of deep focus in the middle and late 1930s that a fully realized visual style involving deep focus was achieved, culminating in Toland's exactingly experimental cinematography for *Citizen Kane* (1941). In chapter 2, I discuss the collaboration between Toland and William Wyler, in which we see a gradual development in Toland's technique of deep-focus photography. Toland's six-film collaboration with Wyler—which spanned the decade from 1936 to 1946—was a partnership that allowed Toland the freedom to perfect his technique. Although deep focus was a single technique rather than a more general shift in photographic style, it was a development that contributed to significant changes in the visual style of American films. I will therefore suggest that deep focus—more than any other filmic technique—marks the transition between the more conservative studio style of the 1930s and the more actively foregrounded style of the 1940s.

In the third stage of cinematography—which begins in the early 1940s with *Citizen Kane* and continues through the 1940s and 1950s—the developing sophistication of filmmaking technologies, including deep focus, allowed for a greater emphasis on stylistic innovation than had been possible in Hollywood productions of the 1930s. This shift toward greater stylization was the result of several interlocking factors: changes in audience preferences and expectations, advances in technologies such as the speed of film stocks and the coating of lenses, a decrease in the centralization of studio control over film style, and a decrease in the emphasis on glamour lighting. The impact of these changes can be seen across a number of genres, but it is most clearly visible in the film noir. Abandoning the glamour lighting and high-key approach that characterized 1930s Hollywood filmmaking, film noir was marked by its low-key lighting, frequent use of shadows, and disturbingly off-center compositions.

In chapter 3, I focus on the collaboration of Billy Wilder and John Seitz as a case study of 1940s cinematography, and in particular a study of noir cinematography. Wilder and Seitz collaborated on four black-and-white films, each of which exhibits an extraordinary awareness of the possibilities of film as a visual medium. In *Double Indemnity,* their second film together, Wilder and Seitz perfected the visual language of what would later come to be called film noir. In their third film, *The Lost Weekend,* they combined elements of film noir style with an almost documentary realism. In their final collaboration, *Sunset Boulevard,* Wilder and Seitz used many of the visual conventions of noir to create a visual masterpiece that is balanced between gothic stylization and photographic naturalism.

The fourth major stage of American cinematography begins in the 1950s with the more widespread use of color film, the introduction of widescreen processes by all the major studios, and a greater proficiency in the use of special effects. The dramatic increase in both color filmmaking and widescreen production during the 1950s was a response to the growth of television and the resulting need to differentiate the cinematic experience from that of the small screen. If the black-and-white photography of the 1940s and early 1950s represented the high point of a certain form of graphic stylization that was ideal for representing the tense urban dramas of film noir, the lushly designed and photographed color films of the 1950s and 1960s—whether they were shot in widescreen or standard format—achieved a very different form of stylization, one based less on the intricacies of lighting and framing and more on the ability to use greatly improved color processes such as Technicolor and Eastmancolor, along with the wider screen and more sophisticated special effects. Whereas the emphasis of the 1940s film noirs was on the creation of striking compositional designs and mood-driven lighting, the emphasis of color films of the 1950s and 1960s—most vividly realized in the epic, the musical, the Western, the melodrama, the adventure film, and the psychological thriller—was on presenting an entertaining or awe-inspiring spectacle.[33]

Chapter 4 turns to one of the most successful collaborations of the 1950s and early 1960s: that of Alfred Hitchcock and his cinematographer, Robert Burks. Along with other key members of Hitchcock's filmmaking team such as production designer Robert Boyle, editor George Tomasini, costume designer Edith Head, and composer Bernard Herrmann, Burks played a crucial role in the creation of Hitchcock's films during what many consider to be the period of his greatest creative success. In films such as *Rear Window* (1954), *Vertigo* (1958), *North by Northwest* (1959), *The Birds* (1961), and *Marnie* (1964), Burks used his considerable skills in lighting and camerawork as well as his background as a special effects cinematographer to create a striking visual surface for Hitchcock's intensely idiosyncratic productions. In the dozen films Burks shot for Hitchcock, he worked in every available format, from the black-and-white pseudodocumentary *The Wrong Man* to widescreen (VistaVision) color productions. In chapter 4, I will focus my attention on Burks's contribution to Hitchcock's color films, which display an unusual degree of chromatic stylization along with innovative camerawork.

In the fifth stage in the development of American cinematography—the beginnings of which I locate in the late 1960s and early 1970s—the mediating technology itself becomes an index of the film's authenticity. The art of cinematography, I argue, has come full circle since the days of Griffith and Bitzer: whereas Bitzer found creative solutions that allowed him to escape the limitations of the available technologies, cinematographers of the post-Hollywood era sought to expand the range of their visual style by emphasizing aspects of the medium itself. They did this in any number of ways: by manipulating the film through "flashing" and other techniques that desaturate the colors or give them a more authentically period feel; by shooting in black-and-white rather than color as a way of referencing a particular genre or time period; by using techniques such as handheld camerawork to create a greater sense of urgency or to approximate the filmmaking of an earlier era; by using various kinds of camera movement (zooms, dollies, or pans) as a means of drawing attention to the camera as an interactive element in the filmmaking process; and by combining different film formats (video, 8mm, 16mm, and 35mm) within the same film in order to create a sense of lived historical experience. All these techniques—taken together—represent a process of self-conscious mediation that began to appear with far greater frequency in films of the early 1970s and that characterized films of the 1980s and 1990s, as cinematographers continued to push the medium beyond the limits of what had been technologically possible and stylistically permissible during the studio era.

My fifth chapter contains case studies of three films—made between the early 1970s and the late 1990s—that engage in highly self-conscious manipulations of visual technology. The chapter begins with a discussion of Robert Altman's *McCabe and Mrs. Miller* (1971). Altman and cinematographer Vilmos Zsigmond used the technique of "flashing" the film (exposing the negative to light) throughout nearly the entire film in order to desaturate the colors, providing an analogue for turn-of-the-century photographs. In doing so, they achieved a unique visual style that not only differentiated the film from previous movies set in the American West but also opened the door for a greater range of stylistic experimentation through technological manipulation. Two decades later, in *JFK* (1991), Oliver Stone and cinematographer Robert Richardson made a self-conscious use of the filmic medium itself to reflect on a centrally important historical event—the assassination of President Kennedy—and the subsequent investigation. Stone and Richardson sought a visual means of capturing the lived sense of historical events as they were originally presented in the television news media. In the sequence involving the assassination, for example, Richardson tried to duplicate news coverage as well the famous amateur footage shot by Abraham Zapruder; he then enhanced the footage in Super 8, 16mm, and 35mm formats, using a total of eight cameras and fourteen different color and black-and-white film stocks. I conclude the chapter with an analysis of Steven Spielberg's combat film *Saving Private Ryan* (1998). Spielberg and cinematographer Janusz Kaminski adopted a wide range of filmic technologies in recreating the experience of World War II. Though Spielberg's stated intention was to present the Normandy landing as if it had been shot by World War II combat cameramen, this attempt at greater authenticity was made possible only by a highly advanced array of devices and cinematic techniques that had become available in the 1980s and 1990s.

In the book's sixth and final chapter, I address the rapid shift over the past decade from analog to digital cinematography. I examine the use of the digital intermediate process, a technique first developed in the late 1990s as a way of adjusting the color palette of films in postproduction through digital rather than analog means. I end the book with a discussion of the different ways in which the digital turn in filmmaking has affected both the role of the cinematographer and the collaborative relationship between the cinematographer and the director. Though it is too early to understand fully the effect these changes will have both on the art of cinematography and on the position of the cinematographer within the film industry, it is clear that the cinematographer will continue to play a central role in the creation of films, and that the collaboration of the cinematographer and the director will remain a crucial one as new visual technologies expand the range of stylistic possibility.

1 Pioneers in Babylon

D.W. Griffith and Billy Bitzer

In 1914, one could see a two-reel drama plus a couple of comedies at the better theatres for a dime. . . . Generally, the photographic quality was poor. Highly contrasty and overdeveloped, the highlights were chalk-white and the shadows deep black. Known in the trade as "soot and whitewash," it was the quality most exhibitors demanded because of low-powered projection equipment. The Biograph Company insisted on being different. They refused to make "soot and whitewash." Their films had delicate half-tones and a silvery effect that was the envy of us all. . . . Screen credits were not listed in those days, but I learned from reading motion picture articles in magazines that the best Biograph films were directed by D.W. Griffith and photographed by Billy Bitzer.

Joseph Walker, *The Light on Her Face*

The collaboration of D.W. Griffith and G.W. "Billy" Bitzer began during the summer of 1908, when American filmmaking was still in its infancy, and it continued until nearly the end of the silent era. One of the longest and most productive creative partnerships in the history of American cinema, the Griffith-Bitzer collaboration resulted in the production of more than five hundred motion pictures, including many of the most canonical American films of the silent period. If it is true, as David Cook has suggested, that Griffith did more than any other filmmaker "to establish the narrative language of the cinema and turn an aesthetically inconsequential medium of entertainment into a fully articulated art form," it was Bitzer, as Griffith's gifted and loyal cameraman, who provided him with the brilliant images out of which he was able to fashion his powerful visual narratives.[1]

The long-term partnership of Griffith and Bitzer raises important questions about the status of such collaborations during the silent era, and more specifically during what has been called the "period of transition" between the early years of American filmmaking and the classical period.[2] There is a good deal that we do not know, and will probably never know, about how directors and their cameramen collaborated during the transitional period of 1907 to 1913. How much control did each of them have over matters such as camera placement, shot selection and composition, camera movement, and lighting? To what extent did directors of the period discuss questions of visual style with their cameramen? To what extent was visual style even a conscious consideration for filmmakers, apart from a desire to find ways of telling their stories more clearly and effectively?

The period during which Griffith and Bitzer initiated their working relationship—the summer of 1908—was one in which the power dynamic between directors and cameramen was still relatively fluid. Although each studio functioned under a slightly different system of production, it seems clear that during the years immediately preceding the transitional period, there was a great deal of collaboration in the making of motion pictures. As Charles Musser has noted, the period prior to 1908 was dominated by a "collaborative system of production," particularly in the case of fiction films. This system generally involved "the uniting of complementary skills" in what was roughly "an association of equals." This association could be two directors working together—as in the case of Wallace McCutcheon and Edwin S. Porter at the Edison studio (1905–1907)—or a more complementary pairing such as that of Porter and actor George S. Fleming during an earlier period at Edison.[3] Musser describes the collaboration of Porter and Fleming, which lasted from 1901 to 1903:

> Fleming was an actor and scenic designer. Porter, who had been improving Edison motion picture equipment, joined him as a cameraman, and the two worked together. What we see is a pairing of men with complementary skills. Working together, Fleming constructed the sets and directed the actors while Porter shot the scenes, developed the film, and edited the results. Yet much of the actual filmmaking—the choosing of subjects and planning of actual scenes—was done by both men.[4]

Similar partnerships also existed at studios other than Edison. At Biograph, for example, Wallace McCutcheon collaborated with Frank Marion between 1900 and 1905, while at Essanay the actor and playwright Lawrence Lee worked closely with cinematographer Gilbert P. Hamilton. Lee, whose background appears to have been very similar to Griffith's, led the acting troupe and production crew, but he deferred to Hamilton on questions of camera and lighting. In fact, as late as the summer of 1908—the exact moment when Griffith and Bitzer were beginning their partnership—the cameraman was still considered the final authority over certain key filmmaking decisions. One contemporary account suggested that the photographer "vetoes absolutely the dramatist's suggestion," and that the said "dramatist"—the person we now call the director—must often "rearrange his pawns in the moving picture game and change his system to coincide with the limitations of the camera."[5]

In part, the power still wielded by the cameraman in the transitional period was the remnant of an earlier era, when filmmakers such as Edwin S. Porter were able to combine the roles of cameraman and director.[6] While the position of the cameraman had existed since the very beginnings of the cinema, that of the director was a later invention; it evolved gradually from the much more limited role of stage manager or leader of a company of actors to a position involving significant creative control over all aspects of filmmaking. In this sense, the working relationship of Griffith and Bitzer can be seen as emblematic of widespread changes in the industry, and especially of changes in the way power and authority were beginning to shift from the cameraman to the director. By 1913, the year when Griffith and Bitzer left Biograph, it is clear that the director was emerging throughout the American film industry as the more dominant partner in both organizational and creative terms. What is not so clear is whether this change was happening with equal rapidity at all the studios, or if Griffith's powerful position at Biograph during these years was something of an aberration, giving him the ability to assume creative control more quickly than directors at other studios.

Charles Musser suggests two possible explanations for the expansion of the director's power after 1908. First of all, with the growth in acting companies at each studio, the director had increased responsibility for such matters as casting and performance. Second, with the increasing dominance of fiction films relative to documentaries, directors were of greater importance, since they were responsible for making sure the stories that would go before the camera were clear and logical. In the case of Griffith, there was an additional factor in his ability to take power more quickly. Because Biograph was on the verge of commercial disaster when Griffith took over as director, he had "unusual leverage in the company."[7] This leverage allowed him to assume the position of producer as well as director of his films and to take control of the editing.

For about the first year of their collaboration, the relationship of Griffith and Bitzer appears to have been closer to one of equals, with Griffith responsible for the actors and Bitzer for the positioning and operating of the camera. This also meant that—because these were two very strong-willed individuals—open disagreements on the set were not uncommon. Bitzer wrote in a 1939 letter to Seymour Stern, he and Griffith had "had differences of opinion . . . from the start," and these differences sometimes led to heated arguments.[8] It became clear, however, in the course of the first months of their collaboration, that Griffith and not Bitzer would gain the upper hand in making crucial decisions about how films would be made. "Before [Griffith's] arrival," Bitzer recollected in his autobiography *Billy Bitzer: His Story,* "I, as cameraman, was responsible for everything except the immediate hiring and handling of the actor. Soon, it was his say whether the lights were bright enough, or if the makeup was right."[9] Bitzer's comment, though telling, leaves us wishing for more details about exactly how these changes took place. Did Bitzer complain to Biograph management about Griffith's attempt to gain greater control? If so, was the company receptive to his complaints? Or did Bitzer simply back down when it became clear that Griffith would have the upper hand?[10]

There are several facts we do know, some of which support my contention that Bitzer was a central collaborator in Griffith's films rather than a mere technical supporter. One of the strongest arguments in favor of Bitzer's central importance to Griffith's films is the fact that Griffith, prior to his appearances in films at Edison and Biograph at the end of 1907, had been an unsuccessful playwright and modestly talented actor, with little exposure to film and even less knowledge of filmmaking technique. Griffith's lack of filmmaking experience is suggested by Bitzer's claim to have taught him the rudimentary aspects of filmmaking—such as how to frame a shot and how to organize a scenario into scenes—prior to his directing his first film, *The Adventures of Dollie.* Further, directors of the pre-Griffith era were essentially glorified stage managers, whose sole purpose was to move the actors into their places for the camera and give minimal instructions about how they should perform their scenes. As Richard Schickel notes, there was not much for the director to do once he had chosen his actors "except [to] make sure that, in carrying out such bits of business and action as he might devise for them, they did not step outside the guidelines, marked on the floor, which indicated the limits of what the lens could record."[11]

Bitzer's situation as Biograph's lead cameraman seems to have been quite secure. Employed as a professional cinematographer since 1896, he had shot over five hundred films by the time he began his collaboration with Griffith, and he had directed at least some of Biograph's films prior to Griffith's arrival. Though it is difficult to say with any certainty how many films Bitzer had directed—given the lack of a clear distinction between cameramen and directors in the early years of the twentieth century—he is credited with directing films such as the 1906 short *The Impossible Convicts* in which trick photography creates the effect of prisoners walking backward into their cells, Since Bitzer was the cameraman for a number of other

Biograph films for which there is no known director, we can also consider him to be at least one of the principal authors of those films.[12] Bitzer was, put simply, one of the most experienced and accomplished filmmakers in the business at a time before the position of director even existed.[13]

Another factor in support of the central importance of Bitzer's contribution is the contemporary attitude toward film photography during this period. Both the industry and the trade press recognized the importance of cinematography to the success of Biograph's films during the period from 1908 to 1913. A 1910 editorial in *Moving Picture World,* the most influential film journal of the period, noted that "the Biograph releases are distinguished by a certain pictorial quality which is the outcome of patient systematized work in the photographic department," and that the Biograph studio had "a standard of [visual] quality . . . which other makers are laudably endeavoring to emulate."[14] Since Bitzer was responsible for shooting the lion's share of Biograph's films of that year, it seems reasonable to assume that his photographic work was judged to be superior to that of cameramen at most other studios. Charlie Keil seems perfectly justified in listing the presence of Biograph's "two veteran cameramen"—Bitzer and Arthur Marvin—as one of the major reasons Griffith had been able to advance so quickly from an inexperienced filmmaker to one of the most accomplished directors in the industry. After Marvin's death in early 1911, it was Bitzer alone who was responsible for the quality of Griffith's images. But even during the years 1908–1910, when Bitzer and Marvin were the company's two cameramen, Bitzer shot significantly more of Griffith's films than Marvin did.[15]

Another argument in support of Bitzer's importance to Griffith's early career is the fact that when Griffith left Biograph at the end of 1913 and went to work for Harry Aitken and the Mutual Film Company, he lobbied Bitzer vigorously to leave Biograph and join his filmmaking team. Bitzer was reluctant to leave the studio and the security of his position there, but Griffith offered him a salary of $200 a week (far more than Bitzer was making at Biograph, and more than any other American cameraman was earning at the time), as well as a 10 percent participation in the profits of Griffith's independent productions. The battle between Griffith and Biograph for Bitzer's services escalated into a no-holds-barred bidding war, with Biograph offering the cameraman a paid vacation in Florida, and Aitken giving him the use of a car. In his attempt to convince Bitzer to leave Biograph and join his new company, Griffith promised his cameraman that they would bury themselves "in hard work out on the coast for five years, make the greatest pictures ever made, make a million dollars, and retire."[16]

Clearly, Griffith placed considerable value on Bitzer's participation in his filmmaking venture, and considered him an essential collaborator in his films.

Bitzer was also instrumental in Griffith's ability to continue making films after leaving Biograph. When Aitken was unable to provide Griffith with a usable studio space in New York, Bitzer found him a space in a former rug factory in the Bowery, and when Griffith needed additional funds to make *The Birth of a Nation,* Bitzer put up a large part of his personal savings to help Griffith finance the picture. As of 1915, at least, Griffith and Bitzer appear to have been acting as partners in the most literal sense of the word, though their relationship would change quite dramatically in later years.

We can also frame the question of Bitzer's importance to the development of Griffith's filmmaking by asking whether Griffith could have made the films he did without Bitzer. Although this is by no means a simple question to answer—especially given the limited information about the exact circumstances of their collaboration during the Biograph years—I would argue that Bitzer contributed significantly to the aesthetic quality of Griffith's films, and that the rapid development of Griffith's technique as a filmmaker would not have been possible without Bitzer's technical and creative input.

Unfortunately, Griffith himself said very little—at least in writing—on the subject of his collaboration with Bitzer. Like many other self-styled auteurists, Griffith preferred to take credit for the artistic and commercial success of his films for himself. Since we do not have Griffith's perspective on his working relationship with his cameraman, we rely primarily on the information Bitzer conveys to us, with supporting evidence from other firsthand commentators, such as Bitzer's assistant Karl Brown. Bitzer's account of the collaboration with Griffith, contained in his posthumously published autobiography *Billy Bitzer: His Story,* is frustratingly incomplete, leaving significant gaps in the record of his work on Griffith's films. Bitzer's "story" also ends rather precipitously in 1920, thus leaving us with very little information about the final decade of his career. Nevertheless, Bitzer's book remains the single most important source of information about his work with Griffith.

Nearly as important to our understanding of the Griffith-Bitzer collaboration is the testimony of Karl Brown, who provided the most complete firsthand account of Griffith's working methods. Brown gives us the unique perspective of a young man who began as Bitzer's assistant and later went on to become a respected cinematographer in his own right. In a 1943 interview, Brown claimed that "Bitzer deserves a great deal of very real credit for Griffith's success":

> Not that Griffith would not have succeeded with another cameraman, but in Bitzer he had the best in the world. Bitzer had one thing which matched Griffith's art: a sort of distinctive know-how that defied analysis. He was absolutely foolproof in the matter of exposure for effect, as opposed to exposure for photographic correctness. He also knew, to perfection, how to work hand in hand with [lab technician] Abe Scholtz, and [how] to get the most out of that cooperation.[17]

In his memoir, published thirty years later, Brown again suggests that it was Bitzer, as much as Griffith himself, who was responsible for the unusually fine sense of composition we find in Griffith's films:

> Composition. That was the thing. That and an infallible instinct for exposure were the secrets of Bitzer's truly wonderful photography. It was also the secret of how he managed to make slender, short-statured Henry Walthall into the giant he appeared to be in *Judith of Bethulia*. . . . But there was more, much more to it than that. He had an instinct for such things that I couldn't grasp then and couldn't explain now. Things seemed to fall into place for him. . . . Composition. That was everything. Exposure was important, too, but that was a matter of scientific judgment. Art isn't. And Bitzer was an artist first of all.[18]

The fact that Brown so strongly emphasizes Bitzer's role both in the composition of Griffith's shots and in their exposure for maximum artistic effect suggests that Bitzer was in large part responsible for the design of shots—including camera placement, camera angle, and length of focus—at least during the period through the making of *Intolerance.* With regard to more specific technical innovations that have been attributed to Griffith, it is often impossible to say whether they originated with Griffith or with Bitzer. Bitzer described the process this way: "If Mr. Griffith asked for some effect, I tried one way or another to produce what he wanted. When it worked successfully, we were hailed as inventors." The pronoun *we* is significant here: since the two of them worked together so closely and for so long, it is in many cases not clear whether Griffith or Bitzer was primarily responsible for their innovations, or, indeed, whether they both were.[19] In *The Drunkard's Reformation* (March 1909), for example, Griffith and Bitzer achieved an effect that was, if not a milestone in the use of artificial lighting, at the very least a significant improvement on earlier efforts such as that of Edwin S. Porter in *The Seven Ages* (1905). In the final scene of Griffith's film, the reformed alcoholic of the title sits with his family in front of a glowing fireplace. Griffith and Bitzer spent a considerable amount of both time and film experimenting with the lighting of the shot in order to perfect the visual effect, which was created by placing a small arc light inside the fireplace. As the lighting from above was gradually dimmed, the fireplace light cast a warm glow on the family, reinforcing the emotional impact of the film's ending.

Two other techniques that Griffith and Bitzer developed together were the panning shot—which they used with great effectiveness as early as *The Country Doctor* (1909)—and the tracking or traveling shot, which became an important part of their arsenal after 1910 and was used with great effectiveness in action films such as *The Lonedale Operator* (1911) and *A Girl and Her Trust* (1912). Another technique, which Bitzer claims to have discovered accidentally but which can be considered a joint innovation of Bitzer and Griffith, was the backlighting of actors. During a break in filming, Bitzer decided to photograph Mary Pickford and Owen Moore as they sat together eating lunch. With the bright sun at their backs and reflecting off the white gravel at their feet, Bitzer was able to capture a beautiful close-up of their faces with none of the "ugly shadows that usually make hollow masks of faces on the screen."[20] When he showed the shot to Griffith, the director immediately grasped its potential and asked Bitzer to repeat it for the movie. By substituting reflectors for the white gravel, Bitzer was able to capture the same effect in one of the most aesthetically satisfying shots of the film. As with many of Bitzer's innovations, the technique quickly became one of the permanent tools of American cinematographers.

Yet another technique of Bitzer's that became not only part of Griffith's repertoire but a staple of other filmmakers, was the "iris shot." Since shooting outdoors in bright sunlight often created a glare in the image, Bitzer worked to devise a means of shading the lens. He at first tried using his cap, but it would too often flop down over the lens and ruin the shot. He then improvised a shade for the lens out of a glue pot. When the camera's lens was stopped down to create a greater depth of field, the edge of the pot was thrown into focus, and a black circle appeared around the outer portion of the frame. This effect, which was actually a "mistake" in the shot, appealed to Griffith, who saw it as an effective way to vary the screen space while focusing more attention on the image in the center of the shot. Eventually, Bitzer had a device specially made that could be controlled to make the iris any size or shape.

Griffith did not "discover" the techniques of camera and lighting that have often been attributed to him. Instead, there was a reciprocal process in which Griffith would ask for an effect, Bitzer would find a way to make it happen, and Griffith would then use it in his films. Griffith had little interest in technical matters, and it is unlikely that he gave much thought to devising new ways of shooting beyond what was demonstrated for him by his cameraman. Bitzer's solid technical foundation and problem-solving ability gave Griffith the confidence to try out new ideas and explore his own creativity in such areas as shot selection, staging, and lighting.

• • •

The already difficult task of grasping the exact circumstances of Griffith's collaboration with Bitzer is made even more challenging by the fact that a substantial amount of the commentary on Griffith's filmmaking technique is based on inaccurate information, much of it originating with Griffith himself. In an advertisement he took out in the *New York Dramatic Mirror* on September 29, 1913, as he was preparing to leave Biograph, Griffith claimed not only to be "the producer of all Biograph successes" but also to be responsible for "revolutionizing Motion Picture drama and founding the modern technique of the art." Griffith took credit for a number of innovations, including "large or close-up figures," "distant views," crosscutting, and the fade-out. This list of techniques—all of which had been used by other filmmakers prior to Griffith—set the stage for the inflation of Griffith's reputation in subsequent decades.[21] The widespread exaggeration of Griffith's status as an innovator of filmic techniques persisted largely unchallenged until the 1980s, when scholars of early film began to discover earlier precedents for the innovations claimed by Griffith.[22]

In part, the tendency to view Griffith's role in the development of American cinema as more central than it was results from an accident of film preservation. Whereas nearly all Griffith's Biograph films were preserved and were later acquired by the Museum of Modern Art, the vast majority of films by Griffith's contemporaries were either destroyed or lost. In fact, while virtually all the 450 films Griffith directed for Biograph up to 1913 survive, only about three times that number of films survive from *all* the other American filmmakers of the same period combined.[23] As a result, Griffith's films have been far more widely available to film historians than those of his contemporaries, and until recently he was frequently represented as the only significant American director of the early silent era. Over the years, a great deal of scholarly attention has been paid to Griffith's career, while very little material exists on the films made by Biograph's competitors such as Vitagraph, Selig, Lubin, Kalem, and Essanay.[24] The biographical record of directors other than Griffith is spotty at best, and in many cases we do not even know the identities of cameramen for films made before 1915.[25]

This situation has important implications for the analysis of Griffith's visual style. Since so many of Griffith's films are available for stylistic analysis, and so relatively few films by his contemporaries, it is difficult to assess the degree of innovation in Griffith's films within an informed historical context. How, for example, did Griffith's films compare with others of the period in terms of stylistic elements such as shot selection, camera movement, and the use of lighting? Although Griffith was certainly an extremely important filmmaker of the transitional period—and perhaps the most important American director of the silent era—he was not the only filmmaker who worked with innovative techniques. Other film companies also put efforts into enhancing their profiles through stylistic innovation, and many of the "innovations" we see in Griffith's films of 1908 to 1912 can also be found in the films of Edison, Vitagraph, and others.[26]

In reaction to inflated claims by earlier scholars concerning Griffith's status as an innovator, some recent scholarship has attempted to point in the opposite direction, suggesting that Griffith was actually relatively conservative in matters of filmic technique.[27] The truth is no doubt somewhere in the middle. While it is clear from a viewing of his Biograph films that Griffith's filmmaking from 1908 to 1912 steadily increased in sophistication—eventually leading him to become dissatisfied with the one-reel format and to leave Biograph in order to pursue more ambitious projects—it is important to temper our received notion of Griffith as a highly innovative, even experimental director. Griffith's films appear to have outpaced those of his rivals in certain areas, such as editing, but they do not appear to have been significantly outside of the mainstream in other respects, such as set design, shot selection, camera movement, and lighting.

• • •

Johann Gottlob Wilhelm Bitzer was born on April 21, 1872, to German immigrants who had settled in the Roxbury section of Boston, Massachusetts. Bitzer's father, who worked as a blacksmith and harness-maker, was able to secure for him an apprenticeship as a silversmith. Karl Brown attributed Bitzer's unusual skill in working with cameras and film to his early training in metalwork:

> His hands, stubby-fingered and thick, moved with the swift certainty of a born artist, a sort of latter-day Cellini. His working habits were as precisely ordered as the mechanisms he worked with. He could take anything apart, find out what was wrong, correct it, and put it back together again without mishaps of any kind, thanks to his methodical precision of working.[28]

Bitzer was not only a meticulous technician, but also a man of considerable ambition. By his own account, he realized at the age of twenty-two that in order to "make something of Billy Bitzer," he would need to change the direction of his career.[29] Soon after enrolling in a course in electrical engineering at the Cooper Union Institute in New York, Bitzer was offered a job as a mechanic and electrician at the Magic Introduction Company, located near Union Square. Though he earned only half what he could have made as a silversmith, he found the work far more stimulating. Bitzer's job involved thinking up and perfecting the new inventions that the company produced, including a benzene-burning cigar lighter and a process for improving the operation of hotel heating systems.

While Bitzer was working at the Magic Introduction Company, the film company for which he would soon become a cameraman was founded. In 1895, a former lab assistant of Thomas Edison by the name of W.K.L. Dickson, along with three other investors, founded the American Mutoscope Company, an enterprise that would produce both a motion picture camera and a device for displaying films. The new venture would later be renamed the American Mutoscope and Biograph Company, and still later simply Biograph. Dickson had worked with Edison to invent a camera, the Kinetograph, in 1891. Biograph's camera, invented by Dickson and Herman Casler, differed from Edison's Kinetograph in two important respects. First, to avoid infringement on Edison's motion picture patents, the camera was designed so that instead of moving the film through the camera by sprockets, it used continuous-movement friction rollers to move the film into the camera. Second, the camera used 68mm film rather than the 35mm film Edison's camera used, meaning that each frame had a surface area nearly four times as large as the frames in Edison's film.[30] As a result, Biograph's films had a more clearly defined image than Edison's, a feature apparent to early audiences. On the other hand, the system of passing the film into the camera without sprockets and puncturing the film as it passed through the camera was cumbersome and resulted in frequent mechanical breakdowns, which meant that a cameraman who was also a skilled mechanic was indispensable.

By late 1907, when Griffith joined the Biograph company as an actor, Bitzer had been the studio's lead cameraman for over a decade. In that time, he shot documentary films on a wide range of subjects, comedies such as *The Tough Kid's Waterloo* (1902) and *Personal* (1904), nursery rhymes such as *Tom, Tom, the Piper's Son* (1905), and historical dramas such as *A Kentucky Feud* (1905). Serious, critical, and argumentative by nature, Bitzer felt himself every bit the equal of the directors with whom he worked, and he had no qualms about expressing his opinions.

By 1908, the Biograph studio was in serious trouble. Not only was the company $200,000 in debt to its bankers, but it was also suffering from a perception that the quality of its films was in decline. Wallace McCutcheon, who had served as the company's principal director, was on the verge of retirement and would cease making films in July of that year. Both Marvin and Bitzer had shot several films with the company's new actor, then going by the name of Lawrence Griffith. Bitzer had been underwhelmed by Griffith's acting abilities, and had told him so:

> The second time I encountered him, he overacted the part of a bartender; so in order to save myself trouble, I asked him if he was trying to get me fired, or wasn't he aware his mugging was taking the action away from the lead? He confided that a friend had told him that was the way to act in pictures, but now that I had brought it to his attention, he wouldn't do it again. He told me he was a writer, accepting movie jobs for the money. He asked my advice about directing work. I advised him against it, for I couldn't see how a man who wasn't a passable actor could direct a flock of geese.[31]

Fortunately for Griffith, others at Biograph were more favorably impressed by his talents, and he was offered the job as Biograph's new director. Griffith's first directorial effort was the unexceptional one-reel short *The Adventures of Dollie,* for which he was assigned Marvin as his cameraman. Bitzer, as he later claimed, offered Griffith some free advice before the shoot: he showed Griffith how to break down a scenario into scenes by sketching out the story elements on a piece of cardboard, and he instructed him to look through the camera before each scene in order to make sure that "there were no open spaces left on either side."[32] Bitzer's straightforward advice on the fundamentals of filmmaking may have helped Griffith to make what is generally regarded as a competent first film—good enough, at any rate, to persuade the Biograph management to give him a contract for $45 a week as the company's director. Over the next five years, Griffith would turn out over 450 one- and two-reel films for Biograph, the vast majority of which would be shot by Bitzer.

One film that is almost universally cited as one of Griffith's most visually innovative early efforts is *The Country Doctor.* Made in May and June of 1909—nearly a year into Griffith's directorial career—the film tells the story of two families: a doctor, his wife, and their young daughter, and a neighboring "poor family." The doctor's daughter has been taken ill, but he is called away to take care of the sick neighbor girl, and while he is away, his daughter dies. The film is most famous for introducing the highly unusual stylistic device of two symmetrically placed pans, one at the beginning of the reel and the other at the end. The striking opening shot is a long pan from left to right, moving across a field and a grove of trees and ending in front of the doctor's house, as the doctor and his family are seen leaving for a walk in the country. In the closing shot, Griffith and Bitzer reverse the visual gesture, panning in the opposite direction, from the front of the house—now without the family—back to the natural landscape. According to Tom Gunning, this final panning shot serves to enclose the film in "a strongly aesthetic structure":

> [The shot] functions as a lyrical postscript of the sort Griffith had developed in previous films, providing a moment for gathering emotions, or a pictorial languor after narrative resolution. The echoing circular structure of matching first and last shots had appeared in a few earlier Biograph films. . . . But this final shot differs from those which preceded it . . . in its absence of human characters. This absence marks this shot as utterly novel, expressive, and profound.[33]

Whereas most commentators have focused their attention on the novel device of the doubled pan shot, I would also call attention to the pictorial expressivity of other exterior shots in the film, especially in the early sections. The first three minutes of the film are composed of exteriors filmed in the countryside of what was then rural Greenwich, Connecticut, and the bucolic beauty of the physical setting is contrasted with the more static shots of the two interiors (those of the doctor's house and the poor family's house) which take up the remainder of the film. Griffith's highly effective use of filmic space anticipates his even more sophisticated use of such spaces in later films, but it is Bitzer's beautifully composed exterior footage that helps to create an emotional involvement with the doctor's family.

A number of the other films Griffith and Bitzer shot in 1909 and 1910 contain similar elements of pictorialism, from *A Corner in Wheat* (November 1909), with its long-held shots of farmers planting wheat in their field, to *The Unchanging Sea* (March 1910) with its repeated use of expressive tableau shots of human figures framed against the beach and ocean.[34] *A Corner in Wheat* is one of most visually powerful of Griffith's Biograph films. The extraordinary second shot is a clear reference to Jean François Millet's famous painting *The Sower.* Bitzer holds the camera on a field as it is being sown by two farmers (a younger man and his father): the shot lasts for over a minute, during which time we see the two figures approach the camera—followed by a team of horses and a third man—and then turn and walk away again. In its elegant composition, extreme length, and unusually deep staging, the shot is one of the most lyrically evocative to

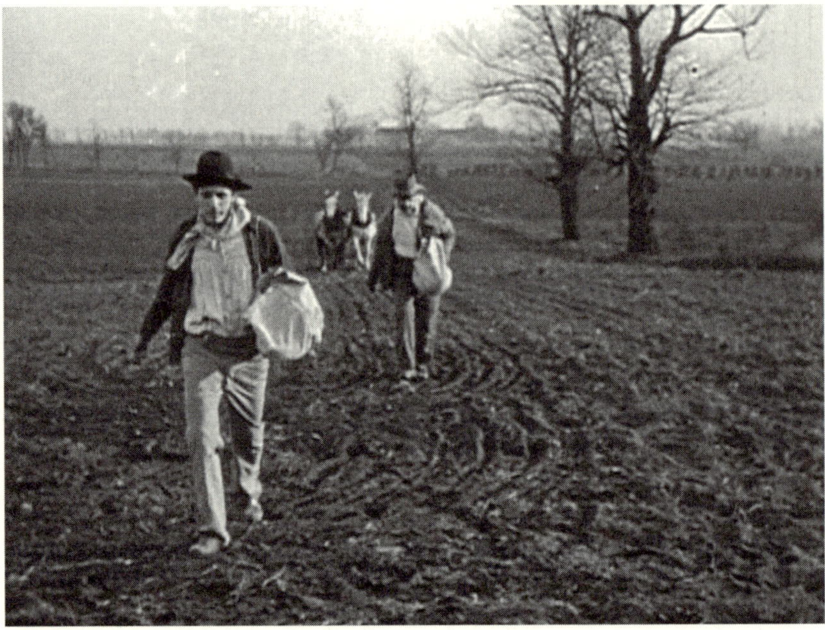

Figure 1. An elegantly composed use of deep space by cinematographer Billy Bitzer. (*A Corner in Wheat,* Biograph, 1909)

appear in any of Griffith's early films; the long take emphasizes the monotony of the farmers' lives as well as the timelessness of their situation.

Although the films of 1909 and 1910 demonstrate the growing assurance of Griffith and Bitzer, their films of 1911–1913 achieve an even higher level of visual sophistication, one that prefigures the visual work of *The Birth of a Nation* and *Intolerance.* The period between 1912 and 1916, encompassing Griffith's later Biograph films as well as his first full-length features, was marked by a general development in American cinematic technique, motivated at least in part by the shift in production from one-reel films to feature-length productions. The ranks of American cameramen were swelled during this period by a new generation of cinematographers who would revolutionize the way films were shot and lit.[35]

Bitzer's films of 1912 include some of the most visually striking that Griffith made at Biograph. Perhaps foremost among them is *The Musketeers of Pig Alley:* shot in the fall of 1912, the film displays what Charlie Keil has identified as "an increased concern for issues of filmic space," both within the individual shot and between shots.[36] The action of the film takes place in a series of iconic urban spaces: a dilapidated tenement, a saloon, a dance hall, and a dead-end alley (the "Pig Alley" of the film's title) in which the climactic gun battle between the two gangs erupts. The primary criminal figure in *Musketeers* is the "Snapper Kid," played by Elmer Booth. Hardly the ambitious overachiever personified in later gangster films, the Snapper is a petty crook whose relatively small gang (it appears to consist of only him, his lieutenant, and a third gang member) becomes involved in a fight with a rival gang over the pursuit of an attractive young woman played by Lillian Gish.

The Musketeers of Pig Alley is not only a masterpiece of silent cinema but also an early example of the highly effective use of cinematography to dramatize action within an urban setting. As Keil suggests, the most obvious of the methods Griffith and Bitzer employ in the film is deep focus. Griffith and Bitzer often intensify the viewer's experience of the depth of the image by telescoping its contents, "funneling the visual material into an inverted cone so that the foreground action occupies a broader field than . . . the background."[37] In the dance hall scenes, for example, groups of people always flank the outer edges of the frame, thus tightening the viewer's gaze toward the background. In order to accentuate this feeling of composition in depth still further, Griffith and Bitzer shoot at an angle that keeps one of the set's side walls visible at all times: this asymmetrical framing not only helps to delimit the screen space, but it also lends the compositions a degree of angularity, offsetting the frontality of the actors' positions. This angularity is further emphasized when the characters enter and exit the frame in a diagonal rather than a horizontal manner, as Keil explains:

> These entrances and exits, because they often operate on a system of diagonals (or even verticals) can, in certain instances, push the frame out toward the camera, thereby extending the depth of the image not only into the background but into the extreme realms of the foreground. Griffith appears to be straining the limits of the frame, severely defining its boundaries to the left and right while simultaneously stretching the area remaining in between. Many shots further impress the viewer with the sheer volume of visual material they provide within such an apparently circumscribed space. . . . By capitalizing on both the potentialities of the depth of his images and the interrelatedness of contiguous spaces, Griffith can imply enclosure without becoming formally static.[38]

The most famous shot in *Musketeers* takes place during the sequence involving the lead-up to the battle between the rival gangs. At one point, Bitzer performs a shot that goes from a medium shot of the Snapper Kid

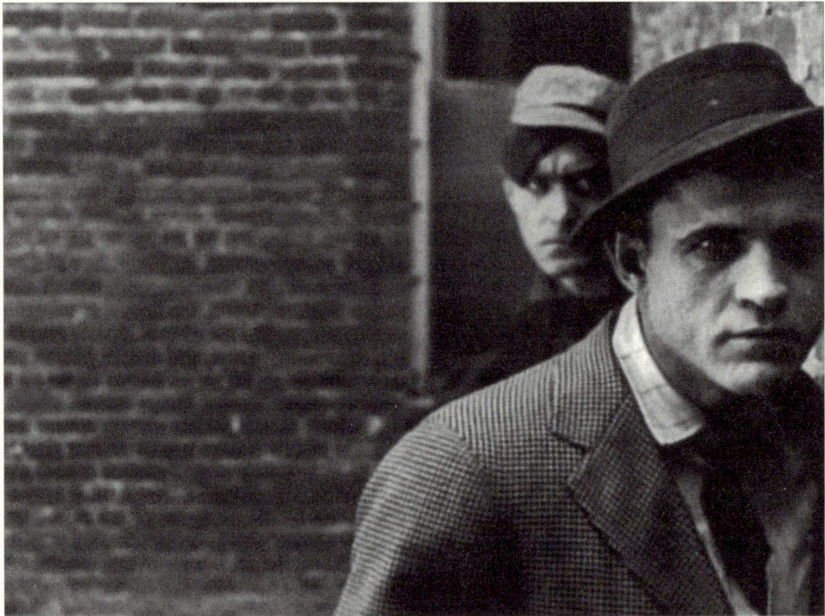

Figure 2. Bitzer's use of rack focus in an innovative shot. (*The Musketeers of Pig Alley*, Biograph, 1912)

into an extreme close-up of him looking directly into the camera. Griffith and Bitzer had used this technique of the direct-to-camera close-up in several earlier films, but with an important difference. In its previous incarnations, the shot had been used to express either menace or mental disturbance; here, Griffith and Bitzer use the shot in a more complex way that reflects their increasingly sophisticated cinematic technique. Bitzer keeps the Snapper in sharp focus at all times by using a technique of rack focus, blurring the other members of the gang in order to follow the Snapper into the foreground of the shot. As Russell Merritt suggests, the shot is "not only a tribute to Bitzer's skill as an operator," but also an indication of how effectively Bitzer and Griffith were able, by this point in their collaboration, to use the camera for psychological effect. Through the visual isolation of the Snapper from his fellow gang members, Bitzer underscores the character's underlying vulnerability.[39]

Another film in which the quality of Bitzer's camerawork is readily apparent is *The House of Darkness* (1913). The film's plot concerns the escape of a violent patient from an insane asylum and his recapture after he has been calmed by the playing of music. Made just six months after *The*

Musketeers of Pig Alley, The House of Darkness uses both mise-en-scène and cinematography to define a distinctive visual style. The film opens with two shots that demonstrate Griffith's use of compositional elements of figure arrangement as well as Bitzer's use of the camera. Keil describes the effect:

> The extreme stillness of the shots, almost tableau-like, coupled with the length of time they are held, reinforces the strange, atemporal quality of asylum life. The first shot in particular, with its aimless background beyond them, communicates through compositional strategies the plight of the disturbed.[40]

Griffith uses the two shots to balance each other in terms of content (one shows male patients, the other female patients), but it is Bitzer's composition of the shots that makes them truly remarkable. In the first shot, which opens up toward the right background, Bitzer uses an extreme depth of focus to show four or five planes of action simultaneously: each plane shows inmates engaging in various kinds of apparently abnormal behavior. In the second shot, the female patients, less kinetically active than the men, are sitting on benches and on the ground, observed by nurses. Here, Bitzer frames the women under a canopy of trees, with a sunny area visible in the background, dappled sunlight in the middle ground, and a shady area in the foreground. These shots—each lasting over twenty seconds—give the film a visual power that we find in few films of the period, adding resonance to the seriousness with which Griffith approaches the topic of mental illness.

• • •

By the summer of 1913, relations between Griffith and Biograph had deteriorated rapidly, eventually reaching a breaking point. The four-reel *Judith of Bethulia* would be the last film Griffith would direct for the company, and by far the most expensive. Griffith had submitted a budget of $18,000, already enough to raise the eyebrows of the Biograph management, but the film's final cost came to twice that amount—the result of expensive rehearsals, elaborate sets, and extra cameras for the battle sequences. Henry Marvin and J.J. Kennedy, the company's managers, were furious with Griffith, not just over the film's length and exorbitant cost but also over the shocking content of some of its scenes, including the gruesome beheading of Holofernes by Judith. Marvin and Kennedy called Griffith into their office and informed him that he would no longer have control over his budgets. He could finish shooting and editing *Judith of Bethulia,* and he would be allowed to supervise the work of other directors, but he would not be given any new projects to direct in the immediate future.

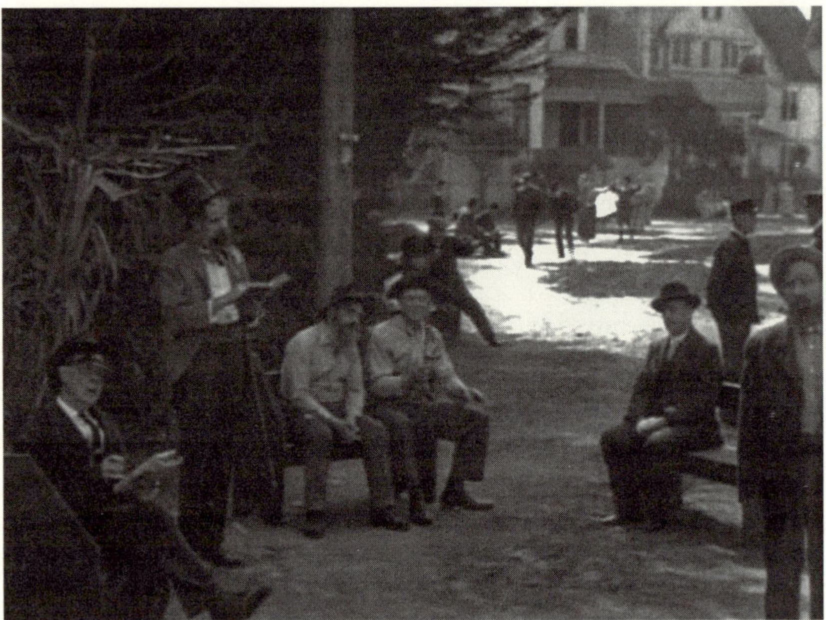

Figure 3. Multiple planes of visual focus combined with natural lighting. (*The House of Darkness*, Biograph, 1913)

Griffith, who had already had disagreements with Biograph over his desire to make longer films rather than continuing to shoot one-reelers, tendered his resignation in October 1913—several months before *Judith of Bethulia* was released—and signed a contract with Harry Aitken and the Mutual Film Company. Griffith was in a strong position to leave Biograph, since he was able to take with him a stock company of actors that included Lillian and Dorothy Gish, Mae Marsh, Henry Walthall, Bobby Harron, and Donald Crisp, as well the writer Frank Woods and assistant director Christy Cabanne. Though it was not immediately clear whether Bitzer would also accompany Griffith, the director was ultimately able to convince his cameraman to join him in his new venture. In December, Bitzer signed an agreement with Griffith and Aitken to leave Biograph, the studio that had been his home for the past seventeen years.

The films Griffith and Bitzer shot for Mutual in the first part of 1914 did not provide much evidence of the inspired filmmaking that was soon to come. Films such as *The Battle of the Sexes* and *The Escape* were intended primarily to keep the company afloat until Griffith had the financing he needed to make more serious films. On the modest budget of $5,000 supplied by Aitken, Griffith shot *The Battle of the Sexes* in five days and nights of furious work in a loft near New York's Union Square. The film was, by Griffith's own admission, little more than a "potboiler." Griffith's next film, *The Escape*—which addressed the consequences of venereal disease—was made in similar "quickie" style. It was soon followed by *Home, Sweet Home,* a sentimentalized version of the life of songwriter John Howard Payne. The last and best of the pre–*Birth of a Nation* pictures Griffith made for Aitken was *The Avenging Conscience.* An adaptation of Edgar Allan Poe's story "The Tell-Tale Heart," the four-reel film is a powerful rendition of the macabre tale in which a young man kills his benefactor, buries him within the house, and then is driven to reveal his crime by the fact that he thinks he hears the dead man's heart continuing to beat. Griffith would later consider *The Avenging Conscience* one of his finest films. Bitzer's cinematography deserves much of the credit for what the critic Gilbert Seldes called its play of "dark masses and ghostly rays of light."[41]

After shooting four films in considerable haste and on shoestring budgets, Griffith was finally able to turn to a project that engaged him on a more profound level. *The Birth of a Nation* was based on *The Clansman: An Historical Romance of the Ku Klux Klan* (1905), a novel by Thomas Dixon, Jr. Dixon's novel recounted a fictionalized version of the Civil War and its aftermath from a strongly Southern perspective. Motivated by the tremendous popularity of his novel, which sold over a million copies, Dixon wrote a theatrical version, which also proved extremely successful. The most controversial aspect of both the novel and the play was, of course, Dixon's blatantly racist account of the growth of the white supremacy movement in the years following the war. Much has already been written about Griffith's racial attitudes and the way in which his racist tendencies informed the making of *The Birth of a Nation,* and it is not my intention to add further to that debate.[42] While it may be true, as Sergei Eisenstein claimed, that "the disgraceful propaganda of racial hatred . . . which permeates this film cannot be redeemed by the purely cinematographic effects of the production," the film's cinematography contains a number of innovations that are significant both in terms of Griffith's development as a filmmaker and in the larger context of the development of American cinematic technique.[43] The film's racial attitudes, as distasteful as they are, have little bearing either on Bitzer's photographic approach or on his working relationship with Griffith. Nevertheless, any scholar who studies *The Birth of a Nation* must acknowledge the problematic nature of the film: in focusing on the style and technique of *Birth,* it is certainly not my intention to defend Griffith's often deplorable depiction of race in the film.

The project of making *The Birth of a Nation* was attractive to Griffith on several levels. First, the film's Southern setting appealed to Griffith's sympathies as a native Kentuckian whose family had pretentions to membership in the Southern aristocracy. Second, it involved the plight of families during wartime, a subject Griffith had addressed in several of his earlier films. Finally, it supplied rich material for large-scale battle scenes and thrilling chase sequences, both of which had become Griffith's trademarks as a director. Griffith and Frank Woods wrote a scenario in early 1914, based mostly on Dixon's novel, with some additional material from the play.[44] In mid-May, Griffith began rehearsing the actors, and on July 4 he began shooting the film, with Bitzer behind the camera. Karl Brown, who served as Bitzer's assistant, was responsible for loading and preparing the camera so that Bitzer could more quickly line up his shots and capture the images he needed. Bitzer, who shot the entire film using a single Pathé camera with only two lenses—a 50mm lens for longer shots and a 32mm for closer shots—was also involved with other aspects of the production, including the rehearsal of the actors.[45]

As both Bitzer and Brown recalled, Griffith's method was to block scenes in several different ways and then disappear into his office, allowing the cast and crew to "get into the mood or attitude of what he expected of them." As rehearsals continued, everyone involved in the production—including prop men, set designers, carpenters, and costume designers—would take notes and draw sketches, working out scenes "to the finest detail." These sketches would then be shown to Bitzer, who would plan out the actual shooting of the scenes. Once Griffith was satisfied with Bitzer's plans, Bitzer would inform the cast, and the scene would be shot.[46]

With his one camera and two lenses, hand-cranking in what he described as three-quarter waltz time, Bitzer was able to produce some of the most magnificent visual effects that had ever been put onto a movie screen. One of the cinematographic effects Bitzer could accomplish with his Pathé was the fade-out, or dissolve. Bitzer did this by cranking the camera with his right hand, while simultaneously using his left hand to loosen the lock knob on the stop lever, thus stopping down the lens.[47] (For a fade-in, Bitzer would do the opposite, gradually opening the stop as he cranked).

Daytime scenes were shot either on location or on the studio lot, which had no electric light equipment. Nearly all the lighting for the film was supplied by the sun, and the stages were built outdoors on the Fine Arts lot in order to take full advantage of the bright California sunlight. Telephone poles and steel girders erected in each corner of the stage supported a network of wires upon which Bitzer laid muslin diffusers that could be drawn up and down like giant window shades to control the amount of sunlight. The sides of the stages were also covered with white muslin stretched over wooden frames. On bright, sunny days the sun was filtered through the diffusers to provide a soft, even quality of light. Nevertheless, the California sun sometimes proved to be too strong for the actors, especially when they had to shoot their scenes at midday, so Bitzer blended a brown powder that could be put on top of their pink greasepaint and would protect them from sunburn.[48]

According to Bitzer, the only artificial lighting used in the production was for the scene of the burning of Atlanta, which required miniature models of the city to be built and illuminated by specially designed lights. However, Lillian Gish recalled that a few other "amazing night scenes" were shot by the light of bonfires.[49] For scenes requiring special lighting effects, Bitzer used large mirrors to reflect strong light onto certain areas of the set. When the scene had to be darkened, Bitzer's crew stretched tarpaulins over the top of the stage and then cut holes in the tarps to allow beams of sunlight to fall onto the set, creating more subtle lighting effects.[50]

In addition to the scenes shot on the Fine Arts lot, a number of sequences were filmed at various outdoor locations around Los Angeles. The sequence in which Gus (Walter Long) chases Flora Cameron (Mae Marsh) among the pine trees during his attempted rape was filmed at Big Bear, as was the love scene between Margaret Cameron (Miriam Cooper) and Phil Stoneman (Elmer Clifton). Bitzer shot the scenes showing the massing of the Ku Klux Klan on back country roads in the vicinity of the Rio Hondo, a tributary of the Los Angeles River. Other locations for the film included Calexico, Idyllwild, and various spots in the San Fernando Valley. The Civil War battlefield sequences were shot in Cahuenga Park in the San Fernando Valley.

The battle scenes contain some of the most extraordinary footage in the entire film, and Griffith went to great lengths to make the Civil War sequences both exciting and visually accurate. He had studied maps of the battlefields, as well as Matthew Brady's photographs and several reference books on the war, and with the help of a number of Civil War veterans he was able to re-create the battle scenes with a strong feeling of reality.[51] Using just six hundred extras (not the 18,000 claimed in the film's advertising), Griffith and Bitzer created the sense of battles involving thousands of soldiers. In order to obtain dramatic overhead views of the action, Bitzer mounted the camera on a 100-foot tower. The battle scenes took about three days to shoot, with Griffith communicating instructions to his assistants—including Raoul Walsh and Donald Crisp—who would in turn use differently colored flags to communicate Griffith's instructions to groups of extras.

Bitzer captured a few unplanned shots that were later incorporated into the film. One day, while waiting for some cannons that were to be used in the sequence involving Sherman's march to the sea, Griffith spotted a family standing in a group on a nearby hill, and he asked Bitzer to capture them on camera. As Bitzer recalled, he "inched the camera unobtrusively up to them," while pretending to be getting shots of the valley below. When that more intimate footage was later combined with a long panorama shot of the battlefield, it created, according to Bitzer, "one of the touches that made *The Birth* so real and convincing to audiences accustomed to stilted acting and stock shorts."[52]

The scene involving the assassination of President Lincoln at Ford's Theater was one of the film's most impressive in terms of its staging and lighting. The scene was staged as a detailed re-creation of period engravings. In order to create the effect of a strong light hitting the character of John Wilkes Booth (played by Raoul Walsh), crew members held a mirror which reflected sunlight onto him like a spotlight. As Karl Brown recalled,

> With Booth dressed in black and creeping along the far side of the wall, it was impossible to pick him out from all the others. So what did Bitzer do? Believe it or not, he had the men bring in a mirror, a big, pier-glass type of mirror made so ladies could admire themselves at full length, and he had this mirror mounted on a high parallel and he had the grips move the mirror to shoot the hot sunlight directly upon Booth and to follow him wherever he went, just like a spotlight in a theater.[53]

Perhaps the most iconic shot of the film occurs during the dramatic scene of the charge on horseback by members of the Ku Klux Klan. Griffith told Bitzer that he wanted the horses shot from below, so that they would appear to be leaping directly over the audience. The shot was rehearsed with expert riders from a local racetrack jumping over Bitzer while he lay on his stomach holding the camera and facing the horses. The shot went well with the stunt riders, but, as Bitzer recalled, it became problematic when the shot was attempted with the actors playing members of the Klan. Most of them were not experienced riders, and they had to do the shot while wearing white sheets and hoods, and with hoods over the heads of the horses:

> Wally Walthall, the "Little Colonel" of the story, was an expert rider, and his horse leaped over me with no trouble, except that a cloud of dust blinded the follow-up. "If they come too close, I can roll out of the way," I yelled to Griffith. Scores of horses were now stampeding past me and swerved to the sides as they saw my camera. But one rider had had to dismount, and the long sheet had blown over the horse's head, blinding it momentarily as it rushed ahead. Griffith ran out, seized the

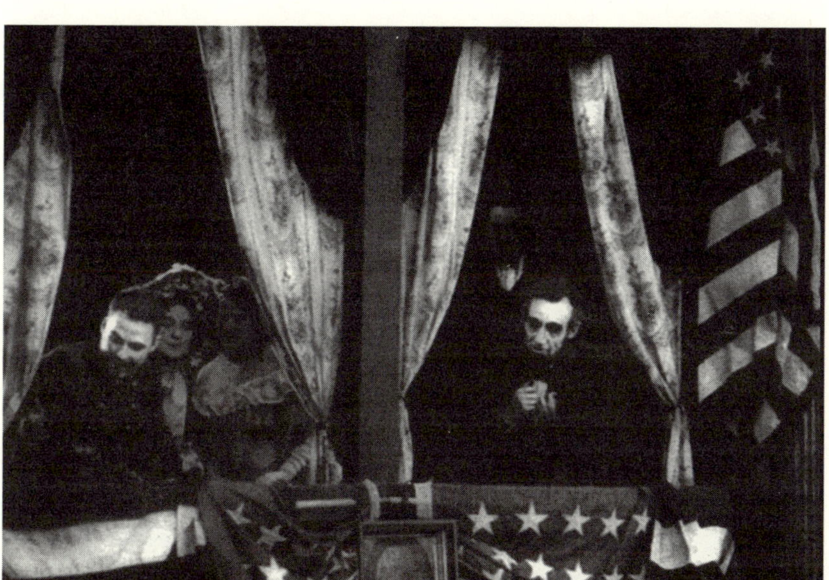

Figure 4. A highly effective visual staging of history: Lincoln's assassination. (*The Birth of a Nation,* D.W. Griffith/Epoch, 1915)

reins of the frightened horse, and nearly had his arms pulled out before he stopped the beast and calmed it down.[54]

Both during the shooting and in postproduction, the negative was treated in what seems today an almost unbelievably casual fashion. Since most of the scenes were shot in only one take, there was only one piece of negative for each shot of the film. This single negative was passed around "from hand to hand," as Karl Brown recalled, and "could be gone through by anyone who wanted to find out something." Griffith, Bitzer, and others involved in the production consulted the negative on a regular basis to check for costume continuity and other such matters. When Griffith was satisfied that a given sequence was completed, the negative was sent to a New York lab for printing.[55]

On its release, *The Birth of a Nation* was phenomenally successful. The film was seen by more people and earned more money in its initial run than any film before it.[56] Bitzer shared in that success to the extent that his personal investment in the film—about $7,000 of the film's total $110,000 negative cost—was returned many times over. In addition, as a result of the film's success, Bitzer's potential earning power as a cameraman greatly

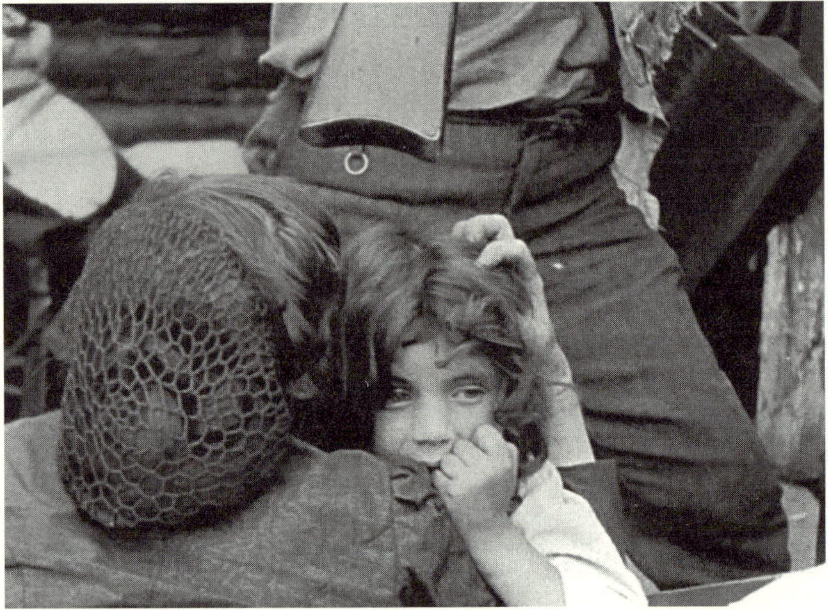

Figure 5. A striking use of the close-up for dramatic effect. (*Birth of a Nation,* D.W. Griffith/Epoch, 1915)

increased: "My services as a cameraman were much in demand," he remembered, "but I decided to stand with D.W."[57]

• • •

If *The Birth of a Nation* was Griffith's first attempt to demonstrate his complete mastery of filmmaking technique, *Intolerance* was an even more ambitious undertaking. Shot in Hollywood between the fall of 1914 and the early summer of 1916, *Intolerance* offered visual spectacle on a scale never before seen in an American film. It also adopted the highly unorthodox narrative strategy of interweaving four separate stories set in different historical periods. The four parts of *Intolerance*—the "Babylonian story" (set in 539 B.C.), the "Judean story" (27 A.D.), the "French story" (1572), and the "Modern story" (1914)—are interwoven through complex crosscutting, resulting in a narrative structure that has been both celebrated as a bravura example of modernist hybridity and dismissed as a "gigantic ruin of modernity."[58]

On an aesthetic level, *Intolerance* was clearly a response to Italian epics such as Mario Caserini's *The Last Days of Pompeii* (1913) and Giovanni

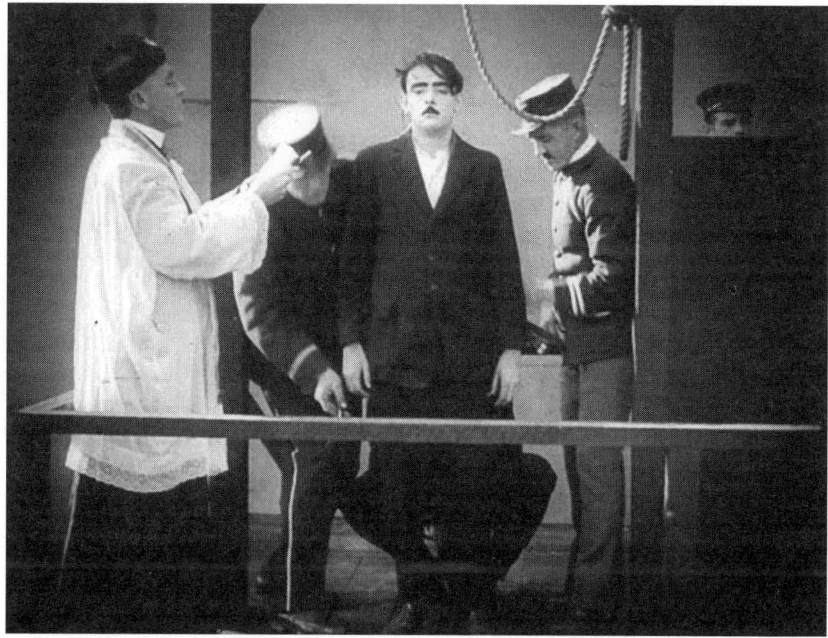

Figure 6. Harsh side-lighting creates a documentary-like effect in the execution scene from the "Modern story." (*Intolerance*, Triangle/Wark, 1916)

Pastrone's *Cabiria* (1914); more importantly, however, it was an attempt to surpass Griffith's own achievement in *The Birth of a Nation.*[59] Bitzer relates a conversation that demonstrates Griffith's desire for his new "Babylonian story" to "top *The Birth*": Griffith asked him whether, given the success of the sequence of the ride of the Klansmen in *The Birth of the Nation,* he could get a similar shot involving a herd of elephants for *Intolerance.*[60]

The first of the four sections of the film to be completed, in the summer of 1915, was the Modern story, also known as *The Mother and the Law.* Both Griffith and his cast and crew thought it was too slight to be released on its own on the heels of *The Birth of a Nation.* For this modern section of what would come to be *Intolerance,* Griffith had been determined to achieve a strong sense of realism. In early 1915, he, Bitzer, and Karl Brown had taken a trip to San Francisco in order to research prison conditions both at the city jail and at the San Quentin prison. The warden of San Quentin took them on a personal tour of the facility and even sprung the gallows trap so that they could fully appreciate the process of executing a condemned man. The company had also shot some sequences in the poorest sections of Los Angeles, where they staged a police raid on a house of prostitution and a battle between strikers and the National Guard.[61]

More than any other American film of its era, *Intolerance* puts in sharp relief the question of visual style. The question of style in *Intolerance,* and of Bitzer's role in creating that style, is a particularly vexed one, since each of the film's four sections is shot in a different stylistic register.[62] Charlie Keil has posed a number of very pertinent questions about the style—or styles—of *Intolerance,* most of which cannot be fully answered without a far longer discussion of the film than is appropriate here:

> Do the four worlds of *Intolerance* represent four [distinct] modes of film style, resulting in the culmination of not only Griffith's Biograph career, but also the achievements of international cinema up to this point? Or do the structural demands of four separate stories create a splintering effect, wherein integral stylistic systems inherent to each narrative line find themselves undone by the film's devotion to a process of alternations? Do the film's aspirations . . . constitute the first stage in what would eventually become the "epic" Hollywood style of DeMille and his successors? Or does Griffith's determination to produce a film that will demonstrate the aesthetic possibilities of the medium inevitably result in a stylistic approach so self-aware that coherence has been abandoned?[63]

Keil's list of questions demonstrates the difficulty of analyzing the visual style of *Intolerance,* Griffith's most complex, perplexing, and arguably greatest film. If the film can be said to have a coherent style that unites the four stories, it lies primarily in Bitzer's camerawork. An anthology of all the techniques Griffith and Bitzer had developed during the seven years of their collaboration, *Intolerance* includes elaborate tracking shots, dramatic crane shots, and unusual framing through unorthodox camera angles. A. R. Fulton observed, nearly a half century after the film's release, that no other film of the silent era equaled *Intolerance* in the variety of shots used:

> From its space-filling distance shot of the Persian Army, to a close shot of the sword of the Mighty Man of Valor, from a view of Belshazzar's feast as the observer looks down onto the court far below to close-ups of the feasters, it contains shots of varying distances and angles. There are close-ups of Margery Wilson's eyes and of just the lower part of Miriam Cooper's face. . . . In the attack on Babylon, the camera moves perpendicularly up the side of the great wall. In the modern story, it tilts up the wall of the Musketeer's room. For the pursuit-of-the-train sequence, it was mounted on an automobile, as it had been for photographing the ride of the Clan in *The Birth of a Nation.*[64]

As with the Biograph films, it is impossible to know to what extent Bitzer rather than Griffith was responsible for the tremendous variety of these shots. Which of the two men had the idea of strategically placing the camera in order to achieve striking compositions framed within architectural elements of the set such as gates and walls? Which of them designed the many different iris shots or partially masked shots that occur throughout the film? How did they decide on certain types of camera movement, such as the backward-moving travelling shot of a camel in the Judean story or the dramatic forward and downward tracking shot in the Babylonian story?

Most commentators have given the credit to Griffith for these stylistic innovations, or at least left the question ambiguous. The film historian Lewis Jacobs, writing in the late 1930s, argued that the "the dramatic framing of the image" in *Intolerance* is accomplished "with a variety and a skill that has never been equaled," noting in particular the "fluid and active participation of the camera." The amount and variety of camera movement in the film, according to Jacobs, "must have strained to the taxing point whatever was known then of camera grace and flexibility." These shots include the combination tracking and panning shot into the French court, the pan across the market of Jerusalem, and the combination pan and iris shot in the Babylonian marriage market sequence.[65] Though he does not mention Bitzer's contribution to the extraordinary camerawork of *Intolerance,* Jacobs was clearly aware of Bitzer's importance to Griffith, writing later in the book that "Bitzer's camera work in *Judith in Bethulia, The Birth of the Nation,* and *Intolerance* . . . awoke cameramen to the possibilities of their craft."[66] Robert Sklar, writing in the early 1970s, made much the same point as Jacobs about the technical accomplishment of *Intolerance,* which he calls "one of the greatest visual experiences in the history of the movies." Like Jacobs, Sklar celebrates "the emotional power and beauty of [the film's] screen imagery" and notes Griffith's "extraordinary ability to compose shots for the maximum effect of movement and spatial form." Also like Jacobs, he fails to mention the collaboration of Griffith and Bitzer that made such shots possible.[67]

Most of the film's scenes were captured, as in *The Birth of a Nation,* with a single Pathé camera operated by Bitzer. Some of the Babylon scenes, however, required the use of up to four cameras running simultaneously. Under Bitzer's supervision, the additional cameras were operated by Karl Brown, William Fildew, and Bitzer's nephew, Louis Bitzer. The extra cameras were needed to capture action on the enormous Babylon set, which measured three-eighths of a mile long, with walls about one hundred and forty feet high, making it the largest set that had ever been constructed in Hollywood. Bitzer recalled his involvement in the building of the spectacular set:

> Imagine laying out what were to be the mammoth stupendous sets for *Intolerance,* without sketches, plans, or blueprints at the beginning. . . . Mr. Griffith, "Huck" Wortman, and myself would have a pow-wow as to how the sun might be, its approximate arc-position months hence—and that was the beginning of the set for *Intolerance*. . . . [E]ventually, these walls and towers soared to a height of well over a hundred and fifty feet, although at the beginning their foundations were intended only for a fifty-foot height, which perturbed Huck a whole lot, and also shot my light-direction plan to pieces.[68]

The most spectacular shot in the film—and one of the most famous shots in the history of filmmaking—occurs during the Feast of Belshazzar sequence of the Babylonian story. Starting from a distance that allowed an establishing shot of the central section of the set, Bitzer's camera moves relentlessly forward, seemingly suspended in mid-air, and then begins a slow descent toward ground level. According to contemporary accounts, the shot as it appeared in initial versions of the film ended with a close-up of Belshazzar (Alfred Paget) and the Princess Beloved (Seena Owen). Griffith and Bitzer had originally planned to have Bitzer take the shot from a hot-air balloon that would be gradually floated toward the set. This, however, proved impossible, both because the shot could not be kept in focus and because Bitzer became sick from the rocking motion of the balloon. Instead, Huck Wortman built a 150-foot-high dolly mounted on six sets of four-wheeled railroad-car trucks, with an elevator in the center to allow the cameraman to be moved up or down during the shot. The pyramidal dolly could be pushed forward or backward along the rails by a team of twenty-five crew members. In order to make a smooth descending shot as the camera approached the set, the elevator had to be lowered very gradually by another group of workers as it ran along tracks starting far away from the set and moving slowly forward.[69]

Karl Brown, who was operating the second camera on the shot, describes it from his perspective:

> People by the thousands, all in gorgeous costumes, were packed everywhere people could be placed, even along the top of the great back wall with its winged god and its twin Trees of Life. We mounted in the elevator. Bitzer and Griffith were on the top level, and I was beside them with my camera. . . . They were ready, the dancers were ready, the light was brilliantly good. . . . The action began, with the bacchanal in

> full swing as the tower glided slowly forward and sank at the same time. The action was beautiful. Everything worked to perfection. The scene had started with a full shot of the entire set, and it continued inward and downward, until it ended with a close-up of the king and his Princess Beloved admiring one another to the rhythm of our great crowd of dancing girls.[70]

Bitzer, in an account written less than two decades after making *Intolerance,* substantially corroborates Brown's description of the shot, noting that it ended "in a close-up of large figures of the Prince and Princess seated on the throne, a pair of doves harnessed to a little golden chariot carrying love notes between them, and the whole thing moving so smooth *[sic]* as to be delightful."[71] In the DVD version of the film produced by Kino (2002), the shot begins with a slow forward and downward movement toward the dancers on the stairs, eventually reaching ground level. There is then a cut to a shot of Belshazzar and the Princess walking in a procession, followed by another cut to a one-shot of Belshazzar's chief guard (the Mighty Man of Valor, played by Elmo Lincoln) stroking a white dove. The forward tracking shot then resumes, moving toward the bottom of the stairs and then sweeping up and over the heads of the assembled crowd. This series of shots culminates in a diagonal pan upward and to the right, taking in the impressive elephant–topped pillars of the city walls.

Despite the spectacle afforded by such shots, however, *Intolerance* was only a mixed success with critics and to a great extent an outright failure with audiences.[72] Of the film's four sections, only the Modern story was truly compelling as a narrative. The other three stories, while they contain moments of excitement and a good deal of epic grandeur, mostly left audiences either confused or bored. Indeed, despite the explanations of the action given in the title cards, the action of the film is difficult to follow on a first viewing, and with the exception of the Modern story the viewer does not identify strongly enough with the characters to care deeply about what happens to them. In the Babylonian section of the film, as has often been noted, the audience has little investment in who wins the dramatically staged battle between the Babylonian and Persian armies: what matters more than the lives of individual characters is the spectacle of the battle itself.

Alexander Woollcott's review of the film in *The New York Times* spoke for many contemporary viewers in contrasting the film's "unprecedented and indescribable splendor of pageantry" with its "grotesque incoherence of design and utter fatuity of thought."[73] The one aspect of *Intolerance* that received almost universal praise was its cinematography. Bitzer's photography, wrote

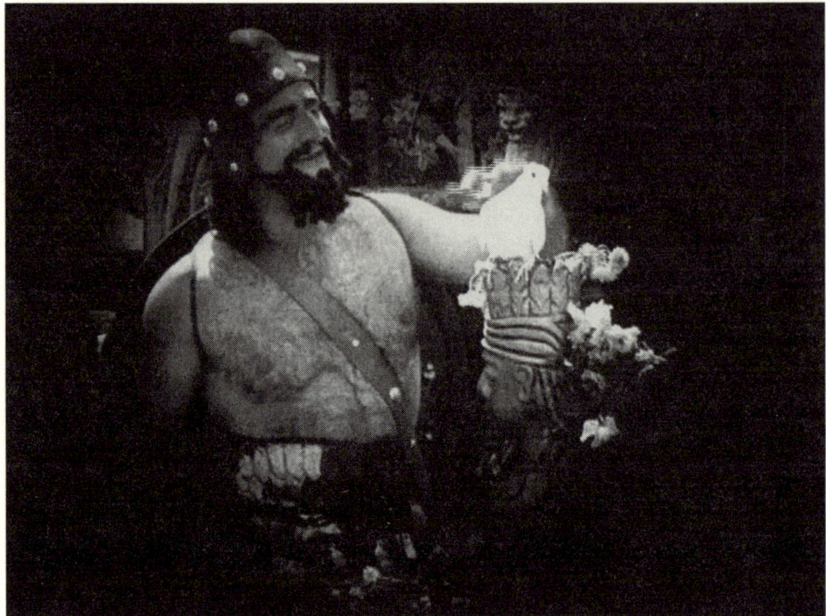

Figure 7. Expressive lighting of the Mighty Man of Valor in the "Babylonian story." (*Intolerance*, Triangle/Wark, 1916)

the *Photoplay* critic Julian Johnson, "flows like the transparent, limpid style of a finished writer ... without tricks, and without imperfections."[74] With *Intolerance*, Bitzer had shot his greatest masterpiece, a film that displays both his virtuosic technique and his visual artistry.[75]

• • •

The argument has often been made that the collaboration of Griffith and Bitzer reached its highest point with the back-to-back successes of *The Birth of a Nation* and *Intolerance* and that the films they made beginning in the late 1910s represent a steady decline both in artistic ambition and in the quality and originality of the films.[76] Although there is much evidence to support this view, the films Griffith and Bitzer continued to produce together from 1916 to 1925 should not be entirely neglected. Griffith's films of the late 1910s and early 1920s—while they may not exhibit either the epic scope or the breathtaking technical brilliance of *The Birth of a Nation* and *Intolerance*—nonetheless represent an important contribution to the development of American filmmaking during the silent era.[77] An entire book could be written on the visual style of Griffith's post-

Intolerance films, which have thus far received far less attention than either the Biograph films or the mid-1910s masterpieces. In this chapter, however, I can offer only a brief overview of the final years of the collaboration of Griffith and Bitzer.

Hearts of the World, photographed in 1917 in France, England, and the United States, was the first Griffith-Bitzer collaboration after *Intolerance.*[78] Though by no means one of Griffith's masterpieces, *Hearts of the World* was one of the director's longest-running and most commercially successful films, enjoying enormous success from its release in March 1918 until the end of the war. Though the film has been justly criticized for containing scenes that do not accurately present the circumstances of World War I combat, as well as for its blatantly propagandistic depiction of German brutality, it combines powerful battle scenes with impressive compositions and meticulously lit interiors. One particularly striking scene presents the character played by Lillian Gish (called only "The Girl" in the film) wandering onto a mist-shrouded battlefield while holding her wedding dress and finding the body of her fiancé.

Over the next two years, Griffith and Bitzer shot an extraordinary number of films, as Griffith tried to fulfill the terms of his contract with Artcraft Pictures.[79] *The Great Love,* now a lost film, was made largely with footage left over from *Hearts of the World. The Greatest Thing in Life,* another lost film, was released in December 1918. In rapid succession, Griffith and Bitzer then shot *A Romance of Happy Valley, The Girl Who Stayed at Home, True Heart Susie, Broken Blossoms, Scarlet Days,* and *The Greatest Question.*

Among these films, the only one with a firm claim to canonical status is *Broken Blossoms.*[80] Starring Lillian Gish, Richard Barthelmess, and Donald Crisp, the film was the first feature on which Bitzer was forced the share the credit with another cinematographer. Hendrik Sartov was a portrait photographer who had taken a series of head-shots of Lillian Gish for *Hearts of the World.* Griffith hired Sartov to take a few close-ups of Gish for *The Greatest Thing in Life,* and based on the success of those shots, Sartov was hired to work alongside Bitzer on *Broken Blossoms,* doing filmed close-ups of Gish.[81] Despite a very limited understanding of the techniques of motion picture photography, Sartov had the ability to shoot effective close-ups with a lens specially designed for that purpose. Karl Brown, loyal to Bitzer and therefore resentful of Griffith's new cameraman, took the opportunity to examine Sartov's "magic lens" and found it to be "nothing in the world but a yellowed old spectacle lens." At over six inches (150mm) long, it required the photographer to be at a considerable distance from his subject. If his f-stop was adjusted to allow a small enough amount of light to enter the lens, Sartov was able to focus on Gish's face in such a way as to leave everything around it in a blur.[82] This soft, hazy image suited Gish's desire to play an ethereal character whose film age was often younger than her actual age. Sartov never mastered the art of hand-cranking, so he was incapable of creating subtle effects in the way Bitzer could, and he knew far less than Bitzer about the mechanics of lighting and shooting.[83] Nevertheless, Sartov appears to have been talented enough as a photographer to represent a threat to Bitzer: Griffith used him on several films, either as the lead cinematographer or as Bitzer's assistant.

Though it is not entirely clear how many of the close-ups of Gish in *Broken Blossoms* were shot by Bitzer and how many by Sartov, Bitzer's own story of how he came to shoot one of the first softly lit close-ups in the history of cinema is one of the great tales of cinematographic lore. Arriving late on the set after having tied on one too many the night before, Bitzer hastily called for the lights to be turned up, focusing his camera on Gish's eyes. The crew had been having trouble lighting Gish's scenes in a way that she considered satisfactory, since she was determined to preserve her beautiful screen image in every scene of the film. On this particular morning, however, Bitzer forgot to stop down his lens after checking for focus. Halfway through the scene, Brown pointed out Bitzer's mistake, but seeing that Griffith was happy with the way the scene was playing, Bitzer continued shooting.

> Now the lens I was using was a Dallmeyr F.1.9 with a large aperture. It was a lens I never would have used wide open, because of its depth and general fuzziness and uncertainty. This was a fast lens, however, and with low-key lighting from directions I would not use ordinarily, and my focus on the eyes as I saw them . . . I made the first beautiful soft-focus head [shot] on the screen. . . . We had a beautiful new atmospheric effect never before seen on film, something that would lend itself to the dull gold sheen I had desired. Throughout the rest of *Broken Blossoms,* I went right on duplicating [that style of] lighting and photography.[84]

It is difficult to know whether Bitzer's account of the making of the shot should be taken at face value. Since Griffith had hired Sartov specifically for the purpose of shooting close-ups of Gish, it seems implausible that Bitzer would have discovered the technique for doing so in such a serendipitous fashion. But whether Bitzer or Sartov created this or other "soft" shots such as those of the Chinese harbor and of Lucy sleeping in the moonlight in the Yellow Man's room, they impressed critics and audiences alike. Julian Johnson called *Broken Blossoms* "the very finest expression on the screen so far," while praising the cinematography in extravagant terms: "The photography is not only perfect, but, with caution, is innovational, and approximates, in its larger lights and softnesses of close view, the details of bright and dark upon the finest canvasses in the Louvres of the world."[85]

The creation of the new "soft style" would have important implications for the work of American cinematographers of the early 1920s. The cinematographer Arthur Miller, for example, was so impressed with the visual style of *Broken Blossoms* that within months he was using a similar technique with the actress Mae Miller in *On with the Dance* (1920). According to Miller, "the fad become so overdone that at times it was virtually impossible to identify the performer on the screen, but the feminine stars demanded it."[86] Sartov continued to specialize in the technique, and Kristin Thompson notes that his cinematography for Griffith's *Dream Street* (1921) exaggerated still further the soft, hazy look that he and Bitzer had created for *Broken Blossoms*.[87] However, it appears that Sartov's aesthetic range was limited to this one style: when its popularity began to wane in the late 1920s, Sartov's services were no longer in demand and he made the decision to retire. After working on several pictures for Griffith in the early 1920s and a handful of films at MGM—including *La Bohème* (1926) and *The Scarlet Letter* (1926)—he disappeared from the rolls of Hollywood cameramen.

Bitzer was less interested in continuing to develop the aesthetics of the soft look, and in the winter and early spring of 1920, he shot his next Griffith film, *Way Down East*, with a sharper, less gauzy focus. It remains to this day a visually stunning film: Bitzer's exteriors are particularly effective, taking full advantage of the natural landscape of New England and New York's Westchester County. An old-fashioned but highly effective melodrama, *Way Down East* reaches its finest artistic expression in its climactic closing sequence: the heroine Anna Moore (Lillian Gish) stumbles blindly through a howling blizzard and then walks out onto the ice floes in the middle of a river, only to be rescued in the nick of time by David Bartlett (Richard Barthelmess). In Richard Schickel's estimation, the sequence "stands alone among the several great climaxes of Griffith's work, and has, indeed, few rivals anywhere in the cinema."[88] Bitzer shot the first part during an actual blizzard that was blowing off the Long Island Sound; he shot the second part—in which the two characters are being carried downriver on the ice floes—in early March near White River Junction, Vermont. As Bitzer shot and reshot the scene, Gish and the crew huddled around a bonfire, hoping the extreme cold would not freeze the oil in Bitzer's camera.

Way Down East was a major success, both critically and commercially, and despite its $800,000 cost (the highest of any picture Griffith had made), it turned a substantial profit, grossing an estimated $4.5 million. Unfortunately, the death of two members of Griffith's acting company—Clarine Seymour and Robert Harron—within months of the film's release put a damper on the company's success. Bitzer claimed that after Harron's passing, "some thread of unity seemed to leave us. . . . [I]t was a falling away and a breaking up of our former trust and friendship [and] it was never the same again."[89] Whether it was the deaths of Harron and Seymour or other factors that led to the end of the "trust and friendship" between Griffith and Bitzer, after *Way Down East,* Bitzer's experience of working for Griffith would never be the same again. It is no doubt significant that the published narrative of Bitzer's career ends in 1920 with the making of *Way Down East,* leaving the last decade of Bitzer's collaboration with Griffith largely undocumented. "We had safely reached the summit, set by Griffith," Bitzer wrote, "and the applause had been mighty. It was now time to relax and rest on our laurels."[90] In reality, however, Bitzer would never have such an opportunity: Bitzer's work as a cinematographer during the 1920s was inconsistent, and he ended his career in fairly ignominious fashion, as the assistant to Karl Struss.

• • •

It is hard to know the exact cause of Bitzer's fall from Griffith's graces. It appears that by the early 1920s Bitzer may have begun to drink, disappearing for days at a time.[91] Bitzer was also openly jealous of Sartov's growing importance to Griffith, remarking sardonically in his autobiography that, "With the entrance of Sartov, I became the pupil." Bitzer did not approve of some of Griffith's other choices either, including his decision to make the actress Carol Dempster his new leading lady. Griffith, understandably, was reluctant to have tensions on the set, and it may have become easier simply to replace Bitzer on those films in which Dempster starred. Another factor may have been that Bitzer's technique—at the cutting edge of American cinematography in the mid-1910s—was now being equaled or even surpassed by younger men. And finally, there is Karl Brown's contention that Griffith simply enjoyed playing one cameraman against another, just as he did with his actors.[92]

In her autobiography, Lillian Gish provides an additional clue as to the reason for Bitzer's decline. During the filming of *Orphans in the Storm,* for which Bitzer and Sartov were hired as co-cinematographers, Bitzer did not meet the standard of collegiality which Griffith demanded:

> Billy Bitzer and Hendrik Sartov were the cameramen on *Orphans.* Sartov had helped with the photography of *Way Down East* and [had]

> photographed all of *Dream Street.* I heard that Billy was becoming embittered by Sartov's rising influence. During the filming of *Orphans,* his resentment of Sartov became apparent. Once, when D.W. asked the two of them to work together on a problem, Billy bristled and refused to help. Another time when Sartov asked him for advice, Billy said, "Why should I help you take my job away?" Then one day, as we were scheduled to shoot a major scene, Billy failed to appear. D.W. waited for a time and then motioned Sartov to begin shooting. Billy was never again the sole cameraman on a Griffith production.[93]

In one of the most surprising passages in his memoirs, Bitzer suggests that it was the ridicule he experienced for continuing to use his old-fashioned Pathé camera that drove him away from Griffith's set in the early 1920s:

> The Pathé camera, which I had worked with throughout so much of my career, was scorned by all but me. Stubbornly I clung to it, and was reviled and ridiculed. I took to staying away from the set as much as possible. When the studio called, I made excuses for not reporting.[94]

Bitzer did, however, report back to the studio often enough to shoot two films for Griffith in the mid-1920s. In 1923, he shot *The White Rose* on location in Louisiana and Florida, assisted by Sartov and Hal Sintzenich. On *America* (1924), Bitzer led a large camera crew that included Sartov, Sintzenich, and Marcel Le Picard. Both of these films exhibit a high level of visual artistry, suggesting that Bitzer had by no means lost his ability to do excellent work. *The White Rose*—rarely seen today—is one of the most visually striking of Griffith's 1920s films. It has a more leisurely pace than some of Griffith's other films of the period, allowing Bitzer's attractively backlit photography to feature in a number of scenes. Jan-Christopher Horak remarks that Griffith seemed to linger more than usual over "the lyric beauty of the images," allowing the story to develop more through composition and lighting than—as had been typical of Griffith's films—through editing.[95] *America,* the last of Griffith's films on which Bitzer served as lead cinematographer, is another masterpiece of visual style. For George Mitchell, the film represents one of the high points of mid-1920s cinematography, containing a number of impressively shot scenes, which include Paul Revere's ride, with shots of Revere's galloping horse taken from a camera mounted on an automobile; the battle of Bunker Hill, shot through the rigging of a British ship; extreme long shots of Fort Sacrifice under British attack; and shots of the Old North Church as seen across a moonlit Charlestown Bay.[96]

Griffith shot his next four films without Bitzer, using Sartov, Harry Fischbeck, and Hal Sintzenich as his cinematographers. When Bitzer returned to Griffith's crew in the fall of 1927, it was as the assistant to Karl Struss.[97] It is significant that the last person to replace Bitzer as Griffith's lead cinematographer was Struss, a member of a new generation of Hollywood cinematographers that had by the mid-1920s almost completely superseded Bitzer and his contemporaries. Struss's masterful lighting—especially on *Lady of the Pavements*—no doubt convinced Griffith that he no longer needed Bitzer as part of this filmmaking team.

In the early 1930s, Bitzer retired from cinematography and moved to New York City, where he took whatever film-related work he could find. For a time, Bitzer worked for a project funded by the WPA that involved preparing filmstrips and recorded lectures to be used in visual education in the city's schools. Later, he served as a technical advisor to the Film Library of the Museum of Modern Art, where he collated and annotated old Biograph bulletins. After suffering a series of heart attacks, Bitzer was sent to the Motion Picture Country Home, a California retirement community for indigent show business veterans. He died there in 1944, at the age of seventy-two. Bitzer's career had spanned the entire silent era from the mid-1890s until the late 1920s, an astounding stretch of time for a cameraman of his generation. During that period, he and Griffith had achieved a uniquely successful pairing of filmmaking talents, resulting in the first artistic and technical collaboration of such importance in the history of American filmmaking.

2 Rebel with a Camera

Gregg Toland, William Wyler, and the Development of Deep-Focus Technique

Toland's acknowledged brilliance has placed him in the most nearly ideal position any Director of Photography has enjoyed since the halcyon days when D.W. Griffith and Billy Bitzer were between them creating the basic technique of the screen.

Walter Blanchard

It is obvious that the relationship of the cameraman to his director must be one of complete coordination. The director will have his own ideas about camera angles, but in the final analysis it is the cameraman who must determine whether those ideas are workable and what the results will be.

Gregg Toland

The collaboration of twenty-five-year-old director Orson Welles and his thirty-six-year-old director of photography Gregg Toland on *Citizen Kane* remains the most celebrated partnership between a director and a cinematographer in the history of American cinema. Toland provided Welles with what many regard as the most inspired cinematography of the studio era, combining elaborate camera movement and striking compositions that involve multiple planes of focus. Toland had experimented with deep-focus techniques in his collaborations with other directors, but his single-film collaboration with Welles allowed him to make his most extreme departure from the conventional style of the period. The radically new techniques Toland used in making *Citizen Kane* enabled him, in the words of David Bordwell, "to consolidate a unified 'look' as his trademark" at a time when most studio cinematographers conformed to a relatively standardized visual style.[1]

Although discussions of Toland's work have been largely focused on his work with Welles on *Kane,* I would argue that Toland's work on Welles's film needs to be understood within the larger context of his career. In fact,

Toland's most significant partnership with a director was not his single-film collaboration with Welles, but rather his six-film collaboration with William Wyler. As an extremely successful collaboration for a number of films between a talented and commercially successful director and a brilliant cinematographer, both operating at the height of their powers, the Wyler-Toland partnership is instructive on at least two levels.[2] First, the collaboration allows us to observe the gradual development of a particular photographic technique—the use of greater depth of focus—from its beginnings in the mid-1930s to its full fruition in the 1940s. Second, the partnership of Wyler and Toland provides an important model of a working relationship in which the director and cinematographer functioned as relative equals, a rare phenomenon in Hollywood studio filmmaking.

Toland's unique status among Hollywood cinematographers has led some to make explicitly auteurist claims on his behalf. Andrew Sarris, for example, made the famous pronouncement: "Subtract Gregg Toland from Welles and you still have a mountain; subtract Toland from Wyler and you have a molehill."[3] If Sarris's suggestion that Toland was primarily responsible for the visual quality of Wyler's films is in part a put-down of Wyler's status as an auteurist director, it is also an acknowledgment of the decisive role a cinematographer like Toland could play in the creation a director's visual style. Toland's privileged position in the history of American cinema can be largely justified on the basis of the consistently outstanding cinematography in the black-and-white films he shot.[4] Toland photographed an extraordinary number of the most celebrated black-and-white masterpieces in the history of American cinema, including *Wuthering Heights, The Long Voyage Home, The Grapes of Wrath, Citizen Kane, The Little Foxes,* and *The Best Years of Our Lives.* But even this impressive list of films cannot fully account for the exceptionally high regard in which he continues to be held both by film historians and by cinematographers. This phenomenon raises the intriguing question: Why does Toland receive so much more attention than contemporaries such as Arthur Miller, an excellent studio cinematographer whose work was just as well regarded by his peers?[5]

Toland's career remains unique in at least four respects, each of which, I would argue, contributes to his exalted status. First, Toland's rise to the top of his profession occurred more rapidly and at a younger age than that of any other studio cinematographer of the sound era. A fully accredited cinematographer by the age of twenty-seven, Toland had, by the time of his death at age forty-four, collaborated with a number of the most talented directors in Hollywood, including King Vidor, Rouben Mamoulian, William Wyler, John Ford, Orson Welles, and Howard Hawks.[6]

Second, Toland benefitted greatly from being able to remain under contract to one producer, Samuel Goldwyn, from the late 1920s until the late 1940s, and to retain essentially the same crew for most of that time.[7] Patrick Ogle explains that "the relative security of employment under the Goldwyn contract and stability of competent operative personnel on his film crew . . . provide[d] Toland the kind of breathing space needed for coherent creative endeavor."[8] On nearly every film he shot for Goldwyn, Toland had the opportunity to spend long hours discussing the photographic plan with the director, writer, and art director, often starting weeks before the production began. Such preproduction involvement by a cinematographer was extremely rare in 1930s Hollywood. Toland's unique arrangement with Goldwyn not only gave him security of employment, but it also provided him with a degree of supervision over sets, décor, and costumes.

Third, Toland's arrangement with Goldwyn allowed him, unlike other studio cameramen, time to experiment with film stocks, lighting, cameras, and lenses and to invent devices and gadgets that would enhance his cinematography. Toland's many technical innovations include a counterbalanced dolly head that allowed the camera to be moved for short distances without the use of a tripod or dolly, special lightweight dolly tracks, a hydraulically operated tripod, and the use of special Waterhouse Stops in his lenses.[9]

Fourth, and most importantly, Toland is indelibly associated with the perfected use of "deep focus," a photographic technique that had a significant, even revolutionary impact on the style of Hollywood films. Toland received an unprecedented amount of attention for his use of deep focus in *Citizen Kane,* an attention which caused him a loss of popularity among his fellow cinematographers after 1941. At the time of his death, Toland was preparing yet another new technical innovation: an "ultimate focus" lens with an aperture even smaller than those he had used on *Citizen Kane,* which he intended to inaugurate on his next film, *Roseanna McCoy.* The ultimate focus lens had an extraordinarily small aperture of f/64, offering the possibility of a depth of field extending from less than six inches to infinity. Unfortunately, Toland never had the opportunity to use the lens in a film, since he died three weeks before the shooting on *Roseanna McCoy* began.

• • •

Born in Charleston, Illinois, on May 29, 1904, Toland was the only child of working-class parents. After his parents' divorce, he moved with his mother to Southern California. At fifteen, Toland was forced to drop out of school and take a job as a $12-a-week office boy and messenger at the William Fox Studios. Intensely anxious both about his lack of formal education and about his diminutive size (he stood somewhere between five feet one and five feet two), Toland developed what his biographer Roger Wallace has called "a nearly obsessive drive to prove himself to anyone and everyone who might question the shortcomings about which he was so self-conscious."[10] These same anxieties later made Toland an extreme perfectionist. He claimed, for example, to have watched *Citizen Kane* twenty-seven times in the projection room before approving the final print. When *The Best Years of Our Lives* was released, Toland personally checked all forty-one release prints of the film and visited all the Los Angeles movie theaters where the film was being shown in order to examine their projection equipment.[11]

By the age of sixteen, Toland was an assistant cameraman earning $18 a week. Working on short comedies directed by Al St. John, Toland moved quickly up through the ranks to a position as one of the highest-paid assistant cameramen in Hollywood, with a salary of $60 a week. In the late 1920s, Toland began working for George Barnes, who took him on as his assistant cameraman and soon promoted him to co-cinematographer. When Barnes was signed to a five-year contract with the Samuel Goldwyn studio, Toland went with him. In 1931, Barnes left Goldwyn in order to shoot films at other studios. Toland, though younger than any of his Hollywood peers, inherited a privileged position as the studio's lead cinematographer.

Over the next decade, Toland was the cinematographer on an astonishing twenty-five of Goldwyn's thirty-five productions, giving the studio's films of the period a consistently high visual quality that no other studio could match. As Leonard Maltin has suggested, nearly every film photographed by Toland during this period is "worthy of detailed attention," though most of them are rarely seen today.[12] Toland photographed a trio of films featuring Goldwyn's glamorous "discovery" Anna Sten (*Nana* [Dorothy Arzner, 1934], *We Live Again* [Rouben Mamoulian, 1934], and *The Wedding Night* [King Vidor, 1935]), as well as two films—*Les Misérables* (Richard Boleslawski, 1935) and *The Road to Glory* (Howard Hawks, 1936)—made while on loan to producer Darryl Zanuck. These mid-1930s films do not yet contain deep-focus compositions, but they do demonstrate Toland's growing technical proficiency, particularly in the use of lighting for dramatic effect. Both *Nana* and *Les Misérables* (for which Toland received his first Academy Award nomination) are distinguished by their mood-driven chiaroscuro effects, while *The Wedding Night* achieves effective use of light and shadow, particularly in the later scenes.[13]

Toland's career as a lead cameraman corresponded closely with the beginnings of the sound era: his development as Hollywood's most successful cinematographer can be seen as paralleling the development of Hollywood cinematography during the first decade of sound. The first and most important change for cinematographers of the early sound era was the drastic reduction in the amount of camera movement. Since cameras now had to be installed in soundproof booths to avoid their noises from being picked up on the soundtrack, any camera movement involving the use of dollies and cranes was impossible. As is readily apparent in Hollywood films of 1929 and 1930, this restriction created a very static visual style. A second problem encountered by cinematographers of the early 1930s was a greatly decreased depth of field. With the camera now enclosed in a booth, longer lenses had to be used, which resulted in a generally shallower plane of focus. In films made between 1929 and 1932, sharply focused foreground figures often stand out against blurred backgrounds to a degree that would have been unacceptable in the late silent era and would also no longer be tolerated just a few years later.

Equally important changes involved lighting. The arc lights that had been the primary source of Hollywood lighting throughout most of the silent era were no longer a viable option, since their distinct "sizzling" sound could easily be heard on the soundtrack. Incandescent lights, which had already begun to be used in silent films of the mid- to late 1920s, would soon replace arc lights almost completely. The advantages of incandescent lights—usually Mazda lamps, a brand of General Electric incandescent lights—were difficult to deny. They were silent; they could be brought in close to the actors without creating excessive heat or irritating the eyes; they could be faded up or down to allow for a wide range of lighting effects; and they used about a third less electricity than either arcs or mercury tubes, thus saving the studios a considerable amount of money on each production. On the other hand, the light the incandescents produced was flatter and less brilliant than that produced by the carbon arcs and thus could not produce the sculptural effects on which cinematographers had come to depend. The use of incandescent lights led to a greater standardization of lighting techniques during the early 1930s, offering less opportunity for creative lighting effects.[14]

Another by-product of the use of enclosed camera booths was that, because of the decrease in camera movement, it became necessary to have several cameras shooting a single scene. Patrick Keating asserts that most cinematographers welcomed the change to multicamera shooting because it allowed the cinematographer to relinquish the role of "manual laborer" (in other words, it allowed him not to operate his own camera) and to serve as the "supervisor for a team of camera operators"; however, this was not universally the case.[15] Joseph Walker, for example, the lead cinematographer at Columbia Pictures and Frank Capra's long-term collaborator, strongly disliked multicamera shooting, which he felt created a bright, undifferentiated lighting scheme and took much of the decision-making authority out of the cinematographer's hands. Walker complained that the quality of the photography generally suffered from this practice:

> No longer would the director ask "How was the camera?" Now, the all-important verdict "OK for sound!" brought an immediate "Print it!" Heretofore, I had had a freedom to create interesting effects with a moving camera. No more! Miserably ensconced in a soundproofed stationary booth, I shot through heavy plate-glass at fixed scenes. It was unbelievably hot and cramped, with barely enough room for myself and a bulky camera. Depression gripped me as I filmed long, uninspiring scenes of "talking stage actors" from my stifling booth.[16]

Other cinematographers, such as Hal Mohr and Bert Glennon, voiced similar complaints about multicamera shooting. Glennon, writing in 1930, noted that cinematography had "never been in a more anomalous or dangerous position":

> On the one hand, [cinematography] has reached a state of great mechanical perfection, but on the other hand, its artistic growth has been arrested in the past year, and on every side we see irrefutable evidence that the art of the camera, upon which all screen art is based, is in danger of being overlooked and becoming stagnant and buried beneath a great maze of ohms, watts, amps, and thoughtlessness. Screen audiences want beauty. They appreciate it. They need it.[17]

Fortunately, the problems caused by the introduction of sound were temporary. In order to liberate the camera from its stationary booth, studios and camera companies worked together to develop various kinds of lightweight blimps that could muffle the sound of the camera while still permitting it to be moved. Though the early blimps were too heavy to be put on tripods, they could be set on rollers, giving them enough mobility for simple tracking shots. Interior shots still had to be made through plate glass, but cameras were quieted enough by the blimp that exteriors could often be shot without additional sound-muffling devices. As the 1930s progressed, cameras were increasingly set on tripods, cranes, crab dollies, and "Rotoambulators" (a combination dolly and crane). Cameramen were once again able to introduce more camera movement into their shots.

If the invention of lightweight blimpless cameras made possible more flexible camera movement in the early 1930s, the introduction of a series of faster and higher-quality film stocks offered the potential for sharper images and greater depth of field. In 1935, Eastman introduced its Super X film, with an ASA rating of 32. By the standards of even a decade later, this was not a particularly fast film stock, but it was a major advance over the stocks available to cinematographers of the era. In 1938, Eastman introduced two other films stocks that allowed further improvements in the quality of black-and-white filmmaking: the Plus X film stock, rated 125 ASA, and the even faster and finer-grained Super XX, rated at 250 ASA.

But improved technology can only take a cinematographer so far. What Toland displayed to a greater degree than any of his contemporaries was a drive to use the available technologies to push the limits of visual style and expression. As he wrote in an article published in *American Cinematographer* in February 1941, the American film industry had so far made only "a few cautious, tentative experiments with . . . technical innovations to produce improved photo-dramatic results."[18] Toland felt that he and other cinematographers were "on the track of something significant," but that instead of using such technical innovations "conservatively" as most were doing in Hollywood films, they should "experiment free-handedly," creating innovative cinematography throughout an entire production. Such experimenting would have been difficult within the highly controlled structure of Hollywood studio filmmaking, but it is nonetheless interesting to consider the direction Hollywood cinematography might have taken in the 1940s had it not been for the interruption of Toland's career with the United States' entry into the war.

• • •

There is a well-developed mythology around the idea that Gregg Toland invented deep-focus cinematography during the making of *Citizen Kane.* In fact, it would be more accurate to say that *Citizen Kane* represented the culmination of a series of films in which Toland experimented with a technique of deep focus, and that at this point in cinema history he had taken the technique further than any other cinematographer. Toland's experimentation with the technique certainly pushed American cinematography in the direction of deeper focus, but the technique itself had existed for at least three decades. A technique of deep focus can be seen in the films of D.W. Griffith and his contemporaries as early as 1910. As Charlie Keil notes in his book on early American cinema, filmmakers beginning about 1910 attempted "a modified version of deep focus," and commentators consistently praised such attempts.[19] A contemporary review of the 1911 film *Captain Kate* suggests that certain films that attempted to carry a depth of focus made it possible to see the actors' faces "not merely in the near foreground but also in the middle [ground] and even in the distance." Such "marvels of camera work" permitted the acting "to carry the audience very effectively."[20] While this kind of cinematography appears to anticipate by several decades Toland's accomplishments in the films he shot for Welles and Wyler, it is important to remember that it was far less complex to achieve such depth in exterior shooting with a silent movie camera than it would be to do so under the conditions of sound filmmaking.

The most often-cited example of the use of deep-focus cinematography in a Hollywood film prior of Toland's development of the technique is *Transatlantic* (1931), directed by William K. Howard and photographed by James Wong Howe. Howe used a 24mm lens and intense lighting to achieve a depth of focus that is impressive when compared with the very limited depth of field found in most Hollywood films of the early 1930s. Nevertheless, as Barry Salt points out, Howe's photography in *Transatlantic* is "far from being 'deep focus' in the modern, post–*Citizen Kane* sense." Howe was able to achieve a sharp focus only in a space between about five feet and thirty feet away from the camera.[21]

Other films of the early 1930s also exhibited a limited use of deep-focus photography in certain scenes. In Frank Capra's *American Madness* (1932), for example, cinematographer Joseph Walker was able to achieve an increased depth of focus by lighting several planes of interrelated action at once. For the first scene of the film, which takes place in the vault of the bank that serves as the central setting for the film's action, Walker lit five distinct spatial planes simultaneously. In the plane closest to the camera, we see the grillwork of the barred cage surrounding the vault, while in the second plane we see the door and passageway leading to the inside of the vault. In the third plane, there is another interior grillwork, followed by a fourth plane of the men inside counting out money, and a fifth plane of the bars surrounding the innermost vault. The camera setups that Capra and Walker used for the scene are not those typically used in a film of the early sound era. Rather than shooting the men inside the vault from a series of different angles, Capra and Walker shot the scene from one central axis, but at a series of different distances, thus anticipating the kinds of deep-focus effects Toland and other cinematographers would achieve nearly a decade later.

As Toland's fellow cinematographers were quick to point out, his experiments in deep-focus technique during the late 1930s were part of an industry-wide shift in photographic style. James Wong Howe noted that "before Gregg Toland . . . came along with his *Citizen Kane,* there was [already] a marked tendency in every studio toward crisper definition and greater depth, sometimes accompanied by increased contrast."[22] Victor Milner described how, in one shot of the 1939 film *Union Pacific,* he was able to use a faster film stock to create greater depth: rather than using half the amount of light he would normally have used, he shot with the same amount of light, stopped down the lens, and "gained in depth and crispness in a way that enhanced the mood of the shot."[23]

On a technical level, there is no doubt that this enhanced deep focus or "pan focus" was made more possible by the use of coated lenses, Super XX film (which could render a sharper image with less light), and very powerful twin-arc broadside lamps. A number of Hollywood cinematographers other than Toland exploited these same techniques. As David Bordwell suggests, several American films of the early 1940s—including Boris Ingster's *Stranger on the Third Floor* (1940), William Dieterle's *The Devil and Daniel Webster* (1941), John Huston's *The Maltese Falcon* (1941), and Sam Wood's *King's Row* (1942)—"displayed a penchant for depth staging and deep-focus imagery."[24] In *King's Row,* released in early 1942, James Wong Howe used an extreme form of deep focus for a shot in which a hypodermic needle is seen in the foreground—at a distance of only eighteen inches from the camera—while the character played by Robert Cummings is seen in clear focus through a doorway at a depth of between fifteen and twenty feet.[25] Nevertheless, such shots were by no means common in early 1940s Hollywood; the deep-focus technique would not become a stylistic norm for American filmmakers until the second half of the 1940s.[26]

Evidence that some cinematographers other than Toland were interested in achieving deeper focus can be seen in Hal Mohr's invention of a novel "swinging lens-mount," which he used in two of his 1936 films—*Bullets and Ballots* and *Green Pastures.* This lens mount allowed the lens to be rotated in such a way that the camera could maintain in clear focus "everything from the immediate foreground to infinity."[27] Although Mohr's invention would seem to have been an important development in Hollywood cinematography, other DPs did not adopt it, and it quickly disappeared from the scene.[28]

Toland began to experiment with depth of focus as early as 1932. According to John Howard Lawson, Toland and his crew studied the bullfighting sequences from Sergei Eisenstein's *Qué Viva Mexico!* while shooting *The Kid from Spain,* and Toland may have learned certain techniques of deep focus from that film.[29] The idea that Toland had been gradually developing his technique throughout the 1930s is further supported by Stanley Cortez, who noted that Toland and his assistant Bert Shipman maintained a darkroom in the old Paramount building on Vine Street, where they would engage in various experiments: "I would dare say that it was here that Gregg really got into shooting in depth. He was experimenting with that [technique]."[30]

In an essay explaining his cinematographic approach to *Citizen Kane,* Toland pointed out that the majority of Hollywood films of the 1930s sacrificed portions of the visual field by focusing the camera on the primary center of interest (usually the star actors), while allowing the parts of the shot lying either in front of or behind the focal point to "fuzz out": this practice, he argued, is contrary to the experience of the human eye, which "sees everything before it (within reasonable distance) clearly and sharply."[31] Toland's justification for deep-focus cinematography on the basis that it more closely approximates the experience of the eye and is thus more "natural" or "realistic" has had its adherents—most notably the French film theoretician André Bazin—but it has also had its share of critics: Robert Carringer, for example, dismissed Toland's claims about the visual style of *Citizen Kane* as "almost comical."[32] Further, it needs to be acknowledged that some of Toland's more extreme deep-focus shots in *Citizen Kane* were done using special effects such as matte work and double exposures. Nevertheless, the use of a deep-focus technique in the camera itself was instrumental in the creation of a visual style that most viewers considered radical, even aesthetically jarring.[33]

Some filmmakers quickly grasped the significance of Toland's deep-focus technique, though not all embraced it. What makes *Citizen Kane* most strikingly different from other films of the period is the sense of all the action taking place around the central character, but including several planes of action simultaneously rather than cutting back and forth between planes of action. Hilton Als explains how this difference functions within a scene of Kane and his wife, Susan, together in the same shot:

> As [Susan] works on a jigsaw puzzle in the foreground, Kane sits in the background of the frame, seemingly bored or oppressed by her plaintive voice, which echoes through the great hall like that of an exhausted toucan. A standard montage might have shown Susan first, then Kane's reaction to her, and then perhaps the hollow fireplace behind them, as the scene faded out. With deep focus, Welles could present all of the "reality" in a single shot.[34]

In order to get such strikingly effective shots, Toland took drastic measures: he stopped down his camera to very small apertures and used coated lenses, faster film, and extremely high light levels. While most Hollywood cinematographers of the period were stopping down their cameras to f/2.3 or f/3.2, only occasionally going as high as f/3.5, Toland shot nearly all the interior scenes of *Citizen Kane* with an aperture of f/8, and a few scenes were photographed at even more extreme apertures of f/11 and f/16.[35] Combining a newly patented system for coating lenses (the Opticoating system, developed at Cal Tech) with the twin-arc broadside lamps and the Super XX film stock, Toland was able to create impressive depth of field even with standard-length 47mm and 50mm lenses. When wide-angle lenses as short as 24mm were used, the effect was even more pronounced, allowing Toland and his crew to hold sharp focus on objects close to the camera up to a depth of 200 feet.

To achieve this tremendous depth of field, light levels had to be much higher than what was common practice for the period. A survey conducted by *American Cinematographer* in June 1940 found that average light levels for interior scenes at major studios ranged from 40 foot-candles for Columbia and United Artists to 150 foot-candles for MGM, RKO, and Fox. By comparison, Toland used 320 foot-candles of light to shoot scenes at f/8, and up to 1,300 foot-candles—nearly ten times the studio standard—to shoot at f/16.[36]

Citizen Kane was Toland's most rigorous attempt to prove to Hollywood that greatly increased depth of focus could be used to intensify dramatic situations. As I will argue in my analysis of Toland's work with Wyler on *The Little Foxes* and *The Best Years of Our Lives*, Toland and Wyler would never go as far in stylistic experimentation as Toland and Welles had in *Citizen Kane*. Nevertheless, Toland's approach would allow Wyler to accomplish things with staging and composition that he would not otherwise have been able to do, thus making his films more visually effective and narratively powerful than they would otherwise have been. The aesthetic possibilities engendered by improved technologies raised the visual quality of films by more conventional studio filmmakers such as Wyler, just as they did those of a more innovative director such as Welles.

• • •

The first collaboration between William Wyler and Gregg Toland was the romantic drama *These Three* (1936). Adapted from Lillian Hellman's stage play *The Children's Hour*—in which a malicious schoolgirl accuses two of her teachers of being lesbians—the screen version changes the accusation of lesbianism to a rumor begun by a student that one of her teachers is having an affair with the fiancé of another teacher. As Wyler's biographer Jan Herman suggests, the "key artistic force" in the making of *These Three*—along with Hellman's screenplay and Wyler's direction—was Toland's cinematography.[37] Toland's lighting and composition allowed Wyler to achieve for the first time the mature visual style that would mark his films of the 1930s. Michael Anderegg describes the result of their collaboration:

> Though Toland had not yet developed the deep-focus technique for which he is best remembered, his rich and careful camerawork already complements Wyler's desire for dynamic and meaningful compositions. With Toland's help, Wyler creates drama by adroitly framing characters and objects, eschewing, as much as possible, constant back and forth cutting between speakers in dialogue scenes.[38]

These Three was shot between November 1935 and January 1936 with few problems other than the constant interference of Sam Goldwyn in the production. But the creative partnership of Wyler and Toland almost ended before it had begun. Wyler, accustomed to working with cinematographers who took a much less active role in the filmmaking process, soon began hearing rumors that Toland was disgruntled and wanted to quit the picture. As Wyler recalled,

> I was in the habit of saying "Put the camera over here with a forty millimeter lens, move it this way, pan over here, do this." Well, [Toland] was not used to . . . being just a mechanic. But making Westerns at Universal, this is what I [had done]. I directed the camerawork. I considered it part of my job. Well . . . you don't do that with a man like Gregg Toland.[39]

Once he had discussed the situation with Toland, Wyler began to engage his cinematographer more actively in the filmmaking process, even asking him to suggest alternate ways of shooting each scene. Wyler's account of this pivotal moment in their collaboration raises the question of how much Toland's involvement in the decision-making process changed the way Wyler shot the film. It seems clear that, although a well-developed technique of deep focus is not yet evident, Wyler and Toland were beginning to experiment with staging in depth in a way that Wyler had not done in his earlier films. Background action, though it at times remains out of focus, is central to the mise-en-scène, consistent with the film's theme of voyeurism and the invasion of private space. In one visually striking scene, Joe (Joel McCrea) and Karen (Merle Oberon) embrace in a long shot in the street outside the school, as the camera remains focused on Martha (Miriam Hopkins), standing inside the building. Here, Wyler and Toland adopt a technique of deep staging that they would use even more effectively in *The Little Foxes* and *The Best Years of Our Lives.*

Toland also used camera movement to establish his stylistic signature in *These Three,* giving the film a sense of visual fluidity that was unusual for a mid-1930s production. A scene in which Toland's camerawork raises the film to a higher artistic level is the one in which Joe has fallen asleep on a couch in Martha's room. Toland first tracks from Martha's face to the bedroom window, and then, after a quick dissolve to show the passage of time, tracks back to a shot that shows Martha watching the sleeping Joe. Later in the same scene, Toland pans away from a weeping Martha and tracks down the hallway to reveal the face of Mary, watching and listening in the shadows. Here, Toland's camera adds a sense of visual drama to what might otherwise have been a relatively static scene.

Wyler's next film, the social drama *Dead End* (1937) was a very different kind of project from *These Three.* For this film, Wyler sought to capture the feeling of a realistic urban environment with a harsher camera style. Wyler had hoped to shoot the film on location on the streets of New York, but this proposal was quickly rejected by Goldwyn, who wanted to retain more control over the production than would have been possible on a film shot on location. The film's huge indoor set—designed by art director Richard Day—was both its most distinctive feature and its biggest liability. From the start of filming, Wyler felt that the set looked "very phony and artificial," but his complaints to Goldwyn fell on deaf ears.[40] The situation was not helped by Goldwyn's insistence on keeping the set completely clean, which made little sense in a gritty urban drama taking place in a poor neighborhood. When the producer came onto the set as Wyler was preparing for the first day's shooting, he noticed that garbage had been strewn about in an attempt to create a more realistic urban landscape. Wyler explained to Goldwyn that the slum depicted in the picture was *supposed* to be dirty, and that the decoration of the slum section of the set was intended to contrast with the fancy new apartment building that had been constructed at the other end of the street. Goldwyn, apparently missing the film's social reformist message, replied that he would not allow there to be any "dirty slums" in his picture. Unfortunately, the almost pristine look of the set detracts from the sense of gritty realism Wyler wanted to convey in the film.

Though the film was shot during the summer—between May and July 1937—the fact that it was filmed on an indoor set necessitated the simulation of daylight throughout the shoot, a difficult challenge for Toland and his crew. Toland solved the problem by bunching eight large arc lamps on a single huge parallel, achieving the effect of a harsh sunlight that continually beats down on the city. "We didn't try to make anyone look pretty," Wyler recalled.[41] The strong lighting allowed Toland to achieve a greater depth of focus than he had on *These Three,* but it did not solve the problem of working on a fundamentally artificial set. The set's artificiality is made even more pronounced by the film's soundtrack. Even though the action is supposed to be taking place in the midst of a busy city, we hear almost no city noises of any kind. Unlike Hitchcock's *Rear Window*—which also takes place on an artificial set but which resonates with the sounds of the living city—*Dead End* suffers from a sonic deadness that detracts further from its realism.

The cinematographic technique of *Dead End* cannot be described as one of deep focus, though the film does contain a number of shots in which Toland succeeds in capturing both foreground and background action. In one scene, we see Baby Face Martin (Humphrey Bogart) and another gangster in a restaurant plotting to kidnap the child of a wealthy family. The men are profiled in close-up, while outside the window a woman wheels a baby carriage across the street. The woman is too far away to be kept completely in focus, but the fact that she occupies the center of the frame and is the only moving figure in the shot gives her an important symbolic presence. Another example of this kind of staging in depth is the scene in which Kay (Wendy Barrie) comes to visit Dave (Joel McCrea) at his tenement. The camera shoots from a high angle down on Kay and beyond her to Dave standing at the bottom of the stairs: Dave is completely in focus and Kay very nearly so. The presence of such shots indicates Toland's desire to develop a more precise deep-focus technique, and it may also suggest that the technology available to Toland had not yet caught up with his artistic ambitions.[42] Even so, Toland's work was clearly considered to be exceptional by his peers: *Dead End* was one of only three nominees for best black-and-white cinematography of 1937. Wyler himself was so appreciative of Toland's cinematography on the film that he inscribed Toland's copy of the script "your co-director, Willy Wyler."

• • •

Wuthering Heights was a prestige project for the Goldwyn studio. With a cast of British actors including Laurence Olivier, Merle Oberon, and David Niven, and a screenplay by Ben Hecht and Charles MacArthur based on Emily Brontë's novel, it was unmistakably the kind of "quality" film Sam Goldwyn liked to produce. The film's cinematography is surely its most remarkable achievement, and Toland's award for best black-and-white cinematography was the only Oscar the picture would win. In an early essay on Toland, Douglas Slocombe identified *Wuthering Heights* as the first in a series of extraordinary films shot by Toland in the late 1930s that, for the first time, "allowed him to develop and exploit his talent fully."[43] Toland shot many of the film's scenes in extremely low-key light, creating beautiful chiaroscuro effects that captured the novel's romantic mood. Toland's lighting helps to establish the visual distinction between the two houses in

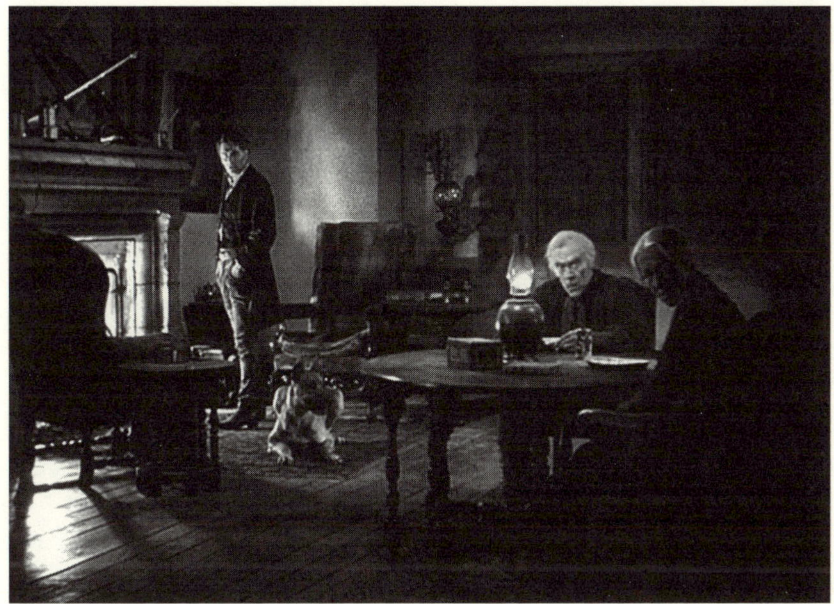

Figure 8. Gregg Toland's masterful use of chiaroscuro lighting to create tonal anxiety. (*Wuthering Heights,* Goldwyn, 1939)

which most of the film's action occurs: whereas Wuthering Heights is shot in mostly low key—giving it a dark and threatening feel—Thrushcross Grange is shot in a relatively high-key style, producing an effect of light and airiness. In the scene early in the film in which Lockwood arrives at Wuthering Heights and stays in what had once been Cathy's bedroom, the flickering candlelight created by one of Toland's miniaturized lighting units allowed him to control with great precision the amount of "flame" thrown around the room, resulting in very atmospheric effects.

A fully developed deep-focus technique is still not apparent, but depth of field is a more important element than it had been in any of Toland's previous films. In some scenes, Wyler and Toland use extremely deep sets and objects placed in the foreground to emphasize the use of deep space. In one particularly effective scene, as the young Cathy and Heathcliff peer into the Grange to watch a dance, the camera tracks past them and through the window to reveal the party going on inside. The penetration of the shot into the depth of the room expresses Cathy's fascination with the life of the wealthy and sophisticated people attending the ball. It was also a way for Wyler to harness Toland's developing technique for a thematic purpose.

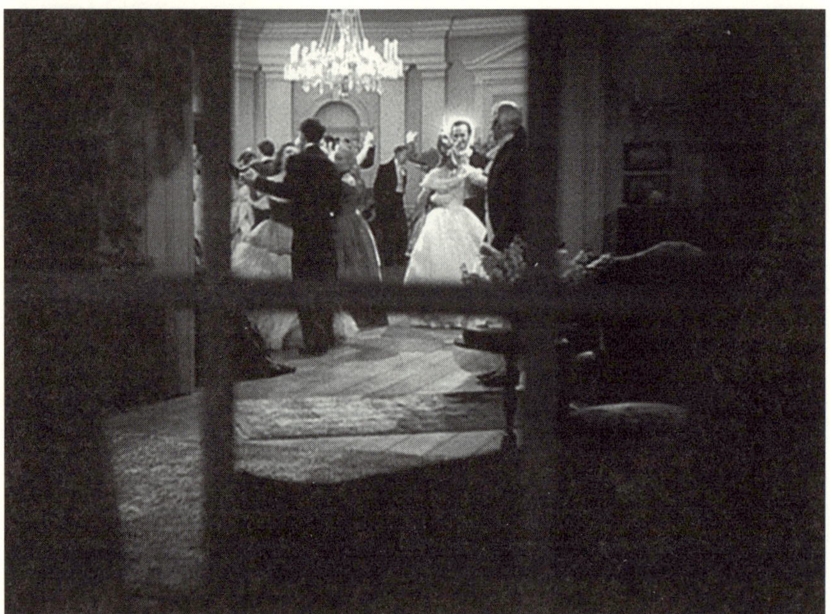

Figure 9. The technique of deep focus allows the viewer to look through a window from the perspective of Cathy and Heathcliff. (*Wuthering Heights,* Goldwyn, 1939)

Although Toland would continue to refine his technique over the next two years, *Wuthering Heights* can be seen as the beginning of the phase in his career during which he did his most strikingly original work. Between 1939 and 1941, Toland would be responsible for the cinematography on a group of extraordinary films that are remarkable both for the quality of their production and for the originality of their visual style. Either of the two films Toland shot for John Ford—*The Long Voyage Home* and *The Grapes of Wrath*—would have been landmark achievements in the career of any cinematographer. *The Grapes of Wrath* is one of a handful of the most brilliantly photographed films in the history of American cinema, while the low-key work of *The Long Voyage Home* is a tour de force of mood lighting. In addition, in those three years, Toland shot *Citizen Kane* for Orson Welles, *Ball of Fire* for Howard Hawks, *Intermezzo* for Gregory Ratoff, and *Wuthering Heights, The Westerner,* and *The Little Foxes* for Wyler.

Toland completed photography on *The Grapes of Wrath* shortly before shooting *The Westerner,* and certain sequences of Wyler's film seem photographically very similar to the style of Ford's Depression-era masterpiece.

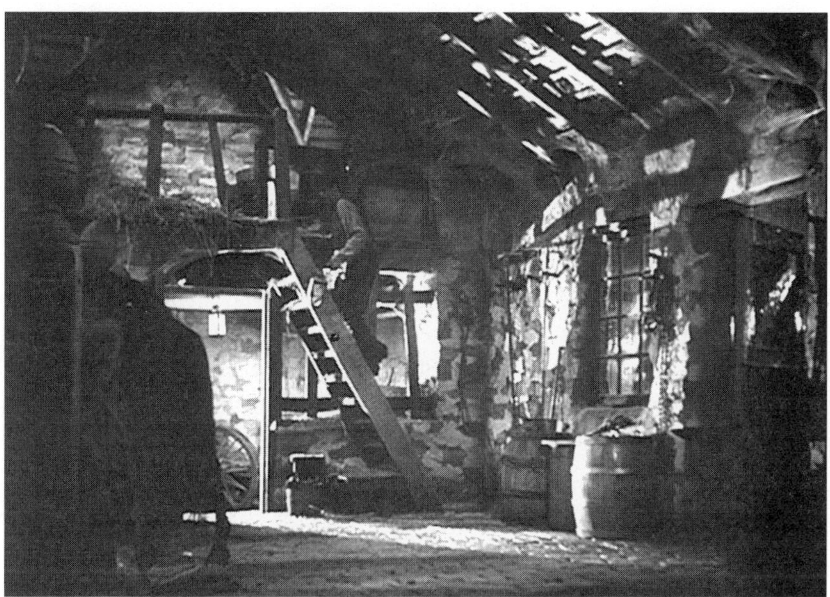

Figure 10. Low-key lighting with localized sources of light to create atmosphere. (*Wuthering Heights*, Goldwyn, 1939)

Based on a rather unsubstantial script about the legendary Texas lawman Judge Roy Bean, *The Westerner* was an unusual project for Wyler, who had not shot a Western since the "quickies" he made for Universal in the 1920s. The story was a simple one, based on a combination of history and semi-fictional Americana. Judge Bean (Walter Brennan), the hanging judge who controls everything that goes on in a small Texas town, is infatuated by the beautiful English actress Lily Langtry. When a saddle bum named Cole Hardin (Gary Cooper) rides into town and is accused of horse-stealing, he is sentenced to hang in Bean's barroom court. A smooth talker, Hardin is able to gain a reprieve from the hanging by promising to bring Bean a lock of Langtry's hair, which he claims to have acquired from the actress herself. Hardin is soon drawn into a range war between the cattlemen, led by Bean, and a group of farmers who attempt to settle in the area. The film ends with a gunfight between Hardin and Bean in the Fort Davis Opera House, in the course of which Bean is killed.

The Westerner was shot on location outside of Tucson, Arizona, in November 1939, but it was not released until October of the following year. Goldwyn spared no expense in trying to capture the atmosphere of the Texas frontier, and the film's budget of slightly over $1 million was a hefty sum for a late-1930s Western. The production rounded up seven thousand head of cattle, more than had ever been put into a Hollywood film, and art director James Basevi built an exact replica of the Fort Davis Grand Opera House for the final shootout. Though the film is not one of Wyler's masterpieces, it is an underrated film that deserves more attention than it has received. In part, the film's lack of status may have to do with the fact that it does not fit neatly into the Western genre as it was being defined by Hollywood in films such as John Ford's *Stagecoach.* As Patrick McGee has noted, the photographic style of *The Westerner* differs from that of most studio Westerns, emphasizing "the stark yet familiar Depression-era landscapes" rather than the "mythographic" space of a Fordian Western.[44]

In some of the film's interior shots—such as those inside Judge Bean's barroom—Toland seems to be consciously experimenting with depth of focus, at times holding focus on the faces of all the men in the bar and at other times letting either foreground or background blur out of focus. It should be noted that the barroom is a ceilinged set, like those of both *Stagecoach*—shot by Bert Glennon earlier the same year—and *Citizen Kane,* which Toland would shoot the following winter. In terms of its photographic style, *The Westerner* is clearly a transitional film for Toland, one that would come very close to a fully realized deep-focus technique but not quite achieve it.

In one scene, Toland shoots down the bar, with a whisky bottle in the foreground and all the men's faces in focus as Brennan walks down to talk to one of the men at the end of the bar. In another stunning shot, one of a group of gamblers places a whisky bottle on a table a short distance from the camera, and Toland keeps both the bottle and the action of the men in the background in clear focus. Since the effect does not seem important in dramatic terms, the shot seems to have been deliberately designed to highlight Toland's camera technique.[45] In yet another shot, the body and face of a man who has been killed in the street are artfully framed through the wheel of the undertaker's hearse. Taken together, these kinds of carefully framed, sharply focused shots seem to be the beginnings of a signature Toland style, and they anticipate the kind of camerawork he would soon perfect in both *Citizen Kane* and *The Little Foxes.*

• • •

By the time he shot *The Little Foxes* in the spring and early summer of 1941, Toland had become the subject of considerable notoriety.[46] Many of his fellow cinematographers resented his extreme approach in *Citizen Kane,* finding it to be in conflict with other photographic ideals such as the glamorous presentation of actors and the illusion of roundness. As a result Toland found himself, as Patrick Keating suggests, both inside and outside Hollywood norms: "inside because he was exploring and improving a functional option that was a recognized component of the Hollywood style, [and] outside because his fellow cinematographers worried that such obsessive attention to one technique was bound to upset the delicate balance that a multi-functional style required."[47] A contemporary article in *American Cinematographer* referenced the way in which Toland's work on *Citizen Kane* created a significant split within the cinematographic community: "Some feel that [Toland] has made a tangibly worthwhile contribution to camera technique. Others feel just as strongly that the '*Kane*' technique is reminiscent of methods discarded before cinematography reached its present maturity."[48]

Although Toland would not go to anything like the extremes in *The Little Foxes* that he had in *Citizen Kane,* he did make ample use of deep-focus technique in creating the film's distinctive look. For André Bazin, the difference between the two films is one of emphasis: while depth of focus was itself "an aesthetic end" for Welles, in the case of Wyler deep focus was "subject to the dramatic demands of the mise-en-scène, and in particular to the clarity of the narrative."[49] For Douglas Slocombe, the cinematography of *The Little Foxes* is an elaboration and fine-tuning of the technique of *Citizen Kane:* Toland maintained the depth of focus he had achieved in Welles's film, while avoiding "the forced perspectives, inseparable from wide-angle lenses," and replacing the "harshness" of *Citizen Kane* with "pleasant, warm modeling."[50]

Toland began working with Wyler, art director Stephen Gooson, and set decorator Howard Bristol six weeks before the start of shooting, an exceptionally long period of preproduction for a film of the time. Toland's description of his discussions with Wyler and other members of the team suggest the extent of his involvement in nearly every aspect of the production:

> Discussions with the director involved a complete breakdown of the script, scene by scene, with an eye to the photographic approach, considering the various dramatic effects desired. While this advance discussion pertained to the art ingredient, it was also of economic benefit because it meant the saving of much time and money once actual photography began. We built knock-down miniature models of the most important sets and juggled the walls about for the purpose of fixing upon the best angles, the best places to set up the camera. We took into consideration color values, types of wallpaper, the color and styles of the costumes to be worn by the principals, the furnishings and investiture. We set the photographic key for various sequences—the light or gay ones dramatically speaking, in a high key of light, and the more somber or moody scenes in a low and more "contrasty" key.[51]

The most significant aspect of Toland's cinematography in the film was his ability to achieve an even greater depth of focus than he had on the other films he had shot with Wyler. Wyler acknowledged that in *The Little Foxes,* Toland's technique of using a stopped-down wide-angle lens with increased light changed the way in which he directed the film:

> Well, that [technique] influenced my direction to some extent. You see it in . . . *The Little Foxes,* where groups of people are together, and normally you have close-up, close-up, close-up, here and there. By [using] his technique, I was able, by keeping the people close together, to have them all in the picture together and have both action and reaction from all the members of the scene at the same time.[52]

Wyler's acknowledgement of the fact that Toland's technique influenced his method as a director is revealing, both for what it tells us about the radically new possibilities for the cinema opened up by deep-focus cinematography, and for what it says about the nature of this particular director-cinematographer collaboration. The depth of focus Toland was able to achieve pushed Wyler to be more creative in his direction of actors, and it also necessitated changes in the way the camera moved. In the dinner table scene near the beginning of the film, for example, we see a combination of deep focus and camera movement used with great effectiveness. Wyler explained the challenges to achieving this:

> It was not easy, physically, putting three, four, or five people in [the shot] in such a way that you could see them all. Somebody had to have his back to the camera, somebody else had to be less prominent than others, which meant camera movements were often very intricate. There had to be a great deal of rehearsing [in order] to have what was not natural appear very natural. Actors had to be very close to each other, for example, because the deep-focus lenses made people in the distance look too far away.[53]

What is singularly striking in *The Little Foxes* is the way in which the possibilities introduced by deep-focus cinematography opened up Lillian Hellman's stage play into what is a more fully cinematic experience in the film. In Hellman's play, and in her screenplay for the film, a number of scenes involve stationary groups of people. Under normal circumstances, such scenes would have risked becoming static, their rhythm determined by the need to cut back and forth between different characters as they deliver their lines. With the help of Toland's deep-focus technique, however, Wyler is able to keep more of the characters in the frame in the same shot—regardless of whether they are in the foreground, middleground, or background of the action—and thus to achieve a more potent form of cinematic artistry.

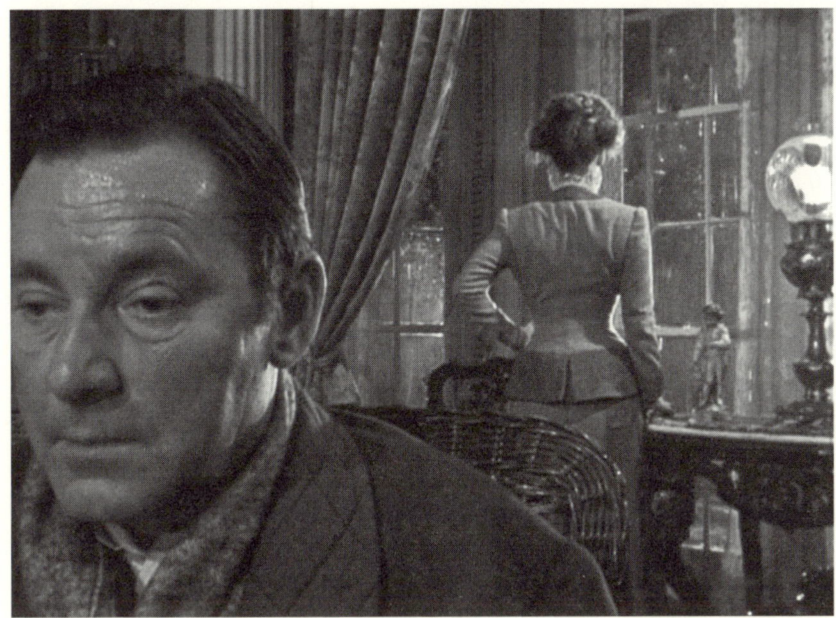

Figure 11. Toland's extreme use of deep focus, with Herbert Marshall in the foreground and Bette Davis in the background. (*The Little Foxes,* Goldwyn, 1941)

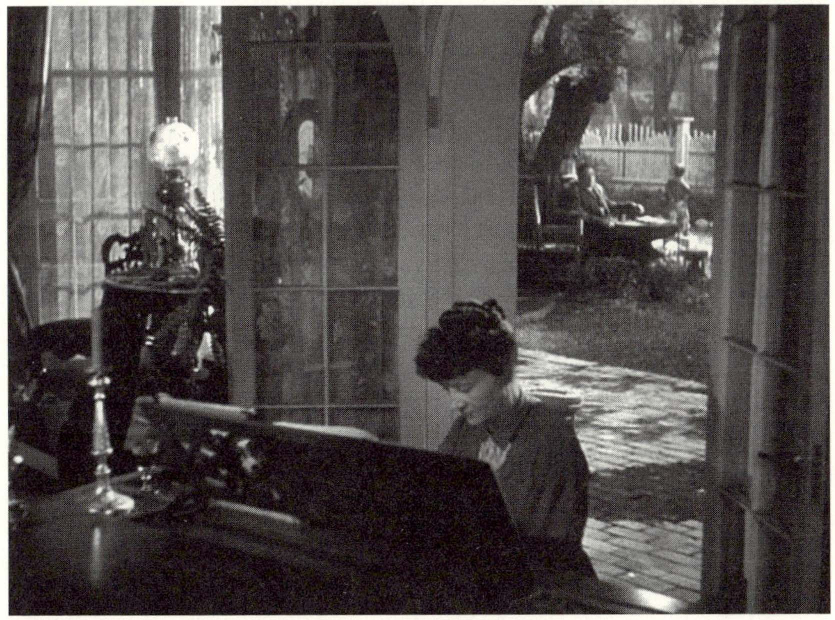

Figure 12. A complicated shot using deep-focus technique to move from interior foreground to exterior background. (*The Little Foxes,* Goldwyn, 1941)

If the style of *Citizen Kane* is expressionistic, that of *The Little Foxes* is closer to a form of cinematic naturalism. There are, in fact, relatively few shots in *The Little Foxes* that employ extreme depth of focus in the distorting way in which it occurs in *Citizen Kane*. This stylistic difference, I would argue, is the result both of the different subject matter of the two films and the different aesthetic preferences of the two directors. Unlike *Citizen Kane*, in which Welles's portrait of a powerful and eccentric individual benefits from the kinds of extreme effects Toland provides, *The Little Foxes* is an ensemble piece about a dysfunctional Southern family, requiring greater balance between the central characters. Unlike Welles, who valued Toland's technique for the increased stylization it provided, Wyler valued Toland's ability to maintain a clear focus on groups of people in the close and middle distance, thus increasing the film's sense of visual and social fluidity. In fact, it is significant that Wyler consistently refers to Toland's technique as "sharp focus" rather than "deep focus," suggesting that what mattered to him was less the extreme distance from the camera at which focus could be maintained and more the camera's ability to keep all the characters in clear focus in the same shot.

Howard Hawks, who worked with Toland on *Ball of Fire*, an ensemble film in which it was necessary in a number of scenes to keep the faces of all seven male characters in focus simultaneously, made a similar observation about the possibilities suggested by Toland's technique:

> He lit it the way you would light an ordinary shot and then he increased the exposure three times. Then he closed his diaphragm down three times to carry focus and he got exactly the effect [he wanted]. It wouldn't have worked too well with a beautiful girl or anything, but it certainly worked in that. We had scene after scene of these great actors who were playing. And that was Gregg's contribution. He was the only [cinematographer] who knew how to do that.[54]

One remarkable scene in *The Little Foxes* that was reputedly admired by Sergei Eisenstein involved a cleverly staged dialogue between Oscar Hubbard (Carl Benton Reid) and his son, Leo (Dan Duryea). The two men are standing back to back, catching glimpses of each other in opposing mirrors as they shave. At one point, Toland introduces a double-mirror shot in which the image of Duryea's face is reflected in his mirror, which is in turn reflected in Reid's mirror. Though the shot might at first glance appear to be simply an attempt to inject visual variety into an otherwise fairly static scene, it is also a commentary on the dramatic situation of *The Little Foxes*, suggesting the narcissistic self-involvement of nearly all the film's characters. Michael Anderegg notes that the use of multiple mirrors "allow[s] Wyler to stage the early parts of the conversation so that Oscar and Leo

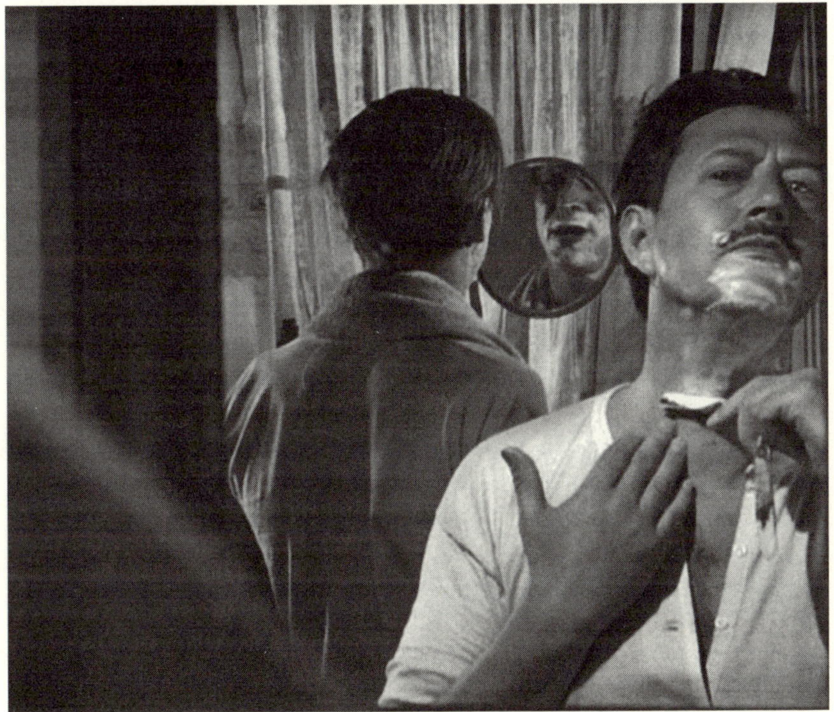

Figure 13. The famous double-mirror shaving scene. (*The Little Foxes*, Goldwyn, 1941)

never directly look at each other, even as they appear to be doing so; the Hubbards are as devious among themselves as they are with strangers."[55]

Another scene that is often cited as an illustration of Toland's artistry is the one in which Horace Giddens (Herbert Marshall) feels the onset of a heart attack and begs his wife Regina (Bette Davis) to fetch his medicine. Ignoring her husband's pleas, Regina continues to sit on the couch in the foreground of the frame as Horace attempts—in the background—to rise from his wheelchair and climb the stairs. Wyler wanted the primary focus of the shot to be the reaction of Regina sitting on the couch rather than her husband's attempt to climb the stairs. In the scene, Toland begins with a deep-focus shot of Horace, and then to allows him to be deliberately thrown out of focus. In this way, Wyler gives visual emphasis to the decision to highlight Regina more than the action going on behind her.

The Little Foxes was a major success for both Goldwyn and Wyler. Reviews were almost uniformly enthusiastic, with most critics rating the

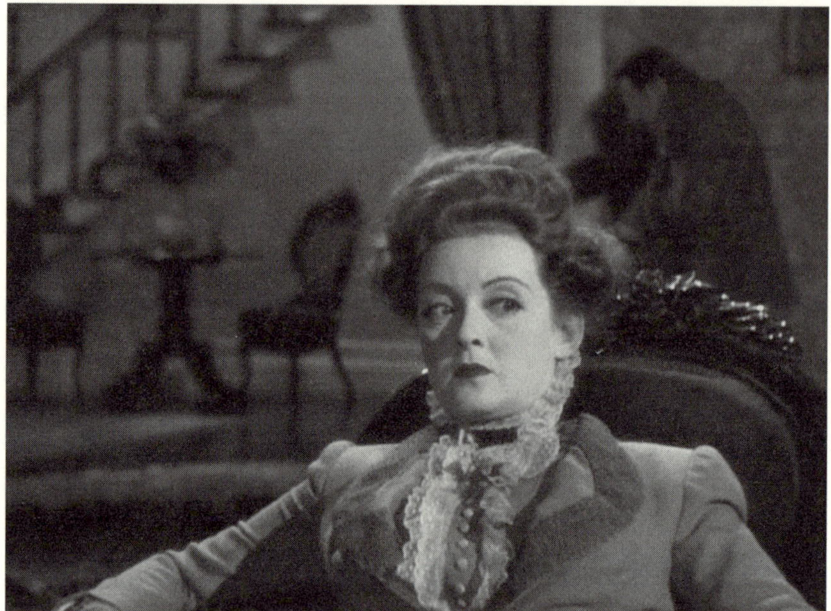

Figure 14. Visual narrative: Bette Davis remains in focus and brightly lit, while the figure of Herbert Marshall is reduced to a dark blur in the background. (*The Little Foxes*, Goldwyn, 1941)

film better than the Broadway production. The film received nine Academy Award nominations, including best picture, best director, best actress, and two nominations for supporting actresses (Teresa Wright and Patricia Collinge), as well as best screenplay, art direction, editing, and score. *The Little Foxes* did not receive a nomination for Toland's cinematography, a curious omission given that the film's cinematography is the single most important stylistic departure from the stage play. Perhaps the members of the Academy felt, as some contemporary critics did, that the style of the film was overly calculated, and that Toland's meticulously claustrophobic framing was a flaw rather than a virtue. Only later did viewers—led by the French critic André Bazin—identify the film as a masterpiece of both cinematography and mise-en-scène.

• • •

During the second half of 1941, Toland entered negotiations with Goldwyn to revise his contract. Toland wrote to Goldwyn requesting a contract that would allow him to shoot two pictures a year for Goldwyn as well as one for himself "on the outside."[56] Toland argued that because he had offers from other studios to shoot films for up to $20,000 per picture, Goldwyn should give him a better deal than the one in his current contract, which provided for an annual salary of $60,000 with no limit on the number of films to be shot. Toland's demands would have been unthinkable for any other cinematographer, but Goldwyn, realizing the tremendous value of Toland's work to his productions, agreed to most of his conditions.

In an ironic twist of fate, however, the outbreak of World War II prevented Toland from exercising his new contract and becoming the highest-paid cinematographer in Hollywood. A few days after the Japanese attack on Pearl Harbor, Toland was inducted into the Navy as a lieutenant and assigned to John Ford's Navy Photographic Unit. When Ford was given the assignment of making a film about the Pearl Harbor attack, he put Toland in charge of the project. In early 1942, Toland began assembling footage from the actual attack and combining it with newly shot footage re-creating scenes from the day of the event. Toland approached the film with great enthusiasm, but his apparent disregard for military protocol soon put the project in jeopardy. Of the completed film, only a condensed 32-minute version was released to the public. Though the film would be awarded the 1943 Academy Award for best documentary short, the censorship of the full-length version was deeply upsetting to Toland, who became depressed. On his request to be sent overseas, Toland was assigned to head the Field Photographic Station in Rio de Janeiro, Brazil, where he remained until the end of the war.

The Best Years of Our Lives, shot in the spring of 1946, was the last film that Wyler made for Samuel Goldwyn, and also his last collaboration with Toland. Based on MacKinley Kantor's verse novel *Glory for Me, The Best Years* tells the story of three GIs returning home after the war: Captain Fred Derry (Dana Andrews), a bombardier returning to an errant wife; Al Stephenson (Fredric Marsh), a middle-aged sergeant who has not seen his wife or children in four years; and Homer Parrish (Harold Russell), a young sailor who lost both his hands when his ship was bombed in the Pacific and is returning to an uncertain future with his girlfriend.

In some respects, *The Best Years* represents the pinnacle of Toland's collaboration with Wyler. More than in any of their previous collaborations, Wyler and Toland worked to achieve a straightforward aesthetic, using mostly high-key lighting and a relatively restrained camera style. As Wyler remembered,

> We had a clear-cut understanding that we would avoid glamour close-ups, and soft, diffused backgrounds. No men in the cast would wear

> makeup, and the makeup on the women would be kept to a minimum so that we could really see our people and feel their skin textures. Since Gregg intended to carry his focus to the extreme background of each set, detail in set designing, construction, and dressing became terribly important. But carrying focus is not merely a stunt; it is to me a terribly useful technique. In *The Best Years of Our Lives,* the sharp and crisp photography, filled with good contrast and texture, is one of the key factors in establishing a mood of realism.[57]

In keeping with the more realistic approach, Wyler asked costume designer Irene Sharaff not to create any fashions for the actors, but instead to buy their clothes off the rack at the kinds of department stores where the characters themselves would have shopped. The director also asked the actors to wear the clothes for several weeks before the scenes were shot, so that they would not look overly new. The uniforms and medals worn by servicemen were researched meticulously: there was an authentic serial number on the B-4 bag carried by Fred Derry, while Al Stephenson wore authentic Army medals including a Bronze Star and a Purple Heart.[58]

The production also created a sense of realism through the use of both exterior locations and interior sets. In addition to the documentary-style shots out of the B-17 bomber at the beginning of the film and the street scenes seen from the taxi as the men are taken to their respective homes, there are location shots using the Long Beach Municipal Airport and exteriors of houses and apartment buildings shot on streets in and around Los Angeles. The interior sets were designed by art directors Perry Ferguson (who had worked with Toland on the sets of *Citizen Kane*) and George Jenkins. In order to emphasize the everydayness of the interiors, the art directors actually designed them to be smaller than normal, going against the Hollywood practice of designing interior sets far larger and grander than their real-life equivalents. Ceilings averaged only eight feet high, and doors only six feet four. The relatively small size of these interior sets is apparent both in the scenes shot in the breakfast nook of the Stephensons' apartment and in the cramped apartment where Fred and Marie live. The latter set, in particular, gives a claustrophobic feeling to the scenes that take place there, adding to our sense of Fred being trapped in an unhappy marriage.

For the film's cinematography, Toland maintained a sense of "simple, unaffected realism" both by using a 40mm lens throughout nearly the entire film and by avoiding crane and dolly shots whenever possible.[59] Toland explained his and Wyler's approach to Lester Koenig:

> [Wyler] had seen a lot of candid photography [during the war], and [had shot] lots of scenes without a camera dolly or boom. He used to go

> overboard on [camera] movement, but he came back with, I think, a better perspective on what was and wasn't important. . . . Willy knows that I will sacrifice photography any time if it means a better scene. I, in turn, know that he will listen to any suggestion. *Best Years* was well photographed because the photography helped to tell the story. It wasn't breathtaking. It would have been wrong to strive for effects. We were after simple reproduction of the scenes played without any chi-chi stuff. The only time I held my breath was in the powder room scene when I thought we might be getting arty and trying to prove how damn clever we were instead of making a scene . . . . If I had to label the photographic style of the picture, I'd call it "honest."[60]

The scene to which Toland refers is the one in which Peggy Stephenson (Teresa Wright) and Marie Derry (Virginia Mayo) find themselves in the powder room of a nightclub while on a double date. Composed of a single shot that lasts a minute and forty-five seconds, the scene was clearly made possible by Toland's artistry. As in *The Little Foxes,* Toland makes effective use of mirrors: the bathroom mirrors allow him to keep both women in the frame, very close to each other, their faces visible but on different planes. The recurrent mirror shots in *The Best Years* were not in the script and were added by Wyler and Toland during the shooting. These shots not only increase the effects of Wyler's deep staging, but they also call attention to the characters' concern with appearances (both of themselves and of others), an important motif throughout the film.

In the bathroom mirror scene, four pans within the shot allow for changes in composition without the need to cut away from the faces. In the beginning of the shot, Marie and her reflected image dominate the frame, while Peggy's image is sandwiched between the two images of Marie. As the shot continues, there is a pan to Peggy, and then, for a brief moment, there is an image of two Peggys and one Marie. In using the mirrors in this way, Toland was able to achieve variety within the shot without sacrificing the intensity of the scene as it is played out in a single take.

The film contains a number of other visually memorable moments, many of them enhanced by Toland's cinematography. One scene that might go virtually unnoticed by today's audiences includes a deep-focus shot in which Al and his wife Milly (Myrna Loy) see each other from opposite ends of a corridor: Al is close to the camera, with Milly in a long shot at the end of the hallway. The shot reveals the emotional distance between the two characters, a distance that will now need to overcome. Other examples of Toland's deep-focus technique are the opening scene at the airport (in which the entire lobby is kept in sharp focus), the drugstore scenes, and

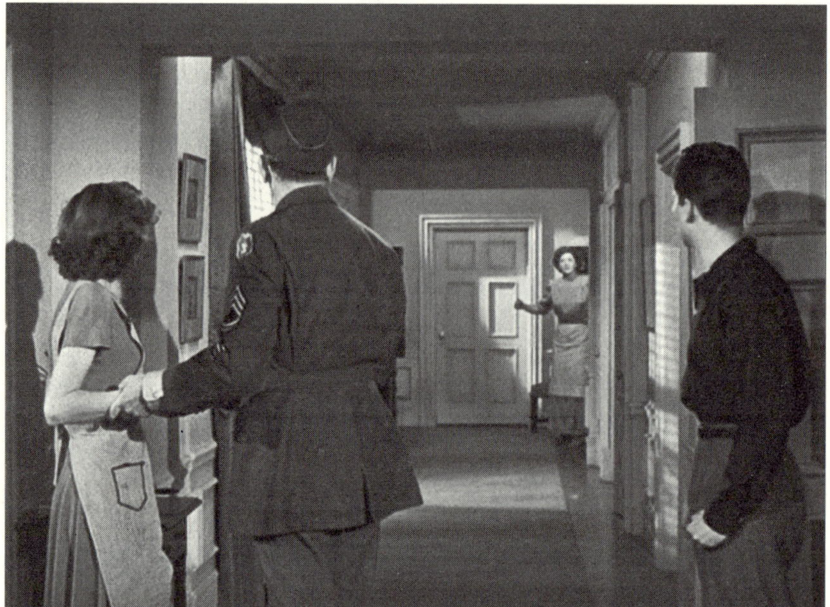

Figure 15. Depth of focus turns an ordinary domestic scene into an artistic composition. (*The Best Years of Our Lives,* Goldwyn, 1946)

scenes involving both Al and Homer reuniting with their families. These scenes use a combination of deep focus, effective staging, and long takes to emphasize the sense of alienation each of the men experiences. In the drugstore where Fred works, for example, the ads and products—all kept in simultaneous focus—"create a sense of commercialism run rampant."[61]

The film's most frequently cited scene is the one in which Al meets Fred Derry (Dana Andrews) at Butch's Bar and tells him he wants the extramarital dalliance with his daughter to stop. As Fred goes to the telephone booth to call Peggy and break it off, Homer enters, sits at the piano with Butch (Hoagy Carmichael), and performs a duet of "Chopsticks," with Al standing behind the piano. Through the use of Toland's deep-focus technique, Wyler was able to capture both planes of action in a single shot. Fred is situated in the phone booth at the top left-hand corner of the frame, with the other three characters in the foreground and to the right side of the frame, so that the audience is able to watch both scenes without the need for cutting back and forth. Further, the audience is able to witness Al's divided attention as he looks back and forth between the two planes of action.

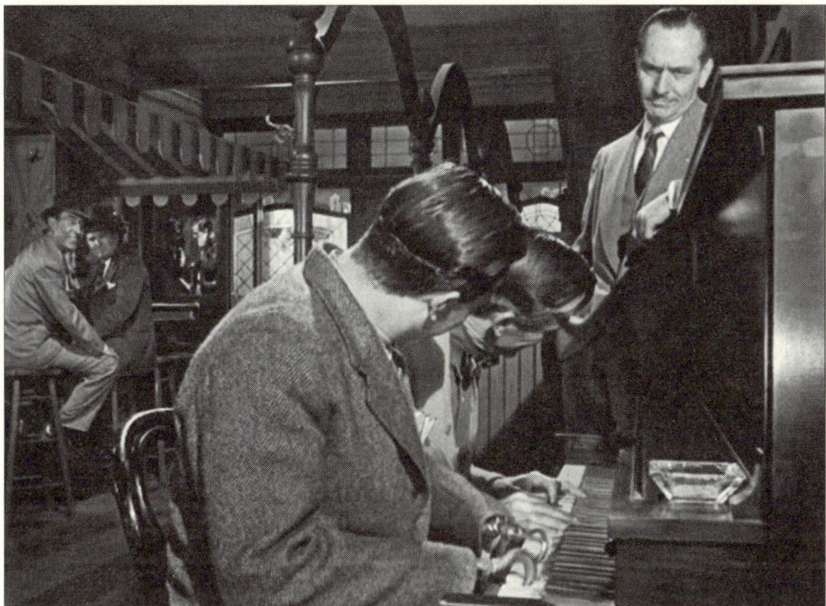

Figure 16. The real action in the phone booth (upper left corner) is juxtaposed against the much more visible foreground action at the piano. (*The Best Years of Our Lives,* Goldwyn, 1946)

In his cogent analysis of the scene, Bazin describes the way in which the more important action takes place in the upper-left corner of the screen, while the less significant action happens in the foreground:

> From time to time, March turns his head slightly and glances across the room, anxiously scrutinizing the behavior of Andrews. Finally, the latter hands the telephone up and, without turning to the men at the piano, suddenly disappears into the street. If we reduce the real action of the scene to the essence, we are left with Andrews' telephone call. This telephone conversation is the only thing of immediate interest to us. The one character whose face we would like to see in close-up is precisely the person whom we cannot clearly discern because of his position in the background and because of the glass surrounding the booth. His words themselves are of course inaudible. The true drama occurs, then, far away in a kind of little aquarium that reveals only what appear to be the trivial and ritual gestures of an ordinary phone call. . . . Forced to wait for Andrews to finish his call in the phone booth and unable to see him well, the viewer is obliged furthermore to divide his attention between this same booth and the scene at the piano. Thus Wyler killed two birds with one stone: first, the diversion of the piano

> allows him to extend as long as possible a shot that would otherwise have seemed endless and consequently monotonous; second, and more important, this parasitic pole of attraction organizes the image dramatically and spatially. The real action at the phone booth is juxtaposed against the action at the piano, which directs the attention of the viewer almost against his will to itself, where it is supposed to be, for as long as it is supposed to be there.[62]

A scene such as the one analyzed by Bazin demonstrates the extent to which Toland's deep-focus technique not only allowed different planes of action to occur simultaneously but also permitted Wyler to achieve longer takes without the shot becoming monotonous for the viewer. In fact, *The Best Years* has an unusually high average shot length: nearly twenty seconds, roughly double that of a typical Hollywood film of the period. Such long takes give Wyler the opportunity to pack more narrative and visual information into each shot, thus allowing him to build an unusually strong identification with the characters and their stories.

Another sequence in which Toland's depth of focus plays a crucial role is the wedding ceremony with which the film ends. While the minister recites the vows for Homer and Wilma, Wyler cuts to a shot of Peggy, first standing alone and then joined by Fred. David Bordwell suggests that this sequence represents a classic example of the way in which "depth composition, editing, and dialogue create an integrated style suitable for the sound cinema."[63] A comment made by Ralph Hoge reveals another aspect of Toland's technique—one not generally noted by film scholars. Toward the end of the scene, Toland slightly lowered the lights on the foreground action while increasing the lighting on the background. The change is subtle, perhaps not so apparent as to be noticed by the average viewer, but it has the effect of drawing the attention back to a deeper plane of focus and thus emphasizing the future pairing of Peggy and Fred.[64]

Both Goldwyn and Wyler recognized the exceptional quality of Toland's cinematography in the film. Toland received his own full title frame in the credits, and his name was displayed prominently on advertising posters. *The Best Years* was also the most highly awarded of any of the films on which Wyler and Toland collaborated, garnering eight Academy Award nominations and winning in seven categories.[65] The fact that Toland did not receive a nomination for best black-and-white cinematography on a film that was nominated in nearly every other major category gives support to the theory that he was being deliberately snubbed by his peers.[66]

Toland's six-film collaboration with Wyler demonstrates the extent to which the style of even a very accomplished director can be decisively influenced by the technique and artistry of an exceptionally talented cinematographer. But Toland's brilliance came at a cost to his own reputation. As David Bordwell suggests, the aggressively innovative cinematography of *Citizen Kane* was seen as too eccentric for an industry that still clung, in the early 1940s, to fairly conservative notions of what constituted good cinematography. Writing in 1942, Walter Blanchard made the telling observation that while most cinematographers continued to rate Toland "very close to the top of the camera profession," they based that judgment "on the many superbly photographed productions he had filmed *before Citizen Kane* and its attendant publicity came along."[67] Blanchard's comment suggests that the "publicity" surrounding Toland's achievements, as much as the technical bravado of the film itself, alienated Toland's fellow cinematographers. Toland's career is instructive not only because it illustrates the very tangible impact a cinematographer could have on Hollywood filmmaking during the studio era, but also because it demonstrates what could happen to a cinematographer's reputation and status when he was perceived as going beyond acceptable aesthetic norms.

3 Peering into Corners

Billy Wilder, John Seitz, and the Visual Style of Film Noir

In their seminal essay on the visual style of film noir, Janey Place and Lowell Peterson argued that "visual style is the consistent thread that unites the very diverse films that together comprise this phenomenon."[1] Although some later critics have taken issue with the notion that film noir constitutes a unique stylistic category, I agree with Place and Peterson that the visual style of film noir, as much as its complicated plots, femmes fatales, and terse, elliptical dialogue, distinguishes it from other Hollywood modes of the period. The highly expressive and strongly stylized aesthetic created by a combination of techniques involving lighting, composition, camera angles, camera movement, and depth of staging first emerged in film noirs of the early 1940s, and it continued to develop throughout the decade and into the 1950s.[2]

Film noir was an extremely widespread phenomenon during the decade from 1945 to 1954. Produced by every Hollywood studio, film noirs represented as much as ten to fifteen percent of the total output of films made in Hollywood in the late 1940s and early 1950s. No doubt there were a number of reasons, both economic and cultural, why so many film noirs were produced during this era. One economic factor encouraging the production of film noirs was a change in distribution practices during the period. The packaging of an "A" movie with a "B" movie, or "program picture," in a double feature was gradually being phased out in the immediate postwar era, creating a strong incentive to produce relatively low-budget films that could be shown on their own rather than on a double bill. Consequently, many of the studios produced films with budgets between an A picture's and a B picture's, a category that film historian Lea Jacobs has named "intermediates." A number of film noirs fell into this category, with budgets of between $250,000 and $500,000.[3] The characteristic look of such films is to some degree determined by their budgets, which were too small to allow the glossy, high-key treatment typical of major studios' A pictures yet large enough for the relatively good production values a stand-alone film required.

Another reason for the production of stylized black-and-white Hollywood films during the postwar era was the need to justify shooting films in black and white at a time when color production was on the rise. Many color films of the period exploited widescreen processes such as CinemaScope and VistaVision, but film noirs signaled their differences from the look and design of 1950s television in a very different way, using location shooting, striking lighting effects, and complicated camera techniques to create a recognizable style.[4] A reason for this film noir style, Marc Vernet suggests, is that films shot in black and white during the 1950s needed a justification for *not* being made in color; they therefore required "an aesthetic supplement that would allow [them] to hold up their end of a comparison with color films."[5]

A final reason for the industry-wide shift toward the production of film noirs was neither economic nor cultural, but more broadly historical. As both Robert Sklar and Sheri Chinen Biesen have argued, World War II had a profound impact on American filmmaking during the 1940s, when films were both thematically and stylistically darker than studio productions of the 1930s had been.[6] The exigencies of wartime production included a 25 percent reduction in the allocation of film stock to the film industry, as well as restrictions on the amount that could be budgeted for set design. Perhaps most importantly, there was an outright ban on the use of high-watt Photofloods in studio film production. Overall, films had to be made on lower budgets, with less elaborate sets, less extensive lighting, and a more efficient use of footage. These restrictions led to the production of films that could be made relatively cheaply, either on location or, if in the studio, using low-key lighting and unusual camera angles to disguise inexpensive sets.

These cost-cutting measures were largely offset, however, by improvements in technology that allowed cinematographers to do more with less. In some cases, wartime austerity measures encouraged directors and cinematographers to use real locations instead of sets; the austerity may have also helped to accelerate the technical innovations that allowed cinematographers to shoot more effectively in smaller spaces and with lower light levels. The technological innovations of the postwar era included faster film stocks with less grain, as well as new lenses—assisted by advanced techniques of lens coating—that allowed greater light transmission, while permitting wider lenses to be placed close to light sources without a loss of focus. These advances in film stock and lenses made it possible to use a single light source placed in almost any position, thus cutting down significantly on the number of lights required for shooting a scene.[7] These new lighting techniques, along with the increasing use of lightweight cameras, allowed cameramen to shoot from previously inaccessible positions, so actions could now be staged at very close range or in very confined spaces. The introduction of the crab dolly—a camera dolly that could be steered by all four wheels and thus could go instantly from a forward dolly movement to a sideways, crab-like movement—also permitted more fluid movements of the camera. From an economic standpoint, these new technologies were especially attractive to producers of both low-budget and mid-budget films. On an aesthetic level, they allowed directors and cinematographers far more flexibility in terms of both lighting and camerawork.

In short, the new photographic technologies of the 1940s enabled cinematographers to become much more innovative in the use of such techniques as low-angle shooting, staging in depth, camera movement, and tilting the camera to create unusual angles. In *Body and Soul* (Robert Rossen, 1947), James Wong Howe used a handheld camera to capture the boxing scenes, while Russell Harlan used lightweight cameras developed for World War II combat coverage to shoot *Gun Crazy* (Joseph Lewis, 1950). For *Sunset Boulevard* (Billy Wilder, 1950), John Seitz devised a reflecting mirror to capture a shot (apparently taken from underwater) of the protagonist floating face down in a swimming pool. In *The Blue Gardenia* (Fritz Lang, 1954), Nicholas Musuraca used a crab dolly to move the camera more quickly through interiors and become a more active participant in the action as it follows the guilt-ridden heroine.

By the late 1940s, faster film stocks and higher-speed lenses also allowed for more daring and effective location work. In films such as *T-Men* (Antony Mann/John Alton, 1947), *They Live by Night* (Nicholas Ray/George Diskant, 1948), *The Naked City* (Jules Dassin/William Daniels, 1948), *Thieves Highway* (Dassin/Norbert Brodine, 1949), *Act of Violence* (Fred Zinneman/Robert Surtees, 1949), *Panic in the Streets* (Elia Kazan/Joseph MacDonald, 1950), and *Side Street* (Mann/Joseph Ruttenberg, 1950), the collaboration of the director and the cinematographer produced visual styles that were both unique expressions of the filmmakers and part of the larger phenomenon of film noir.

Film noir offered the greatest contrast with conventional studio style in its techniques of lighting. The typical studio style of the 1930s involved unobtrusive use of lighting, placing actors in bright light that would allow them to remain the center of attention. Lights were generally hung from above the set, thus eliminating dark corners, removing shadows, and making strong lighting effects difficult to achieve. The preferred style of "three-point lighting"—with a strong key light, a somewhat softer fill light, and soft back light—filled in actors' faces in order to make them look more attractive and separated them more clearly from their background.[8] Lenses were generally kept very open, creating a shallow depth of field and a relatively soft focus.

In film noir, on the other hand, lighting is generally low-key rather than high-key, while the use of fill light is deliberately restricted and sometimes eliminated altogether. More efficient lenses allowed greater depth of focus, and the use of wider lenses enlarged the frame, thus revealing the ceilings of rooms on interior sets and actual locations. Because it was no longer possible to hide the existence (or nonexistence) of ceilings, the ceiling became a design element of film noir, creating a greater sense of the characters being caged or trapped within their (usually urban) environments. This also meant that lighting needed to be placed closer to the floor rather than hung from the rafters, resulting in dramatic contrasts between narrow areas of the frame that are harshly illuminated and surrounding areas that are obscured in deep black shadows. Along with this more contrasty lighting came the tendency to light actors and other objects in a similar way rather than using glamour lighting to focus the viewer's attention on the star.

The cinematographers who achieved the greatest success in film noir combined several essential qualities: the ability to shoot effectively with lower light levels, the willingness to operate on more limited budgets, and the capacity to combine studio and location shooting in an effective way. Those who were the most successful in creating the noir aesthetic were not necessarily from the highest ranks of Hollywood cameramen. In fact, a number of cinematographers of film noir had either been recently promoted to the rank of director of photography or had been working in relative obscurity prior to the advent of film noir. Joseph LaShelle, who would become one of the most important Hollywood cinematographers of the postwar era, became a full cinematographer only in 1943, a year before shooting the Academy Award-winning *Laura* for Otto Preminger. Burnett Guffey, who would shoot film noirs for a number of directors including Fritz Lang, Joseph Lewis, Nicholas Ray, and Don Siegel, was promoted to the rank of cinematographer only in 1944, just in time to participate in the creation of the new style with films like *My Name is Julia Ross* (Lewis, 1945) and *Knock on Any Door* (Ray, 1949). Joseph MacDonald, who achieved the status of full cinematographer in 1941, became a mainstay at Fox with film noirs such as *The Dark Corner* (Henry Hathaway, 1946), *Call Northside 777*

(Hathaway, 1948), *The Street with No Name* (William Keighley, 1948), and *Panic in the Streets* (Elia Kazan, 1950). Milton Krasner had been a cinematographer at Paramount since 1933 but had been assigned to mostly forgettable B movies until the mid-1940s, when his excellence in low-key black-and-white photography was finally recognized in film noirs like Fritz Lang's *Scarlet Street* (1945) and Robert Siodmak's *The Dark Mirror* (1946). Nicholas Musuraca, now celebrated as one of the most important cinematographers of the film noir cycle, had been a member of the RKO staff since the late 1920s but gained status in the industry only by lensing such noirs as *The Stranger on the Third Floor* (Boris Ingster, 1940), *Cat People* (Jacques Tourneur, 1942), *The Fallen Sparrow* (Richard Wallace, 1943), *The Spiral Staircase* (Robert Siodmak, 1945), and *Out of the Past* (Tourneur, 1947).

Perhaps the most famous cinematographer whose full potential was realized only with the advent of film noir was John Alton. Alton spent most of his early career shooting films in Argentina and then spent several years working on negligible B movies for small producers in the United States. He became an established Hollywood cinematographer only when he teamed up with director Anthony Mann in the late 1940s to shoot a series of visually striking film noirs. Like Musuraca, Alton received little official recognition from his peers during his career: his only Academy Award for best cinematography, as John Bailey has noted with some irony, was "not for his signature lighting and compositions in the noir films of Anthony Mann and Joseph Lewis—but for a single dance sequence in the beloved Technicolor musical *An American in Paris*."[9] The turning point in Alton's career came when he was assigned to shoot his first film noir with Mann. The director, who had also been working on B movies since the early 1940s, had recently signed with Eagle-Lion, a small production company run by Arthur Krim. For his first film with the company, the noir-styled crime film *T-Men* (1947), Mann needed a cinematographer who could work effectively with dramatic low-key lighting. He requested Alton, whose work he had seen and admired.

Alton's cinematography was quickly to become a primary force in Mann's filmmaking. *T-Men* begins in the semidocumentary manner that was fashionable in crime and spy films of the late 1940s, but it soon plunges into a highly stylized form of noir cinematography. *T-Men* is marked by Alton's use of disconcerting camera angles, extreme close-ups, deep staging, and expressionist lighting. So effective is Alton's cinematography that we are drawn forcefully into the story, despite the rather intrusive voiceover structure. In Todd McCarthy's view, "Alton and Mann didn't invent film noir, but they created some of the most indelible examples of it, pushing the style further than anyone had dared to up to that time."[10]

A comparison of Alton and Mann's partnership with that of Wilder and Seitz reveals several interesting points. Although both collaborations were important multifilm partnerships of the mid- to late 1940s, there are at least three differences between them. The most obvious difference is that, while Mann's collaboration with Alton involved relatively low-budget films made for independent producers, Wilder's partnership with Seitz took place within the structure of one of the largest and wealthiest Hollywood studios and involved budgets that were relatively large for the period. Moreover, the budgets of the films Wilder shot with Seitz at Paramount grew with each successive picture: from $850,000 for *Five Graves to Cairo,* to $980,000 for *Double Indemnity,* to $1.25 million for *The Lost Weekend,* and to $1.75 million for *Sunset Boulevard.* Mann and Alton, on the other hand, worked with budgets that were more typical of B-movie productions: $425,000 for *T-Men* and around $500,000 for their subsequent films. This difference in budgets can easily be seen in the production values of Wilder's films as compared with those directed by Mann.

Another important difference between the two collaborations has to do with the reception of the films within the Hollywood community: Alton received little public recognition from his peers, while Seitz was nominated for an Academy Award on every one of the four films he photographed for Wilder. This is not necessarily a reflection of the relative skills of Seitz and Alton; it is, instead, a statement about the near impossibility of films made outside the major studios receiving Academy Award nominations, especially in the technical categories.[11]

The third distinction I would draw between the two partnerships has to do with the degree to which the director and cinematographer can share credit for the visual style and, ultimately, for the artistic success of their films. In the films Alton shot for Mann, the quality and originality of the cinematography is readily apparent, especially in relation to the quality of other aspects of the filmmaking such as the writing, acting, and editing. There is no question that the cinematography of these films plays a dominant role. Or, to put it another way, there is a sense in some of the Mann-Alton collaborations that Alton, and not Mann, is the true "auteur." In Wilder's films shot by Seitz, on the other hand, the quality of the cinematography—as perfectly calibrated as it may be—is nearly always balanced by the high quality of the writing, acting, editing, and other elements of the production.

• • •

If Gregg Toland is almost universally acknowledged as the most influential cinematographer in the history of American film, the work of his contemporary John F. Seitz has been too often neglected. During a career that spanned much of the silent era and nearly the entire studio era, Seitz served as the cinematographer on nearly 160 feature films, collaborating with many of the most successful directors in the industry.[12] With the exception of a few years during the mid-1920s when he worked with director Rex Ingram in the south of France, Seitz spent his entire career in Hollywood, crafting films that were as visually impressive in their own way as those of Toland. Seitz has the distinction of having photographed more films that are listed on the National Film Registry of significant American films than any other cinematographer.[13] And yet, although his work has been discussed in passing by a number of commentators, his name is less often mentioned than those of other Hollywood cinematographers such as Toland, James Wong Howe, or John Alton. There have been no monographs devoted to Seitz's career, and there is no autobiographical account of his life and work.[14]

The films for which Seitz earned his reputation as one of the great American cinematographers fall into two categories: the twelve silent films he shot with Ingram in the 1920s and the two dozen or so films he photographed with Billy Wilder, Preston Sturges, and other directors at Paramount during the 1940s. Among aficionados of black-and-white Hollywood cinematography, Seitz is associated more specifically with the lighting and photographing of film noir. His stylistic signature—evident in many of his black-and-white films but most prominent in his noirs—is his use of low-key lighting to create an edgy, threatening, or sinister mood. Seitz's comfort in working at extremely low light levels—combined with his rare skill in composition and use of shadows—allowed him to establish himself as one of the most influential cinematographers of the film noir cycle, to which he contributed iconic films such as *This Gun for Hire, Double Indemnity, The Big Clock,* and *Sunset Boulevard.*[15]

Born in Chicago, Illinois in 1892, Seitz began his career in the film lab at the Essanay Film Manufacturing Company, the same company where Charlie Chaplin would make his short comedies a few years later. By the time he became a cameraman—cranking out shorts for the American Film Manufacturing Company in Santa Barbara, California—Seitz had spent seven years working in the lab, where he had gained an unusually adept understanding of what could be done with a black-and-white negative. Graduating quickly from shorts to features, Seitz was assigned, in 1917, as lead cameraman on a series of films directed by Henry King. In 1920, Seitz received the opportunity to collaborate with one of the most gifted directors in the industry. Rex Ingram, who had fired Steven Norton as cameraman from his film *Shore Acres,* was looking for a new cinematographer.

Before hiring Seitz, Ingram tested the young cameraman's abilities by having him shoot both exterior and interior footage. Seitz used his laboratory skills to full advantage, reducing the development time on the interiors by about 40 percent. "On running these the following evening Rex Ingram said he had for the first time seen an interior scene on the screen which he liked," Seitz reported.[16] Ingram agreed to hire Seitz, who served as his cinematographer on a dozen films over the next six years.

The most famous Ingram-Seitz collaboration is *The Four Horsemen of the Apocalypse* (1921). The film not only showcased Rudolf Valentino in his first leading role, but it was also a career-making production for Seitz, who contributed the movie's strikingly original cinematography. In the course of shooting this and other films for Ingram, Seitz established himself as one of the most inventive cameramen in Hollywood. For *The Four Horsemen,* Seitz mounted his camera on a dolly which could be rotated freely, so that he could photograph a tango performed by Valentino with greater fluidity. In doing so, he developed a technique of camera movement that became part of the standard repertoire of Hollywood cameramen only decades later. Seitz also experimented with low-key lighting effects, inventing a system known as "core lighting." This technique used bright key lights to the side of and slightly behind the figure being lit, with only weak fill-light to the front, thus creating the effect of a vertical band of shadow down the center, or "core," of the actor.[17] The following year, when shooting *Trifling Women* (1922), Seitz developed an elaborate system of matte shots, combining full-scale objects with miniatures and masking part of the lens. To create a castle, for example, he used a real tower with miniatures in the foreground, and he also used the system for scenes in which an orangutan appears to be seated at the dining table with human actors.

Ingram moved his operations to France in 1924, setting up a small studio in Nice. In 1926, as Ingram was preparing to shoot *The Garden of Allah,* Seitz decided to part ways with the director in order to return to the United States and pursue a career in Hollywood. At MGM, where he was assigned to shoot the films of the studio's rising star Marion Davies, Seitz became the highest-paid cinematographer in the industry, achieving considerable success with films like *The Patsy* (1928), a Davies vehicle directed by King Vidor, and *The Divine Lady* (1929), a romantic historical drama directed by Frank Lloyd. For the latter film, Seitz earned an Academy Award nomination for best cinematography in the second year the award was given. In 1931, Seitz joined the photographic department at Fox, where he worked with directors such as Frank Lloyd (*East Lynne*), Henry King (*Marie Galante*), and William Beaudine (*6 Hours to Live*). Seitz also shot five of

Shirley Temple's films, more than any cinematographer except Arthur Miller. In 1937, he returned to MGM, where he collaborated with directors such as Sam Wood (*Madame X*), Richard Thorpe (*The Adventures of Huckleberry Finn*), George Seitz (*Thunder Afloat*), and Joseph von Sternberg (*Sergeant Madden*). In 1941, Seitz made what would be his most important career move, joining the photographic staff at Paramount, where his friend Buddy DeSylva was the new head of production.

At Paramount, Seitz was given more interesting assignments than he had been granted at either Fox or MGM. He had been somewhat overshadowed during the 1930s by cinematographers such as Arthur Miller at Fox and William Daniels at MGM, but he found at Paramount a studio that was more suited to his style of lighting. At Paramount, Seitz had the opportunity to work with a number of major Hollywood directors in long-term collaborative partnerships: in addition to Wilder—on whose films he received four consecutive Academy Award nominations for best black-and-white cinematography—he enjoyed multifilm collaborations with Preston Sturges, Frank Tuttle, John Farrow, and Lewis Allen. Other directors with whom Seitz was teamed at Paramount included Robert Siodmak (*Fly-by-Night*), Albert Lewin (*The Moon and Sixpence*), Sidney Lanfield (*The Well-Groomed Bride*), Elliott Nugent (*The Great Gatsby*), Tay Garnett (*The Wild Harvest*), Leslie Fenton (*Saigon*), and Mitchell Leisen (*Captain Corey, USA*). Seitz also established successful working relationships with actors, including Veronica Lake (whose unique visual presence he captured very effectively in four films) and Alan Ladd (with whom he made over twenty films in the 1940s and 1950s). Seitz's films of the 1940s show an impressive range, from screwball comedies to noir thrillers to elegant literary adaptations.

Although Paramount made fewer films in the noir style than some of the other studios, it was one of the first majors to produce films in the noir cycle. Beginning with *Among the Living* (Stuart Heisler, 1941)—a Southern Gothic drama with distinctively noirish stylistic features—the studio released a steady stream of noirs, including three in 1942: *This Gun for Hire* (Frank Tuttle), *The Glass Key* (Stuart Heisler), and *Street of Chance* (Jack Hively). Paramount differed from the other majors in displaying a greater openness to innovation as well as a greater willingness to allow independent collaboration between its directors, cinematographers, and production designers. The studio's supervising art director Hans Dreier valued stylization as a way of creating more interesting films while at the same time cutting production costs.

The studio was also fortunate in employing two cinematographers who were unusually sophisticated in their approach to lighting and visual style.

In addition to Seitz, the studio had Theodor Sparkuhl, a German émigré who had worked with stylistically motivated directors such as Ernst Lubitsch and G.W. Pabst. Sparkuhl contributed to the development of noir style in *Among the Living* and developed it still further in *Street of Chance.* The latter film exhibits several features that would come to be identified with noir, including the use of rooms with low ceilings, the use of forced perspective and deep staging, and the tendency to break up lighter areas of the frame with patterns of diagonal and vertical lines.

Even more than Sparkuhl, Seitz would establish the Paramount brand of film noir. In *This Gun for Hire,* Seitz's first foray into the noir aesthetic, he used mirrors, odd angles, low-key lighting, and fog to create a sense of the entrapment and paranoia of the outlaw couple played by Alan Ladd and Veronica Lake. This film exhibited many of the defining stylistic traits of what would come to constitute film noir, including the combination of studio and location shooting, gritty urban locations, and a preponderance of expressionistic lighting. Seitz's mastery of low-key lighting assured that he would be assigned to film noirs by a number of different directors, including Tuttle, John Farrow, Roy Rowland, and, most importantly, Billy Wilder.[18]

Wilder was a young and relatively inexperienced director when he began his partnership with Seitz in the early 1940s. A decade younger than Seitz, Wilder was practically a novice, having directed only the wartime comedy *The Major and the Minor.* It would not be an exaggeration to say that Seitz played a vital role in Wilder's early directorial career, lending both his long experience and his technical acumen to Wilder's films and contributing importantly to the growth of Wilder as a visual director. The growing assurance of Wilder's visual style is evident between *Five Graves to Cairo*—his first film with Seitz—and *Sunset Boulevard,* their fourth and final film together.

According to Seitz's son, John L. Seitz, Wilder and Seitz "got along well," notwithstanding some fairly heated arguments: "They were both pretty cantankerous guys. And my dad was very sure of himself. He'd been at it a long time."[19] Wilder also exhibited a large measure of self-confidence, but he had come into directing through writing and had relatively little knowledge of the intricacies of lighting and camerawork. In each of the four films he shot with Wilder, Seitz provides a strong sense of location and mood. In *Five Graves to Cairo,* Seitz contrasts the bright light of the desert with pitch-black footage; in *Double Indemnity,* he renders the world of late 1930s Los Angeles a shadowy, dusty setting for moral and legal turpitude; in *The Lost Weekend,* he recreates the urban grittiness of contemporary

New York City for the story of an alcoholic on the skids; and in *Sunset Boulevard,* he fashions a world of eerily decadent luxury for the story of a young screenwriter and an aging former movie star.

Five Graves to Cairo is a film that, as Dale Pollock notes, "has been largely overlooked and critically dismissed by all but a few Wilder scholars."[20] When it is mentioned at all, the film is usually cited in reference to the acting performance of Erich von Stroheim as Field Marshal Erwin Rommel. Pollock suggests, however, that a number of other aspects of the film—including its visual style—deserve closer attention: Wilder's first collaboration with Seitz "significantly challenged the traditional studio look for a war picture . . . mixing a realist documentary approach and stylized German Expressionist lighting, set design, and camera framing."[21] In other words, the collaboration with Seitz was already pushing Wilder towards a style he would exploit with even greater effectiveness in *Double Indemnity* and *Sunset Boulevard.*

The action of the film takes place in a bombed-out former British hotel in the Libyan Desert during Rommel's North African campaign. By the time Wilder and Charles Brackett wrote the screenplay in the summer and fall of 1942, the fortunes of the Allied forces in North Africa had improved, but the situation was still uncertain. In the film, a British soldier named John Bramble—played by Franchot Tone—is the sole survivor of a British tank crew that has engaged in a major battle with Rommel's troops. Delirious, Bramble stumbles across the North African desert into the small, isolated Empress of Britain Hotel, which the war has reduced to only two staff members: its owner Farid (Akim Tamiroff) and the French maid Mouche (Anne Baxter). Shortly after Bramble's arrival, the swiftly advancing German forces requisition the hotel as a headquarters for Rommel and his officers. In order to hide his true identity, Bramble pretends to be one of the hotel's former employees, Davos. However, when Rommel summons him for a private chat, Bramble is stunned to discover that Davos was not a hotel worker, but an undercover German spy. Bramble convinces Rommel that he is, in fact, Davos, and he manages to piece together the fact that Rommel, disguised as an archaeologist before the war, had secretly prepared five hidden supply dumps, the "Five Graves to Cairo" of the film's title, for use in the conquest of Egypt. The final piece of the puzzle falls into place when Bramble discovers that Rommel's cryptic references to points Y, P, and T refer to the letters of the word "Egypt" printed on his map. During an Allied air raid, a German officer discovers the body of the real Davos in the hotel's basement. In the noise and confusion of the raid, Bramble and the German play a deadly game of hide and seek in the darkened hotel before Bramble manages to kill his opponent. When the dead man's body is found, Rommel accuses Mouche of killing him, and Mouche, in order to protect Bramble, does not deny the accusation. Bramble leaves for Cairo, instructing Farid to present evidence the next day that Bramble and not Mouche had committed the murder. Bramble's information allows the British to blow up the dumps and thus thwart Rommel's plans. When he returns to the hotel, he learns that the Germans have executed Mouche.

For *Five Graves to Cairo,* Wilder was teamed with a talented group of Hollywood professionals, including assistant director C.C. Coleman, art director Hans Dreier, film editor Doane Harrison, composer Miklos Rosza, costume designer Edith Head., and Seitz as cinematographer.[22] Seitz was largely responsible for the visual style of the film, which, as Ed Sikov notes, is marked by a kind of "brutal lyricism."[23] As is often the case in Wilder's films, the opening sequence is also one of its most visually stunning. Filmed in the sand dunes outside Yuma, Arizona, the opening shots present a tank rolling up and down a stretch of grey and white dunes. Here, Seitz's photography takes on an almost surreal quality: when Bramble falls from the tank, ridges of light and shadow in the sand around him form abstract patterns, adding to the visual complexity of the image. Most of the film's remaining scenes take place inside the hotel, which was constructed on a single stage consisting of twelve four-walled, interconnecting rooms. Seitz found the set one of the most "shootable" on which he had ever worked, although the four-walled rooms and the somewhat static staging of many of the film's scenes gave him more limited options than he would have on the subsequent films he shot for Wilder. The set did, however, allow the camera to track along corridors and to crane from floor to floor, thus pushing the action forward and maintaining a clear sense of geography within the hotel. Seitz used a good deal of contrast lighting in the interior shots, employing very limited key light. Further, as Pollock notes, Seitz uses the architecture of the hotel—with its whitewashed brick, dark wooden beams, and idle overhead fans—to great advantage, and his camerawork is "unusually mobile for this period of largely fixed camera technology."[24]

Wilder's primary visual concept for the film's cinematography, which he conveyed to Seitz in their preproduction meetings, was that it should be "very dark." In his interview with Cameron Crowe, Wilder recalled:

> I told him . . . I would like to have it *night,* I would like to have it dark. I did not know myself what I was talking about, [but] I wanted it very dark. So we go and see the rushes. All black, *completely* black. I don't know: he wanted to teach me a lesson on that.[25]

In conversation with German journalist Hellmuth Karasek, Wilder gave a somewhat different account of his collaboration with Seitz on *Five Graves:*

> Above all I had the luck, with John F. Seitz (who had already shot all the Valentino silent films), to have an experienced cameraman. During the shooting, I noticed how courageous he was, and how fond of taking risks was when it was necessary. I had said to him that he should shoot the night footage in the desert so that it would really look like night, and the next day he showed me footage that had not completely succeeded (it was completely black), because he had had to try and see how far he could go. No other cameraman would have had the courage to do this, because of their fear of the terrible disgrace of exposing subpar material.[26]

Seitz's willingness to take risks in order to get the most extreme effect could be an asset to a director who was similarly disposed, though it could also be a liability if it created unusable footage. Seitz was well known in the industry for his extreme approach to lighting and was a source of anxiety to lab technicians who were often unsure how his footage would turn out. As Byron Haskin recalled,

> Fred Gage, lab superintendent at Metro, used to stand anxiously over the developing tanks at night, praying [that] there was something on Seitz's film, because he was a very low-key light man. Fred would say, "Oh, God . . . be something!" and he'd shove it back in the soup and eventually it'd show an image. . . . [Seitz] may have been a problem to the lab, but Seitz's concepts were absolutely revolutionary for the day. In most cases he carried them out with enough light to be able to see them [but] sometimes he didn't—he loved dark effects.[27]

According to Seitz, it had never been his intention on *Five Graves to Cairo* either to teach Wilder a lesson or to take excessive risks. Seitz told James Ursini that he had only wanted to capture as literally as possible the effect the director was seeking: "We discussed the effect. We were trying to simulate heat."[28] Seitz practiced shooting in the Arizona desert night to see how far he could push the Eastman Kodak film stock, and then he used minus reflectors and black velvet, with no key-lighting or backlighting and only a small amount of fill-light.

Whatever discussions Wilder and Seitz may have had concerning the lighting of *Five Graves,* the result was, indeed, a visually dark picture. Though the lighting is effective in some scenes—especially those in which natural light is allowed to come in through open windows or is filtered through latticed windows and slats in the roof—it seems excessively dark in other scenes, some of which take place in complete obscurity. This is particularly disconcerting in dialogue scenes early in the film, when it is impossible to see the faces of the characters as they speak. The fact that Seitz's expressive lighting on *Five Graves to Cairo* earned him an Academy Award nomination for best black-and-white cinematography is somewhat remarkable, given how radically different the film looks from most other Hollywood films of the period.

Though not a film noir, the film's visual style certainly resembles that of noir, as does its predominantly bleak tone. In one extraordinary shot that could have come from a noir shot by Alton or Musuraca, we see only the illumination of a flashlight's beam as Bramble and the German soldier are trying to kill each other in the hotel's basement. Although Sikov argues that the shot "is as close as Wilder ever comes to overtly aestheticizing the image," I would maintain that the play with a single source of light is a trademark of Seitz's style, and that it anticipates similar visual effects in both *Double Indemnity* and *Sunset Boulevard*.[29] In each of his collaborations with Seitz, Wilder tends toward a greater stylization than he does in his films with other cinematographers. Wilder was, after all, a serious collector of modern art, and it is hardly surprising that, when paired with as talented and daring a cameraman as Seitz, he was willing to go beyond a purely realist vocabulary.

• • •

Double Indemnity, with a script by Wilder and Raymond Chandler based on James M. Cain's novel, tells the story of insurance salesman Walter Neff (Fred MacMurray), whose intense physical attraction to Los Angeles housewife Phyllis Dietrichson (Barbara Stanwyck) causes him to plot and carry out the murder of her husband. Realizing toward the film's end that Phyllis has double-crossed him—she has conspired with her daughter's ex-boyfriend to kill him and keep the insurance money for herself—Neff shoots her and in the process is fatally wounded.[30]

Like many other film noirs of the mid-1940s, *Double Indemnity* benefited from cutting-edge technologies including faster black-and-white film stock, improved lighting equipment, and coated lenses. At the same time, however, the technique used by Wilder and Seitz in the film was a deliberate response to limitations imposed by the Production Code and the exigencies of wartime film production. Sheri Biesen notes that several of the film's production memos reference wartime "dim-out restrictions" that affected the lighting of night-location shoots scheduled at the East Los Angeles and Glendale train stations. Though Wilder and Seitz were ultimately allowed to film those scenes, they had to do so with "very little light." Thus, the film's visual rendering of Cain's novel owes its imposingly dark style in part to "wartime production restrictions."[31] In a bizarre example of wartime hypersecurity, the studio hired plainclothes detectives and officials of the Office of Price Administration to patrol the grocery store location while scenes were being filmed there in order to prevent members of the cast and crew from stealing grocery items. We can only speculate on how such measures contributed to the overall sense of paranoia that pervades the film.

As in *Five Graves to Cairo,* Seitz pushed the limits of Hollywood lighting conventions, though with somewhat less of a penchant for darkness than he had displayed in the earlier film. Wilder suggested that the primary motivation for the cinematographic style of *Double Indemnity* was the desire for a kind of "realism" that he associated with "serious films" and that was the opposite of "the white satin décor associated with MGM's chief set designer, Cedric Gibbons."[32] By way of illustrating his point, Wilder contrasted the more realistic style of *Double Indemnity* with the more glamorous style of MGM's *The Postman Always Rings Twice:*

> Shortly afterwards, MGM made another James M. Cain novel into a picture, *The Postman Always Rings Twice,* with Lana Turner as the wife of the proprietor of a hot-dog stand. She was made up to look glamorous instead of slightly tarnished the way we made up Barbara Stanwyck for *Double Indemnity,* and I think *Postman* was less authentic as a result.[33]

Most commentators have tended to agree with Wilder and cite *Double Indemnity* rather than *The Postman Always Rings Twice* as the quintessential example of noir style. Wilder and Seitz attempted to create a new look for the film, one that combined the rawness of a newsreel style with an aesthetic quality that was based in part on German Expressionism. Wilder explained what they were striving for:

> You had to believe the situation and the characters, or all was lost. I insisted on black-and-white, of course. . . . You could say that *Double Indemnity* was based on the principal of *M,* the very good picture starring Peter Lorre. I had a feeling, something in my head. . . . *M* was a picture that looked like a newsreel. You never realized it was staged. But like a newsreel, you look to grab a moment of truth and exploit it. . . . There was *some* dramatic lighting [in *Double Indemnity*], but it was newsreel lighting. That was the ideal. I'm not saying every shot was a masterpiece, but sometimes even in a newsreel you get a masterpiece shot. That was the approach. No phony setups. I had a few shots in mind between [Fred] MacMurray and Edward G. Robinson, and they happened at the beginning and the end, when the two were together in that room. That was it. Everything was meant to support the realism of the story.[34]

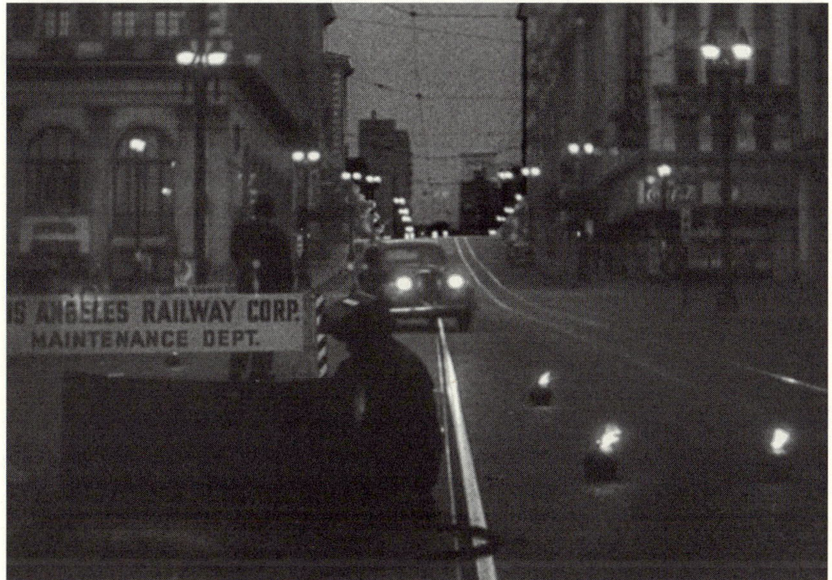

Figure 17. A signature shot by John F. Seitz, lit only by streetlights, a car's headlights, and construction flares. (*Double Indemnity*, Paramount, 1944)

One of the most striking examples of Seitz's cinematography in *Double Indemnity* is the film's opening sequence. A car's headlights can be seen as it speeds down a hill at night, while to the right of the screen the flares used by a work crew provides an additional source of light. The flares, which the car has to swerve to avoid hitting, add a menacing tone to the shot, which otherwise has the look of a documentary image. Later in the film—in the crucial scene in which Neff and Phyllis murder Phyllis's husband—the shot of the flaring torches is echoed. As the camera holds on Phyllis while her husband is being murdered in the car seat beside her, the intermittent flicker from street lamps creates a gothic effect around her face.

Another example of Seitz's artistry is the scene in which Walter first meets Phyllis at her home. Ed Sikov describes the beginning of the sequence, when Neff sees Phyllis at the top of the staircase of the Dietrichson house, a Spanish-style home in the Los Feliz neighborhood of Los Angeles:

> Wilder and John Seitz capture the cheap glamour of Phyllis's dazzling foot in a crane shot that follows her legs as they walk down the length of the stairway. Filmed through the iron grillwork of the railing, this L.A. housewife's shaved and beautifully lit calves take on an even more

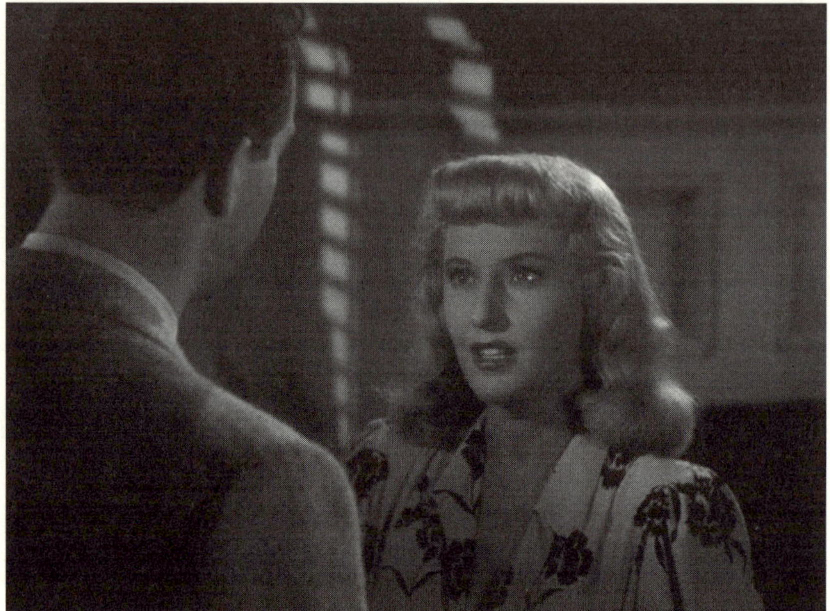

Figure 18. The essence of noir cinematography: light from the venetian blinds casts a distinctive wall pattern, while the glamour lighting of Barbara Stanwyck creates the ultimate femme fatale. (*Double Indemnity,* Paramount, 1944)

fetishized charge, thereby turning a single piece of costuming into one of the most memorable images in the American cinema.[35]

The sequence continues with a memorable dialogue scene between Walter and Phyllis that takes place in the living room. Wilder had told Seitz that he wanted an effect that would show dust as it was reflected in the sunlight coming in through the house's windows:

> I told Seitz what I would like to get on the screen. You know sometimes when the sun kind of slants through the windows of those old crappy Spanish houses, and the house is not too well kept, you see the dust in the air. And he invented a sort of aluminum powder which we blew into the air just before we started shooting.[36]

Seitz's use of metallic powder to capture the look of dust in the Southern California air is his most frequently cited innovation in *Double Indemnity,* but it is only one of many brilliant touches in the film. One of the most impressive scenes is the one in which Phyllis goes to Neff's apartment and tells him of her intention to kill her husband. The scene contains a number of tonal shifts, as Phyllis first feigns innocence, then reveals her murderous intentions, and then convinces Neff to go along with her plan. Seitz's lighting emphasizes each of these shifts, contributing to the sequence's gradually darkening mood.

The scene begins with Neff and Phyllis talking in the living room. Here, the lighting is kept fairly bright as Phyllis insists on her innocence. As they move to the kitchen, and Phyllis hints for the first time at her plan to kill her husband, the lighting becomes more low-key. When they return to the living room for a second time, Phyllis sits on the couch next to a lamp which lights her fairly brightly from one side as she once again denies her intention to kill her husband. As Neff moves from his chair to sit on the couch beside her, Phyllis turns her head away from the lamp and her face is cast in shadow. In the final part of the scene, one of the lamps is turned off, Phyllis is lit only by a table lamp, and Neff is entirely in the shadows. Neff is shown in a reclining position on the couch (suggesting that the two have had sex while the camera was averted), and he seems symbolically to be represented as a more "shady" character as he reveals his own plan for the murder. Seitz resists the temptation to light the entire scene in shadows, following the convention of melodrama. Instead, as Patrick Keating has observed, he "intensifies the expressive effects [of the scene] by tweaking his lighting in almost every shot," bringing the cinematography into "perfect harmony with the moment-by-moment progression of the scene."[37] In doing so, he makes the film's cinematography an active part of its narrative design.

Another aspect of Seitz's cinematography in *Double Indemnity* is the creation of a Southern California that resists the stereotype of the sunny, cheerful place that—at least before the advent of film noir—had been its conventional image. As Sheri Biesen suggests, "*Double Indemnity* effectively utilized its mise-en-scène to reveal the corrupt American city; its sordidness is suggested by scenes shrouded in shadow, fog, and smoke and by light splintered into oblique patterns or glistening reflections on rain-slicked streets, pools of water, shattered windows, and mirrored surfaces."[38] In daytime scenes, we are rarely allowed to perceive bright sunshine, as Wilder and Seitz keep the interior light levels very low, often breaking up soft light with venetian blinds to achieve a dim, hazy effect. Hans Dreier's set design and Seitz's photography make even Jerry's Market, the grocery store where Neff and Phyllis meet twice in the course of the film, seem like an alienating environment, with the overly geometric patterning of its stacks of canned goods, which loom rather ominously behind the two characters.[39]

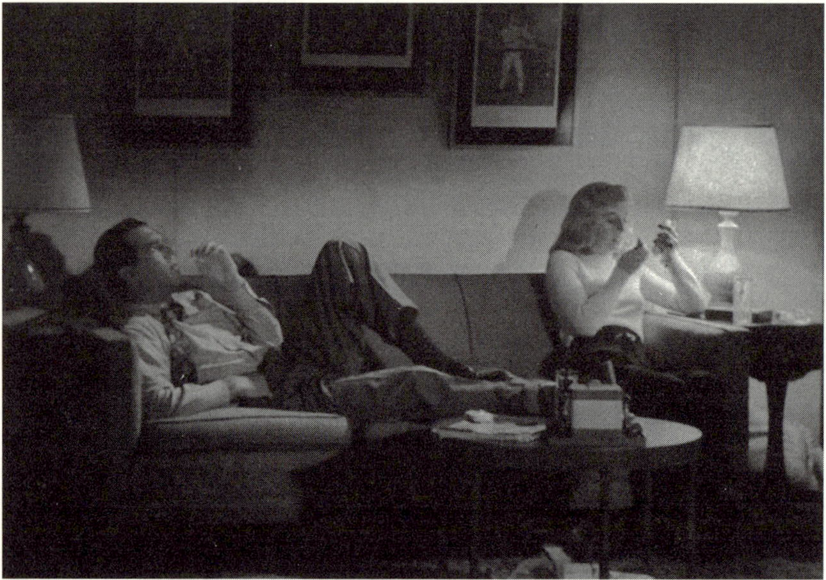

Figure 19. Expressive lighting as visual storytelling: Barbara Stanwyck lit only by a practical lamp, with Fred MacMurray in complete darkness. (*Double Indemnity,* Paramount, 1944)

Double Indemnity was nominated for seven Academy Awards, including best picture, best director, best screenplay, best actress (Stanwyck), and best black-and-white cinematography. Surprisingly—given the legendary status the film has achieved over the years—it did not win in a single category, losing the awards for best film, director, and screenplay to Leo McCarey's *Going My Way,* a sentimental comedy starring Bing Crosby in the role of a Catholic priest. Stanwyck, despite giving one of the most riveting performances of her career, was beaten out by Ingrid Bergman for her melodramatic performance in *Gaslight,* while Seitz lost the cinematography award to Joseph LaShelle for his admittedly impressive work on another stylish film noir, Otto Preminger's *Laura.*

If Wilder's next film, *The Lost Weekend,* does not reach quite the level of subtle artistry he and Seitz achieved in *Double Indemnity,* it is nonetheless an important film in the Wilder canon. *The Lost Weekend* has at times been included in lists of film noir, less for its plot than for its use of urban settings and its creation of an often dark world of apartments, nightclubs, and city streets. Biesen, for example, includes *The Lost Weekend* among Wilder's film noirs, noting that its action takes place within a "noir urban jungle" of pawnshops, urban psychiatric wards, and the gritty streets of midtown Manhattan.[40] More overtly realistic in its stylistic approach than *Double Indemnity*, the film also contains more blatantly expressionistic elements, such as the highly subjective use of the camera in those scenes where the increasingly crazed workings of the protagonist's mind are rendered in shocking visual terms.

The story's central character, Don Birnam (Ray Milland), is an alcoholic writer who has been attempting—with help from his brother Wick (Philip Terry) and his girlfriend Helen (Jane Wyatt)—to stay sober. As the film begins, we learn that Birnam has been on the wagon for ten days and seems to Wick and Helen to be on the way to recovery. In fact, however, it is just the opposite: Birnam's craving for alcohol has only become more desperate with each passing day. In order to get a drink, he avoids going on a country weekend planned by Helen and Wick, and manages to buy enough liquor to go on a serious bender. In a local bar and then alone in his apartment, he consumes so much alcohol that he ends up in the alcoholic ward at Bellevue Hospital. Wearing only his pajamas and a stolen coat, Birnam escapes from the hospital and steals a bottle of whiskey from a liquor store. When Helen returns to the city, he sneaks out to pawn Helen's coat and buy a gun, which he intends to use to kill himself. In the film's melodramatic conclusion, Helen stops Birnam from committing suicide and convinces him to find new meaning in his life by writing his autobiographical novel, *The Bottle*.

Before shooting began, Wilder, Seitz, and screenwriter Charles Brackett held several meetings to discuss ideas for specific shots as well as the overall look of the film. Based on those conversations, Wilder insisted on a number of conditions, each of which he felt would be necessary if the film was to achieve the sense of realism he felt it required. First, the film's street scenes would be shot on location in New York City, rather than on a re-creation of a city street on the Paramount lot. Second, the set for Sam's Bar—in which several scenes take place—would have four walls, so that it would look like a real bar rather than a Hollywood soundstage. (In fact, the set was so realistic that many viewers were convinced it was a real New York bar, and tried to find it in when visiting Manhattan). Third, the Greenwich Village apartment set would be constructed according to the dimensions of an actual New York apartment, including its tiny kitchen. This detail is very effective, as the cramped apartment adds to our sense of Birnam's feeling of claustrophobic confinement. Finally, Wilder insisted that Seitz be able to do one tour-de-force shot that would include the skyline, the garden, the exterior of the apartment building, and the window, so that at the end of the shot, Birnam's whiskey bottle could be revealed hanging from a string.[41]

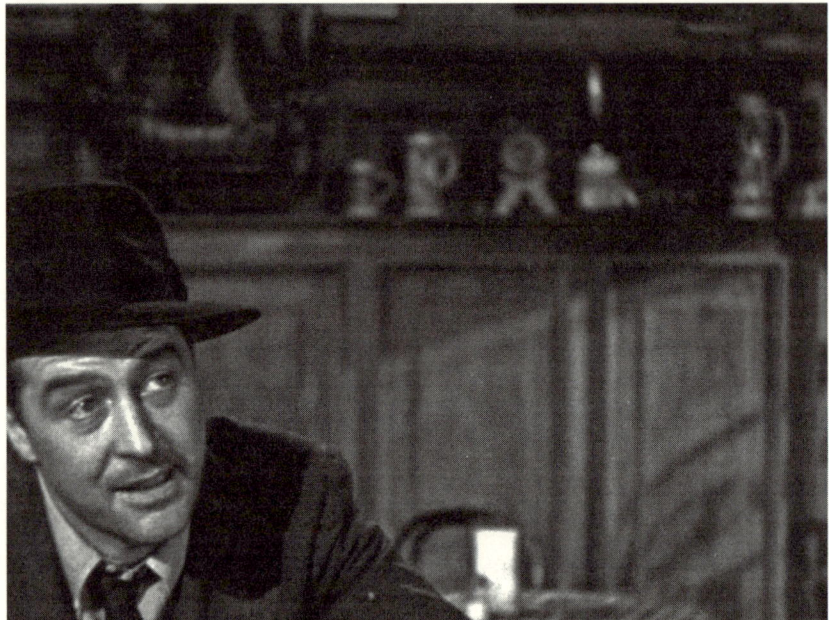

Figure 20. Wilder and Seitz use disturbingly off-center compositions to emphasize the disoriented state of alcoholic writer Don Birnam (Ray Milland). (*The Lost Weekend*, Paramount, 1945)

The naturalistic style of *The Lost Weekend* is sustained throughout the film by exterior shots of Bellevue Hospital and of the city's pawnshops, bars, and grimy streets. In order to shoot the sequence of Birnam walking down the city street after escaping from the alcoholic ward, Wilder and Seitz hid the camera in different places, including a box in the back of a delivery truck and an empty piano packing case on the sidewalk. Passersby had no idea they were being filmed, adding further to the film's sense of almost documentary realism. For one shot of a drunken Birnam falling down a flight of stairs, Seitz strapped a small camera to a stuntman's chest and had him do the fall, thus capturing the event from Birnam's perspective. In a scene in the bar, Seitz shoots Birnam with his head off to the left of the frame, suggesting his growing intoxication.

Overall, the somber look of the film is appropriate to its grim storyline. Seitz increased the effect of Birnam's gradually worsening condition by adjusting the lighting as the film went on, shooting the later scenes in a much harsher style than the earlier parts of the film. Beginning in the sequence where Birnam escapes from the hospital's drying-out ward, Seitz

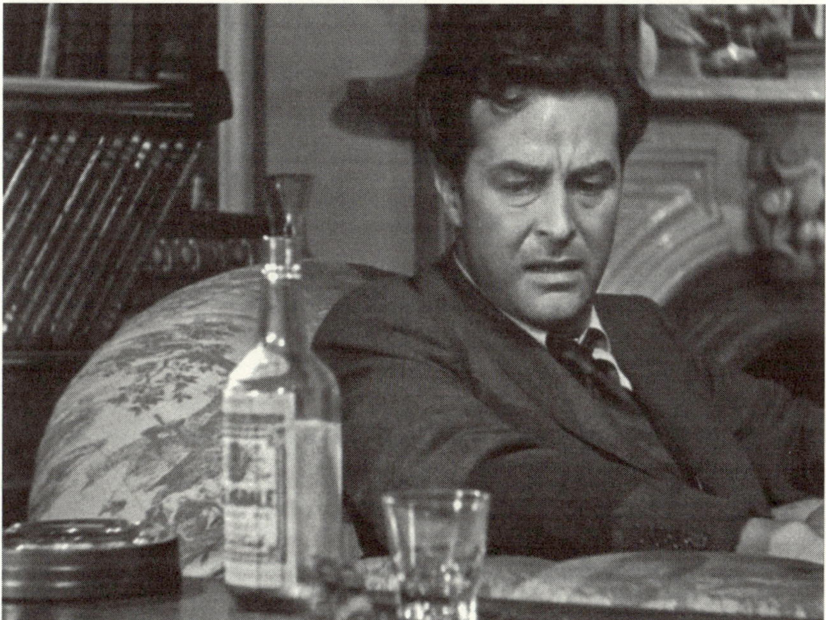

Figure 21. Objects placed in the foreground increase the feeling of depth. (*The Lost Weekend,* Paramount, 1945)

used an orange-yellow filter to give Milland's character a particularly sallow complexion. In the scene where Birnam demands a bottle from a clerk in a liquor store, Seitz used both makeup and lighting to render the close-up of Milland as harsh as possible, caking his face with chalky makeup and shining the most severe light he could on the actor. While watching the rushes of the scene, Milland visibly shuddered at his unglamorous appearance, but Wilder immediately sensed the power of the image. Though Milland complained that the shot made him look "God-awful," the effect added a further layer of realism to his character, contributing to his Oscar-winning performance.

In several sequences, Seitz and Wilder used the technique of placing an object in the foreground in order to create a greater feeling of depth. Such shots are motivated not only by Seitz's desire to keep the film visually interesting but also by the theme-driven decision to emphasize Birnam's troubled psychological state. In one shot, a row of bottles arranged on the shelf of a liquor store are placed between the camera and Birnam, powerfully emphasizing his fixation on their contents. Outside a pawnshop,

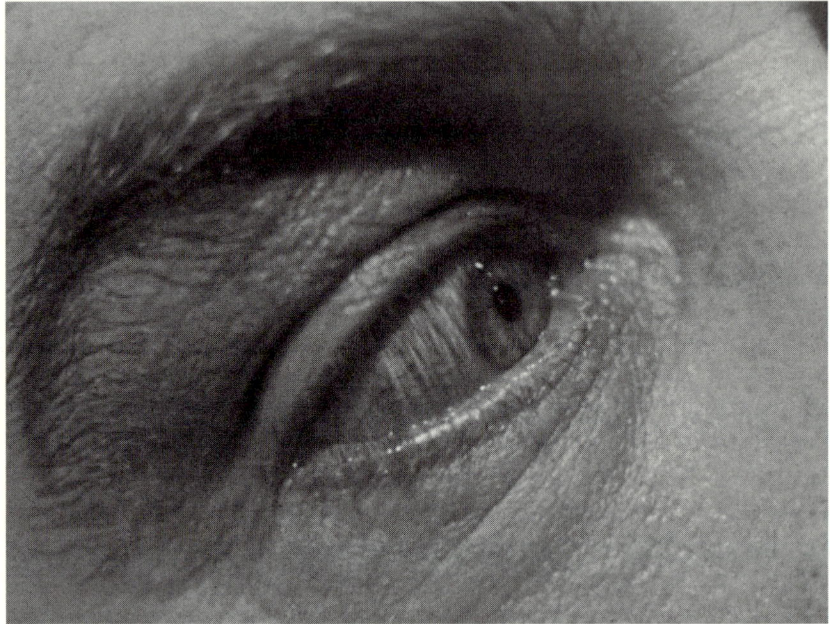

Figure 22. Technical virtuosity: an extreme close-up of Birnam's eye. (*The Lost Weekend*, Paramount, 1945)

desperate to hock his typewriter, Birnam stares in through the crisscrossed bars of an iron gate, while behind him the Third Avenue el forms a grid of shadows, symbolically imprisoning him and heightening our sense of his despair.

In the film's most famous sequence, Seitz uses the camera to portray the inner workings of Birnam's mind. While slumped in a chair in his apartment, hemmed in by ominous shadows, Birnam begins to experience disturbing hallucinations. A mouse wriggles in a crack in the wall, while a bat and its shadow circle the room, the bat finally diving on the screeching mouse and killing it. This is followed by an extremely daring camera move for the period (Sikov calls it "the single most extreme close-up ever achieved to that point"): an intense close-up of Birnam's eye as he wakes from his alcoholic stupor.[42] Seitz, Wilder, and Brackett had discussed the shot, deciding to bring the camera lens as close to the actor's face as possible. Attaching a special-effects lens to the camera and placing the camera on a boom, Seitz brought the lens to within six inches of Milland's eyeball. Seitz had to tell Milland not to breathe, since any movement of his face would have destroyed the shot. Once the close-up was completed, Seitz orchestrated a reverse tracking movement with a deliberate change of focus, emphasizing Birnam's disorientation as he stumbles out of bed. Masterful shots such as this earned Seitz his third straight Academy Award nomination on a Wilder film. Once again, Seitz would fail to win the award, which would elude him throughout his career.[43]

• • •

In the spring and early summer of 1949, Seitz was reunited with Wilder on their fourth and final collaboration, *Sunset Boulevard. Sunset Boulevard* tells the story of the struggling screenwriter Joseph Gillis (William Holden), who becomes involved in the life of a long-forgotten and aging silent film star named Norma Desmond. When Gillis parks his car in the garage of Desmond's house in an attempt to escape the repossession men, he finds himself in the presence of Desmond herself (Gloria Swanson) and her butler, Max (Erich von Stroheim). Discovering that Gillis is a writer, Norma asks him to stay at her mansion and help her write a script for a film that she hopes will revive her faded acting career. At a New Year's party—which, as it turns out, is attended only by the two of them—Gillis learns that Norma is in love with him. He escapes to a party at a friend's house, where he falls for Betty Schaefer, a script-reader who had earlier rejected one of his screenplays. Gillis returns to the Desmond mansion and agrees to stay with Norma, but he has secretly begun to work with Betty on a new screenplay. When Gillis tries to move out of the Desmond mansion, Norma shoots him in the back, and he falls face-down into the swimming pool.

In his cinematography for *Sunset Boulevard,* Seitz surpassed even the high level he had established in his earlier collaborations with Wilder, creating one of the most stylistically distinctive films of the late 1940s. As Gerd Gemunden suggests, the film "contains some of the most stunning cinematography in Wilder's oeuvre, breaking with his credo that images should not draw attention to themselves":

> From the pool shot using mirrors to the wide-angle shots with extreme depth-of-field—for example in the scenes when Max's white-gloved hands dominate the foreground when he plays the organ, or when the bandaged wrists of Desmond after her suicide attempt are featured big in the foreground while her soon-to-be-lover is kept in sharp focus in the background—the film presents a daring cinematography.[44]

The film's visual design can be divided into two very different stylistic registers. For such real-life locations as the Alto-Nido apartments, the

Bel-Air golf course, and the Paramount back lot, Seitz shot in a relatively flat, highly realistic, quasi-documentary style. In the sequences shot at the shadowed, secluded estate of Norma Desmond, the lighting and camerawork are far more expressionistic, taking on the characteristic style of film noir. As in *The Lost Weekend,* a number of shots call attention to their artistry, but in *Sunset Boulevard* these shots remain more purely cinematic, in the sense that they are not motivated by any obvious psychological factor such as an alcoholic state of delirium.

The visual style of *Sunset Boulevard* is a departure in certain respects from that of the first three films on which Wilder and Seitz had collaborated. One of the most evident stylistic changes in *Sunset Boulevard* is the number of deep-focus shots.[45] It is Seitz's elegant use of deep-focus technique—nearly a decade after Gregg Toland's pioneering efforts in *Citizen Kane* and *The Little Foxes*—that allows Wilder to move throughout the vast spaces of the mansion while keeping everything in sharp view. In order to achieve such an extreme depth of field, Seitz not only used greatly intensified light levels—as Toland had done in *Citizen Kane*—but he also latensified the film in order to be able stop down the lens aperture even further. The process of latensification—in which the film is pre-exposed to light so that objects that would normally be too dark to appear on the negative can be seen—was used in about 15 percent of the film's footage, adding two stops to the speed of the film.[46] This technology allowed Seitz to be more creative with the lighting, for example using a practical lamp on the set as the key light or creating the gothic gloom of the backyard funeral for Norma's pet monkey. Another scene that exploits the new photographic technologies is one in which Max is seen playing the pipe organ—his white-gloved hands looming in the foreground—while Gillis, furious at having his belongings moved to the mansion without his knowledge, rushes up from behind. Seitz's wide-angle perspective creates the effect that Max's hands briefly hover over Gillis's head, making the butler look like a puppet-master controlling Gillis.

In addition to its use of deep focus, *Sunset Boulevard* features a highly mobile camera, resulting in a visual style that is significantly different from that of *Double Indemnity.*[47] The camera, as Sam Staggs has noted, is "always on the go, looking around and peering into corners . . . tracking in closer [and] then tracking out."[48] The camera movement begins with the opening credit sequence, in which the titles are laid over a tracking shot that moves down the street, and continues throughout many scenes of the film. In comparison with *Double Indemnity,* in which the relatively immobile camera allows Seitz to build scenes out of a series of static shots, *Sunset*

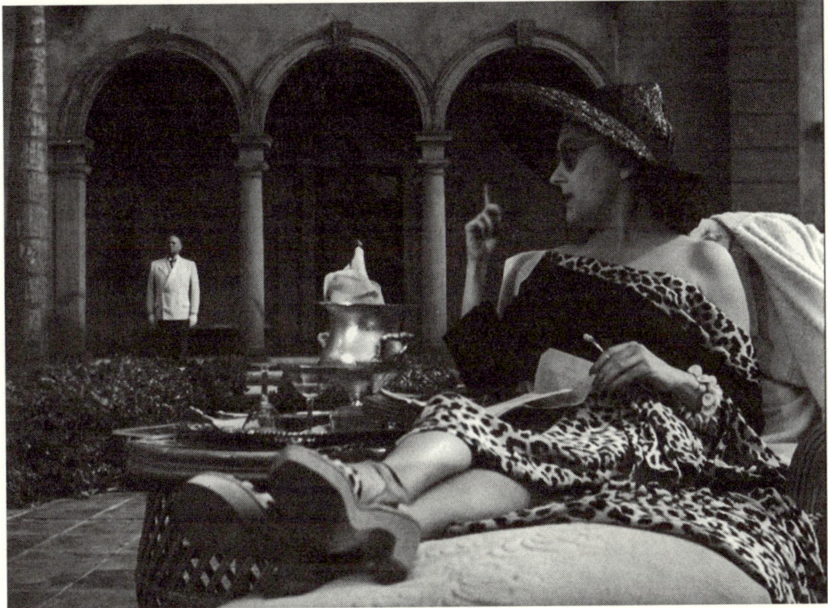

Figure 23. Deep-focus composition, with the aging star Norma Desmond (Gloria Swanson) in the foreground and her servant, Max (Erich von Stroheim), in the far background. (*Sunset Boulevard*, Paramount, 1950)

Boulevard is marked by a far more fluid camera style, in which a combination of different camera movements engenders a feeling of vertiginous mobility. Like Alfred Hitchcock and Robert Burks in *Vertigo*, another film in which a male protagonist comes to be controlled by a mysterious woman, Wilder and Seitz use camera movement to heighten the character's sense of psychological dislocation.

The film is marked by a number of flamboyantly stylized uses of cinematography. One of these occurs in the scene in which Desmond is captured in the beam of a movie projector as she and Gillis are screening one of her silent films. As she postures dramatically, strong side-lighting edges her hair in a white blaze. The shot is both visually effective and cleverly allusive, at once recalling *The Four Horsemen of the Apocalypse*, in which Seitz had used shimmering backlight for the actress Alice Terry, and the silent film career of Swanson herself.

Another multilayered allusion occurs in the scene where Swanson and Holden dance together on the floor of Norma Desmond's mansion. "You know, this floor used to be wood, but I had it changed," Desmond tells

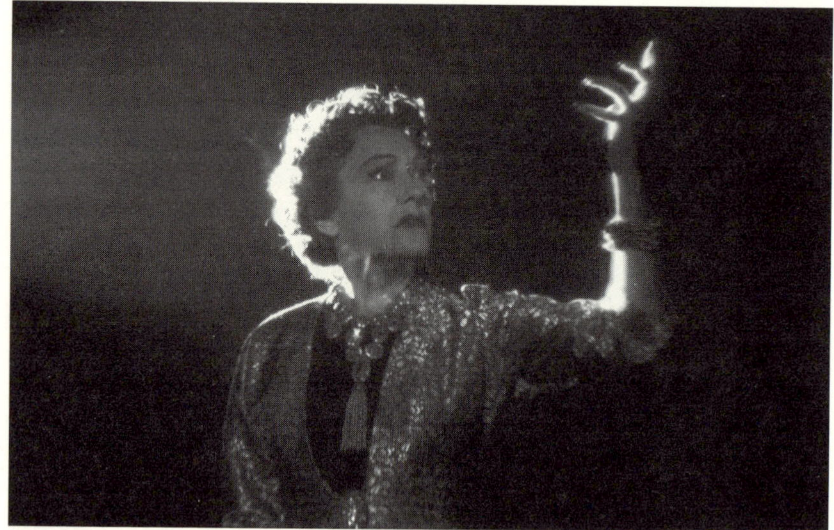

Figure 24. Gloria Swanson is dramatically lit from behind by the film projector as she watches herself on screen. (*Sunset Boulevard,* Paramount, 1950)

Gillis. "Valentino said there's nothing like tile for a tango." It is one of several Hollywood insider moments in the film—along with the sequence in which Cecil B. DeMille plays himself, and the scene in which Norma plays cards with a group of silent-era stars including Buster Keaton. Valentino did in fact appear in a film with Gloria Swanson—*Beyond the Rocks* (1922)—in which they danced a tango. The Valentino reference is made even more complex by the fact that Seitz had shot Valentino and Alice Terry dancing a tango in *The Four Horsemen of the Apocalypse* and had used a variation of the same dolly technique he used in *Sunset Boulevard* to capture a shot of the dancers making a 360-degree turn.

Wilder and Seitz use visual imagery and lighting in ways that are thematically resonant as well as stylistically evocative. When Desmond goes to see Cecil B. DeMille on the Paramount lot, for example, a lighting technician turns the spotlight on her, a sadly ironic reminder of her past glory. In the final scene of the film, this lighting is echoed when news photographers light and shoot Desmond as she comes down the stairs of her mansion after she has been arrested for killing Gillis. Having lost all touch with reality, Norma believes that the news cameramen lighting her for pictures to be printed in the newspapers are in fact movie cameramen and that she is acting on the set of her new film.

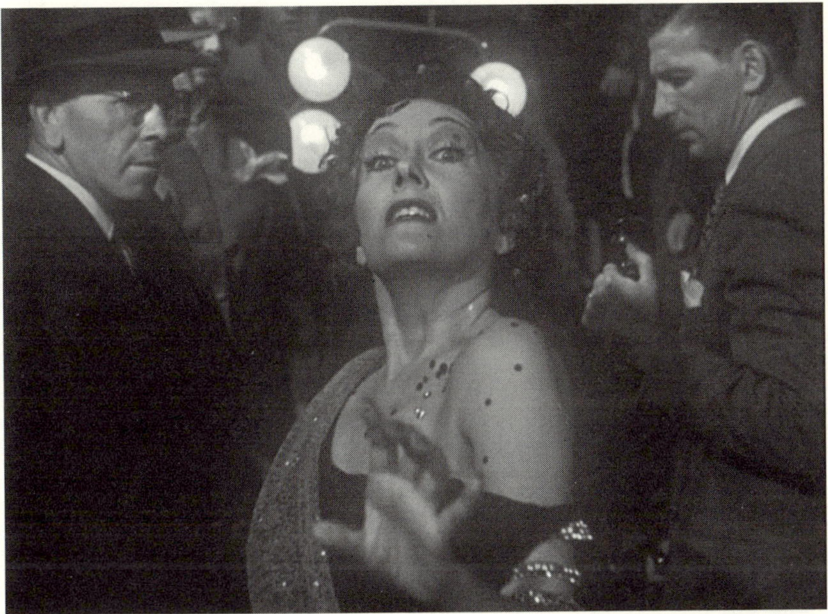

Figure 25. Stylistic innovation to express character: Norma Desmond moves in for her close-up, breaking through the conventional wall separating actor and camera. (*Sunset Boulevard,* Paramount, 1950)

The most famous shot of *Sunset Boulevard*—and one of the most iconic images in all of Wilder's work—is the one in which Gillis floats face-down in Norma Desmond's swimming pool after Norma has shot him in the back. The effect of this shot—the likes of which had never before been attempted—is that of looking up through the water of the pool to see Gillis's face-down body, and beyond it the policemen and photographers standing at the edge of the pool. Merely placing the camera underwater and shooting up would not have created the desired effect, since the water's surface would have acted as a mirror and prevented anything outside the pool from being seen. Instead, a giant mirror had to be placed at the bottom of the pool and photographed from above in order to get the reflected shot.

In *Sunset Boulevard,* Seitz once again demonstrated his desire to push the photographic medium to its furthest limits. The swimming pool shot is not only highly effective in providing closure to the film's gothic narrative, but it is also impressive in its gesture toward an extreme form of visual stylization. The sheer bravado of the shot—its self-conscious play with visual excess—reminds us of similarly hyperstylized images in *Citizen*

Kane, made almost a decade earlier but clearly a model for the cinematography of *Sunset Boulevard.* Like the Welles-Toland film, *Sunset Boulevard* exudes a sense of pleasure in its own visual texture and reminds us of the powerful images that cinematic collaboration—at its best—is capable of producing.

4 The Color of Suspense

Alfred Hitchcock and Robert Burks

[Hitchcock's] entire approach to a picture while preparing it is to visualize it from the camera point of view.

Robert Burks

Alfred Hitchcock's reputation as one of the most important visual stylists in the history of the cinema is based in large part on the twelve films he made in the 1950s and early 1960s in collaboration with cinematographer Robert Burks.[1] Along with art directors J. MacMillan Johnson, Henry Bumstead, and Robert Boyle, it was Burks who worked most closely with Hitchcock during this period to achieve the look of several of his most technically innovative and visually stylish films. If the period from 1950 to 1964 was, in the words of Donald Spoto, the "golden age of Alfred Hitchcock masterworks"—a period during which the director made *Strangers on a Train, Rear Window, Vertigo, North by Northwest, Psycho, The Birds,* and *Marnie*—it was also the era during which Hitchcock enjoyed his most successful and lasting partnership with a cinematographer.[2]

Since coming to Hollywood in 1940, Hitchcock had worked with a series of cinematographers, several of whom lasted for only a single film. In a ten-year period, Hitchcock collaborated with George Barnes (*Rebecca, Spellbound*), Rudolph Maté (*Foreign Correspondent*), Harry Stradling (*Mr. and Mrs. Smith, Suspicion*), Joseph Valentine (*Saboteur, Shadow of a Doubt,* and *Rope*), Glen McWilliams (*Lifeboat*), Ted Tetzlaff (*Notorious*), Lee Garmes (*The Paradine Case*), Jack Cardiff (*Under Capricorn*), and Wilkie Cooper (*Stage Fright*). Whether this rapid turnover in DPs was due to institutional and economic factors or to artistic and temperamental differences is not altogether clear. Nevertheless, Burks was able to become a permanent member of Hitchcock's filmmaking team in a way that no other cinematographer had.[3]

Hitchcock was most effective when working with a stable group of collaborators, and in the 1950s he was able to build a team capable of creating a visual style uniquely suited to each film. Perhaps the key player on this team was Burks, who photographed twelve of the thirteen films Hitchcock directed between 1951 and 1964, moving with the director from Warner Bros. to Paramount in the early 1950s and then continuing as a collaborator until the mid-1960s. Had he not suffered a nervous collapse just before the shooting of *Torn Curtain,* and then died in a house fire in 1968, there is every reason to think that Hitchcock would have continued to use Burks as his cinematographer for the remainder of his films. Collaborating with Hitchcock could not have been easy: as Stephen Rebello notes, the director's unusually good understanding of the camera "often heightened his expectation of the cinematographer," placing additional pressure on even an established DP such as Burks.[4] It appears evident that working with Hitchcock took a physical and emotional toll on Burks and eventually ended their partnership.

In this chapter, I will argue that Burks's participation was of vital importance to Hitchcock's filmmaking. Yet I will also suggest that the partnership of Hitchcock and Burks represents a different model of collaboration from that of Wyler and Toland or that of Wilder and Seitz. In those two partnerships, a cinematographer widely recognized as among the most talented in the industry helped to shape the visual style of a director whose films would very likely not have reached the same level of artistic excellence without his involvement. A close reading of the collaboration of Hitchcock and Burks, on the other hand, poses more questions than it answers. How were the films of the artistically visionary Hitchcock influenced by the contribution of a hard-working, technically proficient, but not widely celebrated cinematographer? Was Burks's role more a matter of passively carrying out the director's ideas than of actively participating in the creation of an aesthetic vision? What would Hitchcock's films have looked like if shot by a different director of photography? Did the presence of Burks on the set have a significant impact on Hitchcock's career? Conversely, what form would Burks's career have taken had he not been paired with Hitchcock?[5]

The details of Burks's career are not as well documented as those of Bitzer, Toland, or Seitz. There are no published articles or books by Burks, and his accidental death at the age of fifty-eight deprived him of the opportunity to do an oral history or a career interview. Although we do have the testimonial of another important Hitchcock collaborator, the screenwriter John Michael Hayes, that Burks "gave Hitchcock marvelous ideas [and] contributed greatly to every picture [he shot] during those years," we have relatively few comments from either Burks or Hitchcock himself about the details of their collaboration.[6] What we do know of Burks's biography is that after being hired by the Warner Bros. lab in 1928 at the age of nineteen, he appears to have demonstrated unusual talent, rising to assistant cameraman in 1929, to operating cameraman in 1934, to special effects cinematographer in 1938, and to full cinematographer in 1944. Burks worked on over thirty films as a special effects cinematographer—including *Kings Row* (1941), *Arsenic and Old Lace* (1941), and *The Big Sleep* (1944)—before moving on to a position as DP. The skills he developed gave him an understanding of the visual technologies Hitchcock's films of the 1950s and 1960s would increasingly require.

At the age of thirty-five, Burks became the youngest fully accredited DP in the industry when he joined a cinematographic unit at Warner Bros. that included James Wong Howe, Sol Polito, and Ernest Haller. Within a few years, Burks would gain a position as one of Warner's top cinematographers, benefiting from the departures of Howe in 1947 and Polito in 1950. In the years from 1948 to 1950, Burks was assigned to a series of prestige projects, including *Task Force* (Delmer Daves, 1948), *The Fountainhead* (King Vidor, 1949), *Beyond the Forest* (Vidor, 1949), *The Glass Menagerie* (Irving Rapper, 1950), and *The Enforcer* (Bretaigne Windust and Raoul Walsh, 1950). In making *The Fountainhead*, Burks worked closely with both Vidor and art director Edward Carrere to plan the visual conception of the film. Burks studied miniature models of each of the film's sets so that he could plan the lighting and camera setups well in advance of the construction of actual sets.[7] This degree of preproduction involvement was still quite unusual for a cinematographer in late 1940s Hollywood, and it presaged a similarly close involvement in each of the films Burks would shoot for Hitchcock. The quality of Burks's work on *The Fountainhead* was impressive enough to be noticed by the Motion Picture Academy, which included the film on its short list of the ten best-photographed black-and-white films of the year.

• • •

Though it is difficult to determine the precise factors that allow for a successful partnership between a director and a cinematographer, it seems very likely that Burks's background in special effects appealed to Hitchcock, who had been incorporating elaborate special effects into his films since the late 1920s.[8] Burks's first film with Hitchcock, *Strangers on a Train* (1951), was an ideal vehicle for a cinematographer of versatile talents, combining both studio and location shooting as well as fairly intricate special effects. According to Donald Spoto, Hitchcock and Burks engaged in long conferences about how

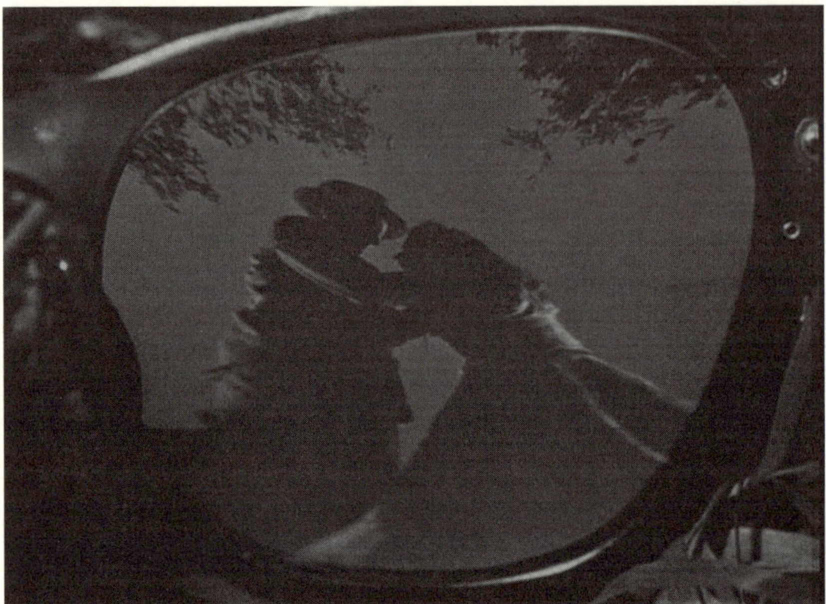

Figure 26. Hitchcock noir: the murder scene as reflected in the victim's eyeglasses. (*Strangers on a Train,* Warner Bros., 1951)

to shoot the film's most dramatic moments, including the scene in which Bruno Anthony (Robert Walker) murders Miriam Haines (Laura Elliot) at the amusement park and the climactic final sequence in which Bruno is killed and Guy Haines (Farley Granger) is exonerated.[9]

The film's most celebrated visual effect—and the shot that no doubt earned Burks his first Academy Award nomination—occurs during the sequence in which Bruno follows Miriam into the amusement park and strangles her.[10] When Bruno grabs Miriam by the neck, her eyeglasses fall to the ground and the entire scene of Bruno strangling Miriam is seen reflected in her glasses. The shot was done using an elaborate system of optical printing: the shot had to be first captured in a concave mirror, with the camera facing the mirror while Elliott turned her back to it so that her reflection could be seen in it and captured on film. Then, as she is strangled and falls to the ground, the image of the murder appears to be reflected in the lens of her glasses.

Another tour-de-force combination of camerawork and special effects is the sequence involving the film's spectacular merry-go-round climax. After completing a tennis match, Guy races to the amusement park to try to find

Bruno before he can plant Guy's cigarette lighter at the scene of Miriam's murder. When Bruno sees Guy, he jumps onto the merry-go-round, and Guy jumps on after him. The scene that follows was, as Hitchcock himself remarked, "a most complicated sequence."[11] As the two men struggle on the merry-go-round (now spinning at top speed), an old man volunteers to crawl under the moving carousel to reach the controls. This scene was not accomplished by trick photography: in an extremely dangerous stunt, a man actually crawled underneath the spinning carousel. When the merry-go-round is finally brought to a halt, the entire machine is destroyed in a massive explosion. The actual collapse of the merry-go-round was done using a miniature, and then Hitchcock had Burks cut back to the real machine, which had been destroyed in advance of shooting the scene.

The cinematography of Burks's second film for Hitchcock, *I Confess* (1952), might at first viewing seem relatively unremarkable when compared to the more visually exciting *Strangers on a Train.* In reality, however, *I Confess* posed challenges that tested Burks's skills in a different way. Hitchcock and Burks engaged in discussions about the style of the film before shooting began, and they screened both documentaries and fiction films shot on location in an attempt to understand what factors created a sense of greater realism in a motion picture. The film's feeling of authenticity, which would be greatly admired by the future directors of the French New Wave, was achieved in large part by shooting nearly the entire film on location in and around Quebec City, Canada: only three of the film's scenes were shot on the Warner Bros. lot. The amount of location shooting was highly unusual for a Hollywood film of the early 1950s, and it presented, as Burks observed, "many handicaps—some of them severe."[12] Since the ceilings in most of the buildings used for interior scenes were too low to permit lighting units to be set above the action—as would have been done on a studio soundstage—Burks and Hitchcock decided to handicap themselves further by shooting the entire film without any overhead lighting or backlighting, using only lights hidden behind chairs or under desks or tables. Further contributing to the film's sense of almost documentary realism were the decision to cast nonprofessionals in many of the smaller roles and the requirement that none of the actors—with the exception of lead actress Anne Baxter—could wear makeup.

I will step briefly out of chronological sequence to examine the third and final black-and-white film Hitchcock made with Burks as cinematographer, since I believe the technical and aesthetic challenges of black-and-white cinematography to be very different from those of color. *The Wrong Man* (1956) was based on the true story of a New Yorker, Manny Balestrero

(Henry Fonda), wrongly accused of a series of robberies. The visual style of this film is difficult to describe, falling somewhere between documentary realism and film noir, with elements of Italian neorealism and moments of modernist expressionism. The account of the film's production contained in an *American Cinematographer* profile implies a style of strict documentary realism, with little in the way of deliberate artistry. Hitchcock is quoted in the article as telling Burks that he wanted the film shot "in a style unmistakably documentary." According to Burks, he and Hitchcock shot nearly the entire film on location in and around New York City, using a newly developed kind of small, portable lamps called Garnelites. The article also suggests that Hitchcock hesitated before assigning the film to Burks, concerned that the film's "stark, colorless, documentary treatment" might damage the reputation for shooting elegant Technicolor films Burks had earned in *Rear Window* and *To Catch a Thief*.[13]

In reality, the story of the film's production was far more complicated. The circumstances under which the film was made reflect Hitchcock's ambivalence about the move toward cinematic realism, a realism he not only appeared to embrace in his choice of story material but also publicly touted as his attempt to produce a form of almost unadulterated documentary.[14] According to art director Paul Sylbert, Hitchcock had originally intended to shoot nearly the entire film on location in New York City, just as he had shot *I Confess* in Quebec City. However, discouraged by the difficult shooting conditions created by an unusually cold New York winter, Hitchcock announced that the production would return to Hollywood to shoot the remainder of the footage.[15]

Clearly, the visual style of the completed film is far from the documentary "newsreel" look claimed in the *American Cinematographer* article. As Paula Marantz Cohen has noted, "the images are as artfully arranged . . . as any in the Hitchcock repertoire." Burks's cinematography contributes "substantially to setting a mood for the film," his frequent use of lighting to create crosshatched shadow invoking "the dominant theme of imprisonment and . . . of crucifixion."[16] The film's shots are highly planned (Hitchcock had carefully storyboarded them), and they are executed with a high degree of technical precision. Many shots were taken either on soundstages or the back lot rather than on actual locations. Overall, the film feels less like a documentary than like a 1950s film noir, with frequent use of extreme camera angles (both high and low) and bravura shots involving wide-angle lenses.[17]

Several of the film's more innovative shots were the result of close collaboration between Burks and Sylbert. The first of these is a shot at the

Balestrero home, a modest New York City rowhouse that had been rebuilt on a soundstage. This home had a movable front that could be rolled to the side so that when Fonda enters the front door, the camera appears to move into the house with him and follow him down the hallway. Another striking shot takes place when Balestrero has been locked up in a jail cell on the night of his arrest. The camera was mounted on a device that functioned as a kind of Ferris wheel, spinning around the stationary face of Fonda, who stands with his back to the wall. The effect, like that of the more famous "vertigo shot" Hitchcock would use two years later, is a feeling of dizziness, reflecting the character's profound disorientation at being unfairly arrested and incarcerated. In a later scene at the Long Island city jail, there is a shot in which the camera appears to go through a small slot in the front of the jail cell door. Burks designed the shot using a wide-angle lens that makes the cell look extremely cramped, emphasizing Balestrero's sense of entrapment. According to Sylbert, a cell about five and a half feet wide was constructed for the scene, allowing Burks to design a shot in which Fonda steps to the window, then quickly steps back toward the closed door and looks out through the slot, his enormous eyes staring out hauntingly at the viewer.[18]

• • •

Dial M for Murder (1953) was the first of Hitchcock's color films to be photographed by Burks.[19] Adapted from a stage play that Hitchcock had seen on Broadway, *Dial M* was the director's only attempt to make a film using 3-D technology. Hitchcock and Burks shot the film in 3-D on the insistence of Warner Bros., even though Hitchcock himself had little interest in the technology. Shot in August and September 1953, the film was "a safety net picture" for the director, during which he "ran for cover while waiting for the muse."[20] The film is probably best remembered as the first of three of Hitchcock's late-1950s films to star Grace Kelly, who recalled: "Hitch felt frustrated and annoyed at having to use the cumbersome 3-D camera, and poor Bob Burks had to tell him, 'Oh, no, Hitch—you can't do this and you can't do that.... We had endless rehearsals, and we were always doing a dance around this enormous machine, which seemed to me the size of a room."[21]

The constraints of shooting in 3-D no doubt contributed to the static nature of the film, which takes place almost entirely within the confines of a stage-set reproduction of a London apartment. As it turned out, the 3-D shooting was almost superfluous: by the time of the film's release, the short-lived 3-D fad had ended, and the film was exhibited almost entirely in normal, flat-screen format.[22] Nevertheless, Hitchcock and Burks did attempt to move beyond the confines of the apartment set. Several overhead views and a series of fluid camera movements take the audience into spaces they would not be able to occupy in a stage play, effectively breaking down the proscenium wall of the theater. As Steven Jacobs has noted, the viewer watches the action of *Dial M* "not only from the wings but also from the center stage, from backstage, from the footlights, the curtains, the rafters, and the balcony, and at times . . . everything at once."[23]

In its use of a highly structured visual space, *Dial M for Murder* served as a useful preparatory exercise for Hitchcock's next film: *Rear Window.* This would be Hitchcock's fourth film with Burks, and the first of their collaborations to be made at Paramount. Hitchcock left Warner Bros. for the more prestigious Paramount lot in the late fall of 1953, bringing Burks with him. At Paramount, Hitchcock would take full advantage of a talented team of collaborators, including Burks, editor George Tomasini, and costume designer Edith Head; he would also avail himself of the studio's physical resources, including its spacious soundstages.

The set of *Rear Window* was unlike any Hitchcock had been able to build for his earlier productions: constructed on one of the studio's largest soundstages, it measured an impressive 184 feet in length, 98 feet across, and 40 feet high, making it one of the largest interior sets ever built in Hollywood. The construction was supervised by Hitchcock himself, along with art director Joseph MacMillan Johnson. An extremely realistic reproduction of a New York apartment complex, with thirty-one separate apartments surrounding a courtyard approximately seventy feet wide, the set was, as Scott Curtis suggests, the real "star" of the movie, arguably "even more central to its success than James Stewart or Grace Kelly."[24] The cost for the design, construction, and dressing and lighting of the set accounted for over 25 percent of the film's total budget, compared to only 12 percent for the actors.[25] In addition to the set's thirty-one apartments—eight of them completely furnished—it included a Manhattan skyline backdrop as well as gardens, trees, fire escapes, working chimneys, and an alley leading to a street behind, which itself was complete with a bar, pedestrians, and moving traffic. The lower levels of the courtyard were built beneath the stage-floor level, and the walls of the apartment inhabited by L.B. Jeffries (Stewart) were movable, allowing for different camera angles in the shots taken from his viewpoint.

The technical challenges of shooting on such a set were formidable. In large part, the difficulties stemmed from the requirement that virtually all shots had to depict the action from Jeffries's point of view, either with the naked eye or as if seen through binoculars or a telephoto camera lens. Many of the shots

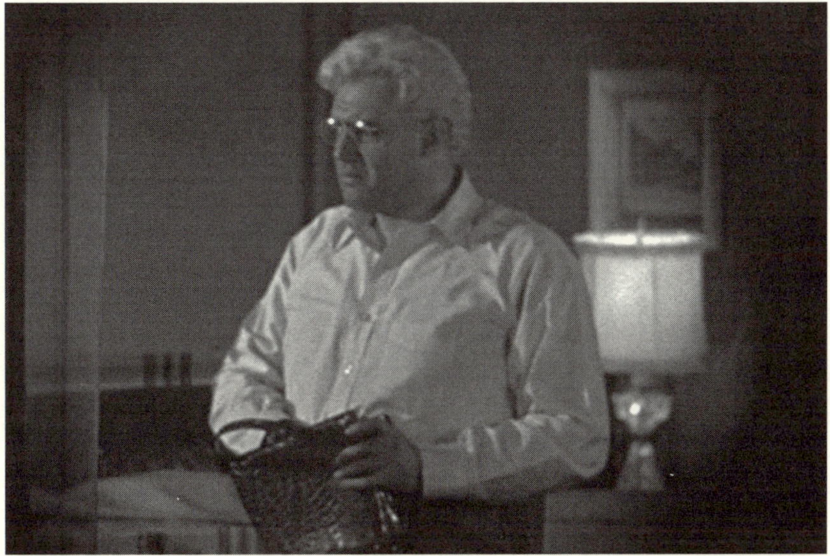

Figure 27. The camera eye as voyeur: Lars Thorwald (Raymond Burr) is in perfect focus as he is observed from across the courtyard. (*Rear Window*, Paramount, 1954)

also needed to pinpoint small objects or convey important action taking place at distances varying from forty to eighty feet from Jeffries's apartment.[26]

The lighting requirements for the film were equally demanding. The set had seventy windows and doors, each of which had to be lit as if they were separate sets. Moreover, since much of the action of the film occurs at night, Burks had to light the entire set for both daytime and nighttime shooting. The rigging of the *Rear Window* set was the most elaborate electrical job ever undertaken at Paramount, and it severely taxed the studio's resources. At one point during filming, almost every piece of lighting equipment on the Paramount lot was in use on Hitchcock's set. James Stewart recalled the consequence of all those lights:

> One day there were several shots where the camera was behind me—that is to say, I was in the foreground, and across the courtyard the action was in focus. Well, you've got a big depth-of-field problem with that. It would need twice the amount of light so that the aperture could be kept small [enough] to keep everything in focus. Paramount took all the lights they had from the stages not in use and it still wasn't enough; then they borrowed lights from Columbia and MGM, and finally they could do the shot; the heat was really intense. Suddenly, in the middle

> of it, the lights set off the sprinkler system, not just a section of it, but on all the stages, and we're not talking about little streams of water but torrents. But it never fazed Hitchcock. He sat there and told his assistant to get the sprinklers shut off and then to tell him when the rain was going to stop, but in the meantime to get him an umbrella.[27]

Given the size of the lighting project, Hitchcock and Burks decided that rather than shoot the film in a conventional manner—moving lights from one part of the set to another for each set-up—they would prelight the entire set, rigging all the lighting in advance and then leave it in place throughout the shoot. A remote switchboard resembling an enormous organ console controlled the lights in each apartment, and a large chart detailed the set-lighting plan and indicated which switches needed to be activated for any given lighting scheme. While adjustments to the lighting were continually necessary in order to shoot different scenes, the prelighting saved an enormous amount of time and money during shooting. The change of set lighting from night to day, for example, could be accomplished in forty-five minutes rather than the several hours it would normally have taken.

A major challenge for Burks was lighting the individual apartments both for night and for day. The goal was to have the artificial lighting of the apartments seem as natural as possible. Attempts to achieve this kind of naturalistic lighting on a large indoor set had been largely unsuccessful in other films: apartments that were lit with enough intensity for night scenes looked exaggeratedly bright during the daytime sequences. Burks's challenge lay in finding a more balanced approach to the lighting of individual apartments, so that there would be enough light to see the action within them from the other side of the courtyard at all times, without the light ever seeming artificially bright. An additional challenge was the need to maintain the required light intensity of the entire set for daytime sequences while not "burning up" the actors with too much light as they approached the apartment windows. In order to avoid this effect, Burks placed graduated scrims below the lighting units, and gradually diffused the lighting of apartments as actors walked toward the windows.[28]

Burks's greatest technical challenge, however, was not the lighting of the set but achieving the many point-of-view shots from Jeffries's apartment. In order to make the image on screen match what Jeffries would actually observe as he looks into the apartments, Burks needed to find a way of shooting the action across the courtyard with perfect definition combined with a very deep focus. One scene in which these requirements were of paramount importance was the one in which Lars Thorwald (Raymond Burr), the salesman who lives across the courtyard from Jeffries and is suspected by Jeffries of having murdered his wife, is seen removing a wedding ring from his wife's purse. Burks was able to show clearly that the object being removed was a wedding band. Most directors would have showed an inserted close-up of the ring. For Hitchcock, however, a simple close-up would have been too simple: the shot had to look as if the ring was being observed through a telephoto camera lens held by Jeffries seventy feet away. Initially, Burks tried to get the shot from inside Jeffries's apartment, using a 250mm lens and increasing the illumination to an extraordinarily high level of 1,600 foot-candles.[29] Even with this much light, the definition was not adequate to show that the object was a wedding ring. Eventually, Burks was able to get the shot by suspending the camera on a boom overhanging the courtyard and using a somewhat shorter 150mm lens.

Having solved the problem of how to get adequate definition on such detailed long-range shots, Burks still had to contend with the fact that shooting at such distances created an extremely narrow depth of field. In other words, there was no room for error: every time an actor took even half a step backward or forward, he or she would be out of focus. As a result, all shooting distances had to be determined in advance and with absolute precision. Although measuring shots in advance was not particularly unusual in Hollywood filmmaking, it was made more complicated by the fact that—because Burks would be shooting across a courtyard—the usual practice of using a tape measure to measure distances prior to shooting was impossible. Instead, Burks had to measure the distance of each shot at the same time that he did the prelighting of the set, creating a thorough chart of the distances from each camera placement to each point of action. For these kinds of precise technical calculations, Burks's experience as a special-effects cinematographer was indispensable, just as it would later be for the exacting technical and special-effects work on *Vertigo* and *The Birds*.

One of the most famous sequences in *Rear Window* is the long expository shot near the beginning of the film that both introduces the apartment building and informs us that Stewart's character is a photographer who has broken a leg while on assignment. The uninterrupted shot—which lasts almost ninety seconds—is a remarkable example of the shot-making skill of which Burks and his operators William Schurr and Leonard South were capable. The shot commences on a couple who, because of the heat wave the city is experiencing, have chosen to sleep on the fire escape and are in the process of awakening. The camera then pans left to reveal the apartment of a dancer (later given the name "Miss Torso"), who can be seen getting dressed, and then pans left again to disclose an alley leading to the street, where a water tanker is spraying the pavement. From there, the camera

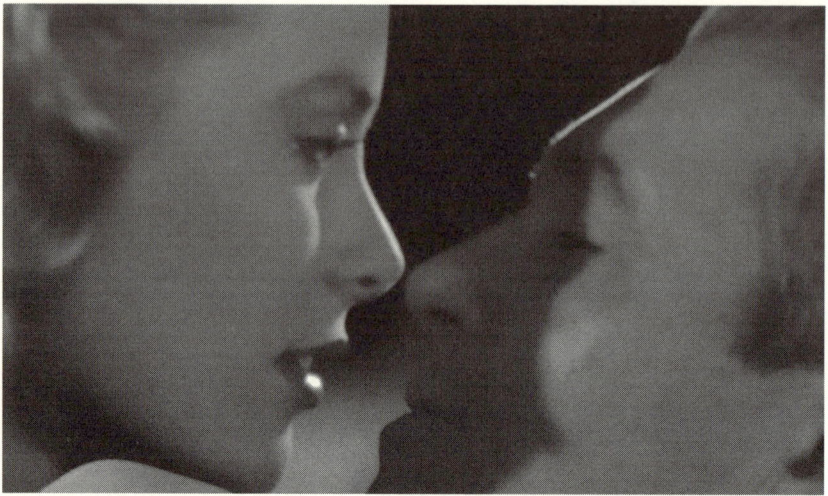

Figure 28. The iconic kiss, captured by Robert Burks in extreme close-up: Grace Kelly and James Stewart. (*Rear Window,* Paramount, 1954)

begins to pull back and eventually enters Jeffries's apartment via a window. There, in close-up, Stewart is shown sleeping in his wheelchair. The name of Stewart's character is revealed via another close-up of the inscription on the plaster cast of his left leg, after which the camera tracks back further to reveal more of the apartment, before panning left to show in turn a smashed camera, a photograph of a car-racing accident, and an array of photographic equipment. In order to film this complicated sequence, Burks had to mount a camera on the biggest boom available on the Paramount lot, which was fitted with an extension. The shot involved numerous focus changes, and it required a good deal of planning and many rehearsals. It took ten takes and half a day of shooting to execute the shot to Burks's satisfaction.

Principal photography on *Rear Window* was completed in January 1954. The film's overall cost was just over $1 million—amazingly low, even when adjusted for inflation, for a film shot on such a large set and involving so much technical complexity. At least some of the credit for the modest budget goes to Burks, whose streamlined processes of lighting and shooting kept the film's below-the-line costs in check.[30]

• • •

To Catch a Thief was the first of Hitchcock's films to be photographed using Paramount's VistaVision wide-screen process. The process—unveiled by the studio in the spring of 1954—involved exposing the film horizontally and then rotating it ninety degrees and reducing it to a standard 35mm negative. This process produced an extremely sharp image with less grain than other wide-screen formats. Hitchcock and Burks were to use VistaVision on five of their films—*To Catch a Thief, The Trouble with Harry, The Man Who Knew Too Much, Vertigo,* and *North by Northwest*—before the introduction of a sharper color negative (Eastman Kodak 5250) made the extra definition afforded by the larger VistaVision negative less noticeable, rendering the process obsolete.[31]

There is no doubt that VistaVision—with its remarkably sharp image—was an attractive alternative to other wide-screen formats. The limitation of VistaVision, as with all wide-screen processes, was that it did not allow the same depth of field as a conventional 35mm format. When the VistaVision lens was focused on images in the foreground, the backgrounds tended to become unacceptably blurred.[32] In order to address this problem, it was often necessary to create rear-projection shots of the background scenery and then combine them with close-ups or medium shots of the actors taken either on location or in the studio. Although rear projection was a convenient technique for studio filmmaking, it could be a distraction for the viewer, especially when the look of the rear-projection footage was noticeably different from that of the actors in the foreground. Because Hitchcock was shooting *To Catch a Thief* on location in the south of France, the studio suggested that Burks shoot all the backgrounds there and then do the close-ups when the production returned to Hollywood. Instead, Hitchcock decided to shoot both close-ups and rear-projection shots on location and then shoot a set of alternative close-ups against the rear-projection plates in Hollywood.[33]

This somewhat cumbersome process did not hurt the film's visual presentation, which earned Burks his only Academy Award for best color cinematography. However, measured against the other films Burks shot for Hitchcock, the cinematography of *To Catch a Thief* was not particularly noteworthy. As Hitchcock's biographer Patrick McGilligan suggests, Burks's Oscar for the film was "miraculous," since the film was created largely through laboratory effects done in postproduction.[34] Nevertheless, the combination of glamorous actors (Cary Grant and Grace Kelly), beautiful scenery, and luscious costumes, all captured on the crystal-clear VistaVision image, was enough to win Burks his only Oscar.

With *Vertigo,* however, he earned a place as one of the most important color cinematographers of the 1950s. Hitchcock first discussed the project that would become *Vertigo* with Burks in August 1956, and by October, Burks was making tests both in the studio and on location.[35] During preproduction, Hitchcock told his cinematographer that he wanted *Vertigo* to have the slightly iridescent quality of a Vermeer painting. Burks managed to achieve this somewhat ethereal quality through a finely calibrated use of lighting, while executing a number of tracking shots that add a sense of fluidity to the film's visual style.

Among the most effectively shot scenes in the film is the one in which Scottie (James Stewart) and Madeleine (Kim Novak) are in Scottie's apartment after he has rescued her from what he thinks is an attempt to drown herself in San Francisco Bay. The scene, which lasts a full nine minutes and contains several complex shots, was one of the most complicated to shoot. It opens with a pan that travels from Scottie, seated on a sofa by the fireplace, toward the bedroom where Madeleine is sleeping. The second pan, later in the same scene, was even more complicated, requiring six takes to execute properly. The shot follows Madeleine as she walks from the bedroom to the fireplace. Hitchcock wanted the shot to match in style a later shot of Judy, Madeleine's alter ego, emerging from the Empire Hotel bathroom.[36]

An even more famous shot is the one that occurs during the first scene at Ernie's Restaurant. Hitchcock had decided to build an exact replica of the famous San Francisco restaurant on a soundstage at Paramount, and art director Henry Bumstead designed the forty- by sixty-foot space down to the last detail.[37] (In a typically Hitchcockian gesture, even the food the extras were served during the scene was prepared by Ernie's chefs.) The scene's complicated crane shot, which took Burks eight takes and over three hours to prepare and shoot, pulls back from Scottie, who is seated at the bar, and then pans across the dining room to discover both Madeleine (or the woman he thinks is Madeleine) and Gavin Elster sitting at a table near the back. As Madeleine leaves the restaurant, Burks captures her in an iconic profile close-up, her face in shimmeringly clear focus with the restaurant's walls a blurry red behind her.

The photographic effect most commonly associated with *Vertigo* has become so imbedded in the history of cinematic innovation that it is often referred to as the "Vertigo Shot." The first use of the effect occurs during the rooftop-chase sequence with which the film begins. A suspect leaps from one rooftop to another across an alley below and scrambles to safety. A policeman follows him across, but when Scottie attempts the jump, he slips and nearly falls, saving himself only by hanging onto a rain gutter. When the policeman reaches out to help Scottie, he falls to his death. Scottie's first episode of vertigo, which occurs just before the policeman's fall, is dramatized by a point-of-view shot aimed down into the alley: as Scottie looks down, the distance seems to stretch and the perspective distorts.

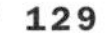

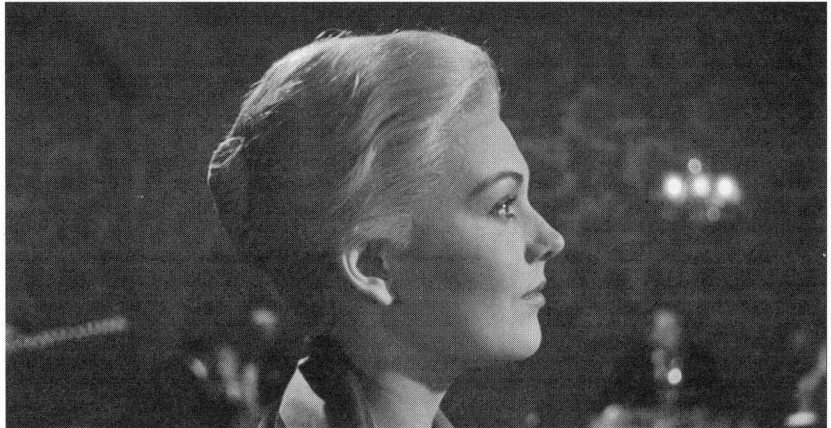

Figure 29. Burks uses shallow focus to capture Kim Novak in a stunning profile shot. (*Vertigo*, Paramount, 1958)

Hitchcock and Burks went to considerable lengths to achieve the complex sequence, which combines location shooting on the rooftops of San Francisco, additional shots made on rooftops of the Directors Building at Paramount and the Security First National Bank in Hollywood, and travelling matte shots made on the process stage by special-effects coordinator John Fulton. The film's crew scouted buildings in Los Angeles to find the best location for the downward shot between the buildings, and then built a wooden bridge between two buildings with an alley between them. Burks set up the camera on the bridge and shot directly down into the alley. The vertiginous effect of the trademark shot was accomplished by the ingenious combination of a forward zoom and a backward dolly track. Though Burks and Hitchcock had discussed how to do the shot, a second-unit cameraman by the name of Irmin Roberts actually perfected the technique.[38] The second and third uses of the vertigo shot occur when Scottie climbs the San Juan Bautista tower, first with Madeleine, and then, in the film's concluding sequence, with Judy. As originally designed, the tower shot would have required building an enormous rig to suspend and operate the equipment at the top of the tower set. Instead, Hitchcock had a miniature scale model of the set built, and the dolly-zoom effect was shot with the model lying on its side.

One of the most striking aspects of *Vertigo*'s visual style is the film's use of color. Throughout the film, the color green is strongly associated with the mysterious Madeleine—who often dresses in green and drives a green car—while the color yellow is just as strongly associated with the character of

Scottie's former girlfriend and loyal supporter, Midge (Barbara Bel Geddes). In Midge's cheerful apartment, the walls are painted yellow; Midge wears a yellow shirt, and she has a bright yellow stepladder that Scottie uses in an attempt to overcome his fear of heights. *Vertigo*'s luminescent color is one of its most extraordinary features, demonstrating both Burks's adeptness in color cinematography and the coordinated efforts of art director Henry Bumstead and costume designer Edith Head to create the appropriate color scheme.

The most symbolically resonant use of the green motif occurs in a scene of Judy and Scottie in Judy's hotel room. When Judy looks in the hotel mirror, half the mirror reflects the green light, indicating that Judy is in fact Madeleine's alter ego. When she steps out of the bathroom and is seen by Scottie, she is bathed in green light, a visual suggestion that she has become Madeleine, back from the dead. Burks achieved this very unusual effect by using a specially designed diffusion filter, which cast Novak's face in a magical greenish glow. Hitchcock considered using the green filter in other scenes as well, but he ultimately decided to use it only for the sequence of Judy at the hotel, thus marking the scene as stylistically distinct from the remainder of the film. Before shooting the scene, the crew shot test footage of the effect, varying the lighting each time. Once the lighting for the shot had been determined, the scene was accomplished in only three takes.[39]

Another of the film's most famous shots also takes place in Judy's hotel room. When Scottie moves forward to embrace Judy, Hitchcock wanted to suggest Scottie's psychological disturbance without resorting to dialogue. As they kiss, the room begins to spin in a slow, vertiginous movement. The room turns in a clockwise direction, as do the two lovers, but because the room appears to spin faster than the lovers, the shot becomes somewhat dizzying. Hitchcock began with a circular set, most of which was identical to Judy's hotel room but one section of which showed a livery stable. Burks first photographed the room with a 360-degree pan, and then Hitchcock stood the two actors on a turntable, set the camera in front of them, and turned them slowly around. Behind them, the shot of the room was rear-projected onto a screen, and then the ensemble was photographed with the lovers spinning in the foreground while the set behind them seems to spin faster. As the lovers spin, the background begins to change and the room disappears, leaving a view of the livery stable. Scottie's kiss with Judy transports him in his memory to the kiss with Madeleine just before she ran up the bell tower to commit suicide. When Scottie returns his attention to his embrace with Judy, the stable disappears and the room comes back into view as the circling continues. Backlit by a green neon sign, Scottie and Judy go into a deeper embrace. In this scene, Burks's lighting and camerawork combine with Hitchcock's ingenious staging to create one of the most memorable moments in any Hitchcock film.

• • •

If *Vertigo* is the most beautiful film Burks shot for Hitchcock, *The Birds* is the most technically impressive. More than any of his other films with Hitchcock, *The Birds* called on Burks's background in special effects. Of the 1,500 shots that were designed for the film—nearly triple the number of a typical Hitchcock production—over four hundred were either trick or composite shots. Knowing that the technical demands of *The Birds* would be particularly intense, Hitchcock brought in two specialists to work on the production's visual effects. Ub Iwerks, who had worked with Walt Disney as a pioneering cartoonist in the 1920s and later headed Disney's special-effects department, was loaned to Hitchcock for the film, and the two men met on an almost daily basis during the production.[40] Albert Whitlock, one of the preeminent matte artists in the industry at the time, painted many of the film's backgrounds.

The largest complication in making *The Birds* involved the birds themselves. Hitchcock had originally intended to use mechanical replicas of different kinds of birds with motorized wings, and more than $200,000 was spent on building and testing bird models. It soon became clear, however, that the models were phony-looking and unconvincing. In one test, where children were running while being attacked by mechanized crows, the mechanical birds looked more like model airplanes than real birds. When Burks saw the tests, he voiced his opinion to Hitchcock that the idea of using mechanical birds would have to be abandoned. The best solution, he argued, would be to use a combination of real birds and optical effects. Working with the studio's optical department, Burks and special effects editor Bud Hoffman were able to modify existing footage of real birds to create acceptable-looking shots of birds and people intermingling.

One of the most difficult scenes in the film to shoot was the dramatic sequence in which thousands of smaller birds—a mix of finches, swallows, and buntings—come down through the chimney of the Brenner house and pour out into the living room, attacking the inhabitants. The set had to be enclosed by a polyethylene wall so that the lights could illuminate the set but the birds could not escape. Placed in cages at the top of the chimney, the birds were then released through trapdoors into the chimney. Air hoses pointed down the sides of the chimney kept the birds from roosting before they reached the bottom. After the scene had been shot, the number of birds had to be multiplied by double-, triple-, and quadruple-printing, using a process known as sodium vapor process photography.

The film's most spectacular sequence involves a mass avian attack on the town of Bodega Bay. The sequence begins immediately after crows attack a group of schoolchildren. Melanie Daniels (Tippi Hedren) enters the Tides restaurant in a frightened state, and an intense discussion ensues between the staff and customers as to what should be done about the increasingly violent bird attacks that are taking place around town. The conversation is interrupted by another attack. A gull knocks the gas station attendant unconscious, and as men rush to the attendant's aid, gasoline that has been spilled from the still-running hose runs along the pavement. Melanie and the others attempt to shout out a warning to a man lighting a cigarette, but he does not hear them and drops his match, setting off a series of fiery explosions. High above, a squadron of seagulls that has been watching the events below begins to descend upon the town, apparently intent on further destruction. It is at this point that the most famous shot of the film occurs. An aerial view of Bodega Bay shows the gas station engulfed in flames as more gulls swoop through the field of the camera at closer range. The "balloon shot," which Hitchcock liked to call a "God's-point-of-view shot," is one of the film's most effective, replicating the point of view of the birds themselves while adding a particularly ominous mood to the scene. To achieve the shot, a cameraman stood on a one-hundred-foot cliff on Santa Cruz Island shooting footage of fish being thrown to gulls on the wing. The travelling matte process was then used to multiply the images of the birds and make them appear to be circling over the town center.[41]

The most complicated sequence from a technical perspective was the film's ending, in which the Brenners drive away with Melanie in her sports car, passing silently through a bird-filled landscape and escaping from Bodega Bay. As Mitch Brenner (Rod Taylor) pulls the car out of the garage, Hitchcock wanted a view of all the birds perched on the house and grounds in an eerie calm, as if waiting for some unseen signal to start yet another wave of attacks. The shot of the actors leaving the house required a combination of thirty-two different exposures as well as one of Whitlock's matte paintings. Although Hitchcock was justifiably proud of the shot—certainly one of the most complicated in any film of the early 1960s—it is Burks who deserves credit for the shot's execution.[42]

Principal photography on *The Birds* lasted a grueling six months, from March to August 1962, with the first two months on location in Bodega Bay and the last four on the Universal lot. As the footage multiplied, simply keeping track of all the shots in the film was a Herculean task. Burks and Hoffman started by recording all the shots on paper, but when that procedure became too unwieldy they adopted what is called a "coloring book"

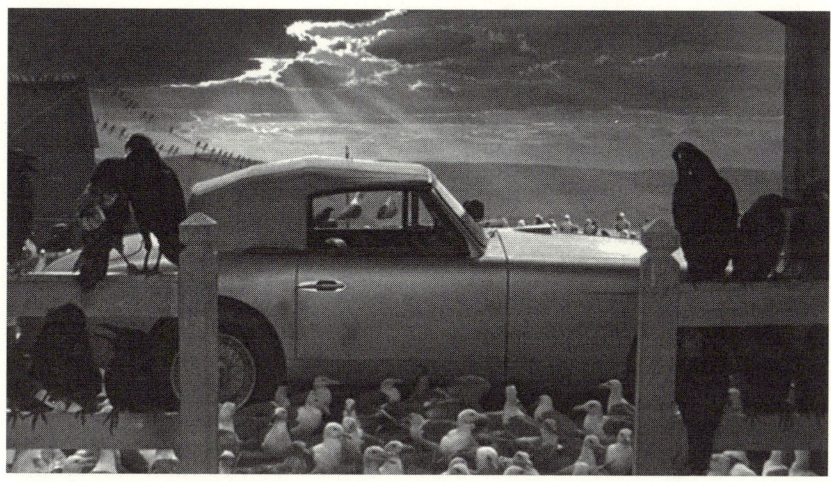

Figure 30. A haunting image of an avian apocalypse, combining cinematography and special effects. (*The Birds*, Universal, 1963)

method: Hoffman would make a black-and-white dupe that could be used to indicate shots that still needed to be finished; it would be replaced with a piece of color film once the shot had been taken. Though principal photography was completed in the late summer of 1962, Burks did not finish his work on *The Birds* until the following February: in all, he spent over a year working on the film. Burks spent much of the fall shooting retakes and overseeing the special-effects footage. In December, when Burks and Hoffman submitted the footage to several optical houses for printing, Burks rejected much of the work for not looking sufficiently real.[43]

In a rare gesture of praise for a member of his crew, Hitchcock singled out Burks for his contribution to the film. "If Bob Burks and the rest of us hadn't been technicians ourselves," he wrote to Peter Bogdanovich, "the film would have cost $5 million [instead of $3 million]."[44] Hoffman went even further, stating that the film "never could have been made" without Burks: "It was his persistence in doing these shots over and over that made *The Birds* the classic it is today."[45] In fact, the role Burks played in making *The Birds* was as indispensable to that film as Billy Bitzer's contribution had been to *Intolerance* half a century earlier.

• • •

The final collaboration of Hitchcock and Burks was a very different project from *The Birds. Marnie* (1964), a psychological drama, features Tippi

Hedren as the title character, a woman unable to escape the psychic trauma of a deeply buried childhood experience. Sean Connery plays Mark Rutland, the wealthy businessman who hires Marnie, catches her committing a robbery at his offices, and marries her.

Though *Marnie* relied far less on special effects than *The Birds* and was filmed in a generally more conventional manner, the film exhibits a visual style that is unique among Hollywood productions of the period, combining unusual camerawork, meticulous composition and framing, and one of the most elaborate color schemes of any Hitchcock film. Perhaps the most striking aspect of *Marnie*'s visual style, at least on a first viewing, is its use of color.[46] Hitchcock's plan—carried out very effectively by Burks and art director Robert Boyle—was to avoid warm and bright colors and to emphasize subdued tones that would allow for the selective use of two primary colors: red and yellow. In the scenes at Marnie's mother's house, for example, shades of grey and dull green predominate, so that a vase of bright red flowers in the living room has a lurid intensity; at the Rutland Company office, the color scheme is varying shades of grey, making any bright color such as the red ink Marnie spills on the sleeve of her white blouse stand out. In the sequence of Marnie's flashback to her traumatic childhood experience, Hitchcock and Burks went even further in the de-coloration of the film, strongly desaturating the colors in order to give the feeling of a deeply buried memory.[47]

It is impossible to know to what extent Burks can take credit for the striking use of color in the film. What seems clearer is his use of the camera to create a distinctive visual style for the film. More than in any of his other films for Hitchcock, Burks alternates between tightly framed compositions shot with 50mm fixed lenses and striking camera moves, including backward and forward zooms, elaborate tracking shots, pans, crane shots, Dutch tilts, and even the combination zoom-and-dolly shot he had developed in *Vertigo.* Hitchcock and Burks also make more striking use of deep staging than in previous films. On board the ship during the honeymoon voyage, for example, an extreme long shot captures Mark as he runs down the corridors of the ship toward the camera, adding to the drama of the sequence as he looks for Marnie.

In the scenes that take place at the Rutland Company office, Burks uses camera movement in particularly effective ways. In the first scene of Marnie in her new job after she has been hired by Mark Rutland, the busy office is shown in a very high-angle shot that pans across the room, gradually moving down to eye level and then turning to the right to reveal Marnie in close-up typing at her desk. Then, after a brief cut to a point-of-

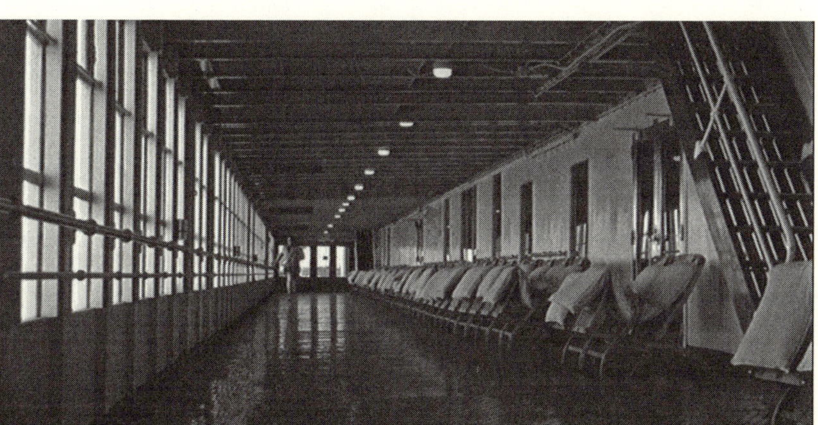

Figure 31. Visual stylization: Mark Rutland (Sean Connery) runs toward the camera, as the long corridor of the ship increases the feeling of depth. (*Marnie*, Universal, 1964)

view shot showing Marnie's apparent interest in the office safe, there is another pan to the right to reveal Mark watching Marnie from behind. On an emotive level, Burks's flowing camera moves create a subtle feeling of tension or unease: as in both *Rear Window* and *Vertigo,* the camera adds to the Hitchcockian motif of the watcher being watched. On the level of visuality, such shots emphasize a sense of circularity that is in contrast with the geometric angularity of the office. One could read the circular patterns of such shots as reflecting, on a formal level, Marnie's periodic need to rob the offices where she works, as well as her recurring nightmares and her repeating episodes involving her fear of storms and of the color red.

One of the film's most innovative shots occurs during the party sequence at the Rutland mansion. The camera begins at the top of the stairs, overlooking the spacious foyer of the house in which dozens of well-dressed socialites are mixing. As the doorbell sounds and a butler opens the front door, the camera moves twenty feet down to the floor level and then forty feet forward to a close-up of the face of Sidney Strutt (Martin Gabel), who has just entered the door. Production manager Hilton Green recalls how several members of the filmmaking team, including Burks and Robert Boyle, watched a similar shot from Hitchcock's *Notorious* in preparation for making the shot in *Marnie.* The shot is, as Peter Bogdanovich notes, an example of tour-de-force cinematographic technique used to underscore the dramatic situation: "The actual movement of the camera creates suspense

. . . because you know it's going somewhere, so you ask, 'Where's it going? Where's it going? Where's it going?' And then it ends up on a close-up of Strutt, and the audience says 'Oh, my god!'"[48] The fluency of such shots suggests that the collaboration of Hitchcock and Burks had by this point achieved not only a prodigious visual technique but also a highly effective synthesis of narrative development and artistic expression.

Despite the sophistication of the film's visual construction, *Marnie* was taken to task by some critics for what they saw as infelicities of style, particularly in the use of obvious rear projection during the horseback-riding sequences and the use of a garish model of a ship in the sequences involving Marnie's visits to her mother. For the latter scene, art director Robert Boyle had designed a cut-out of a ship that would be placed at the end of the street set, but when Burks shot the footage of the street with the ship in the background, he found it to be less than convincingly realistic. After Burks and Boyle discussed the problem, Boyle went to Hitchcock and asked if the footage containing the street could be reshot:

> I . . . said, "Hitch, I've never asked you to do this before, but I'd like to have this retaken." I said, "I think we can fix it." I'd already talked to . . . Bob Burks, and he admitted that he had lit the sides of the street too much. And we both were at fault. And we stayed up all that night . . . trying to figure out some way that we could repair the damage. But Hitchcock wouldn't reshoot it. He would reshoot [a scene] if Tippi Hedren's hair or dress was awry, but not that.[49]

This anecdote, though it may represent a relatively minor detail within the larger context of the shooting of the film, is a significant indication of Hitchcock's attitude toward his collaborators. The fact that Hitchcock was unwilling to make a change in the way a scene was shot—even when asked to do so by his cinematographer and production designer—reveals a good deal about Hitchcock's working relationship with his crew, including even his most highly valued collaborators. Anecdotally, at least, it seems clear that Hitchcock's relationship with Burks was more one-directional than the other collaborations we have examined in this book.

Since we do not have Hitchcock's side of the story, it is difficult to know the precise reasons for his refusal to retake the scene. Although from the standpoint of a purely realistic Hollywood style, the ship does appear visually exaggerated—a fact that would have been a source of considerable frustration to a cinematographer working toward a more realistic representation of the Baltimore cityscape—the street set might also be viewed within the larger context of Hitchcock's changing use of visual style as a means of representation during this period. Hitchcock's interest in European

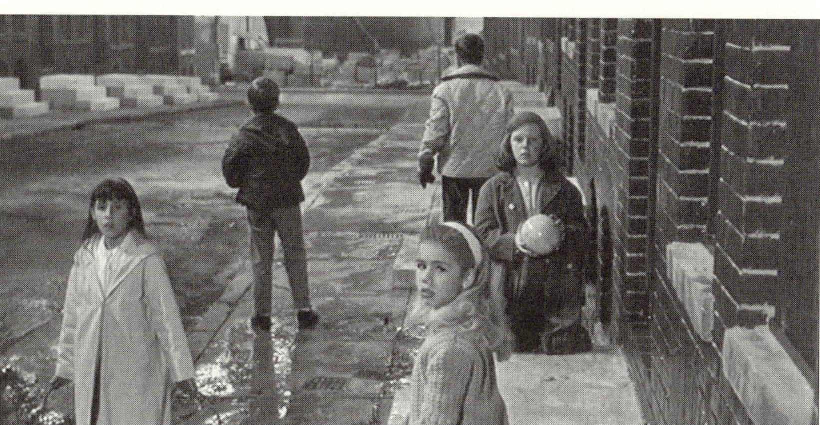

Figure 32. Strong compositional framing and multidirectional lighting give a surreal tone to this shot from the ending of *Marnie.* (*Marnie,* Universal, 1964)

art cinema had been growing since 1962, when he had screened films by Godard, Antonioni, and Bergman prior to filming *The Birds.* Jane Sloan notes that Hitchcock was increasingly interested in the appeal of his films to an "art" audience during this period, and that he had launched a publicity campaign aimed at transforming his image from that of a maker of entertaining thrillers to that of a director of serious art films.[50] Indeed, shots such as the final images of *Marnie* appear to fit into this "art film" model of design, photography, and mise-en-scène. As Mark and Marnie leave the Baltimore house for the last time, several children play on the rain-coated street, framed by the red brick rowhouses on either side, with the ship in the background. When Marnie exits the house, the three girls who are playing in the street turn to stare at her. The strong compositional framing and somewhat garish lighting of the shot give the scene an almost surreal feeling, leaving a hint of uncertainty as to the future of Mark and Marnie.

Considered by many to be Hitchcock's last cinematic masterpiece, *Marnie* was also the last of his films to be made by his team of trusted collaborators. Not only was it the final Hitchcock film to be photographed by Burks, but it was also the last to be made with George Tomasini as editor, Robert Boyle as art director, and Bernard Herrmann as composer.[51] Tomasini, who had died from a heart attack in the fall of 1964, was replaced as editor on Hitchcock's next film, *Torn Curtain,* by Bud Hoffman, and Boyle was replaced by Hein Heckroth. In his most surprising move, Hitchcock replaced Burks with John Warren, a long-term member of Hitchcock's crew who had been the cameraman for the director's *Alfred Hitchcock Presents* television series.

A good deal of mystification has surrounded the replacement of Burks on *Torn Curtain*. Even those close to Hitchcock were puzzled by his decision not to use Burks. Herbert Coleman relates a conversation with Hitchcock shortly after *Torn Curtain* was completed in which he told the director that he thought the film had suffered from not having Burks as cinematographer: "There are qualities missing in this picture that made the others so successful," Coleman told Hitchcock. "The camerawork, for instance. Jack Warren isn't Bob Burks. I thought Bob was all set [to shoot the film]. Why did you drop Bob and Bummy [Henry Bumstead]?"[52] Hitchcock, apparently, did not answer the question when it was posed by Coleman, and in an interview he gave to *American Cinematographer* magazine in the spring of 1967, he continued to avoid revealing the true reason for Burks's absence from the film. "When we were preparing to film *Torn Curtain*," he told Herb Lightman, "I began casting about for a photographic style that would help us tell the story in a more realistic, not so 'glossy' way."[53] Though Hitchcock never mentions Burks specifically, his comments suggest that he had deliberately replaced Burks with Warren for artistic reasons. This, however, was not the case.

What actually transpired had little to do with aesthetic considerations. According to a memo from Hitchcock's assistant Peggy Robertson, Burks was slated to begin work on *Torn Curtain* (then with the working title *Double Agent*) on September 1, 1965, but by mid-September he had not yet begun preproduction tests, and he appears to have been suffering from nervous exhaustion. Robertson wrote in a detailed production memo:

> On Friday, September 17, we called [Burks] at noon (we had tried to reach him about every half-hour but no reply). At noon we got him and he said that he was terribly sick with nerves and would not be able to work for two or three weeks, and could not shoot the tests with Julie Andrews on Monday, September 20th. He said he paid $1,000 in advance to a neurologist/hypnotist/psychiatrist, etc., for a crash course to cure him. On Saturday, September 18, in the morning, he called Mr. Hitchcock and it was decided that it would be too risky for him to do the film. On Saturday afternoon, at 2:30 P.M., Mr. Hitchcock saw Jack Warren at his house for two hours and told him he would do the picture.[54]

It is difficult to know, based on this memo, the exact circumstances of Burks's illness, but it would appear that he suffered some form of nervous collapse. Perhaps Burks's nervous exhaustion was related to the emotional toll of working closely with Hitchcock over the course of a dozen films, some of them involving significant postproduction work as well as production shooting. According to John Michael Hayes, Burks "had a very tense time with Hitch . . . and by the end of every picture was emotionally worn out."[55] Over the long term, the pressures of working with the director on twelve films in fourteen years may have contributed to the emotional breakdown Burks experienced in the mid-1960s, a breakdown that appears to ended their creative partnership.[56]

The question remains, however, why Hitchcock would have mischaracterized Burks's withdrawal from *Torn Curtain* as an artistic decision to replace him. Perhaps Hitchcock simply wanted to shield Burks from unwanted scrutiny about the real reason for his withdrawal from the picture. Or, more likely, Hitchcock saw this as an opportunity to assert his own auteurist credentials by taking credit for the creation of a new style of filmmaking. In either case, it is unfortunate that Hitchcock felt the need to characterize the films shot by Burks as "glossy." It was, in fact, Burks's nuanced and exacting approach that had helped Hitchcock to fashion several of his most successful films, none of which could be considered "glossy" in relation to most other color productions of the period.

If the importance of Burks as a collaborator on Hitchcock's films has been generally underestimated, it is in part because Hitchcock was notoriously reluctant to give credit to those who assisted him in the creation of his films. Although Hitchcock certainly could have made the films he did with other cinematographers, I would argue that the intricacies of his films of the 1950s and early 1960s—especially *Rear Window, Vertigo,* and *The Birds,* which called for meticulous planning and execution—required a DP with Burks's particular background in special effects as well as his excellent eye for lighting and composition. No director of Hitchcock's stature collaborates with the same cinematographer a dozen times without good reasons, and in the case of Hitchcock and Burks those reasons appear to have involved personal affinity as well as technical proficiency and artistic integrity. The technical and creative partnership of Hitchcock and Burks made it possible for Hitchcock to take greater artistic risks, and by doing so to create motion pictures that remain among the most visually compelling ever made.

5 What Rule Are You Breaking?

Collaborating in the New Hollywood

> The rule of thumb is you have to know what rule you're breaking. . . . You must know what [shooting a scene] a stop underexposed looks like on the screen, or what [shooting] a half stop under looks like. . . . You have to understand what happens when you underexpose or overexpose, because that's another way to paint, another way of making emotional statements on the screen.
>
> **Gordon Willis**

In the early 1960s, the ranks of Hollywood cinematographers were still dominated by an old-guard establishment that had changed little in the past quarter century. By the mid-1970s, the profession had undergone a sea change: between 1965 and 1975 most of the older generation of studio cinematographers either died or retired, leaving the field open for a significant influx of new talent.[1] The departure, within a relatively short time, of many of the cinematographers whose camerawork and lighting had defined the style of Hollywood filmmaking for decades represented a major watershed not only in the history of cinematography but also in the development of visual style in American cinema. The cinematographers who replaced them—members of what came to be known as the New Hollywood—were an extremely talented group that included John Alonzo, Bill Butler, Michael Chapman, Jordan Cronenweth, William Fraker, Conrad Hall, László Kovács, Andrew Laszlo, Owen Roizman, Haskell Wexler, Gordon Willis, and Vilmos Zsigmond. Less tied to traditional studio methods than their older counterparts, these younger cinematographers were more willing to engage in innovative practices that challenged or revised industry norms.[2] As Gordon Willis put it, being a successful cinematographer was no longer a matter of learning how to work within the established rules but a matter of knowing what rules to break and of finding the technical and technological means to break them.

Several factors played a role in the dramatic change in photographic style that characterized films of the late 1960s and early 1970s. Perhaps the most important was the influence of European cinema on American filmmakers. The visual style of films photographed by cinematographers such as Raoul Coutard and Henri Decae in France; Vittorio Storaro, Carlo Di Palma, and Gianni Di Venanzo in Italy; and Sven Nykvist in Sweden was increasingly a source of inspiration to young American cinematographers, who sought to emulate their methods. A number of European cinematographers would later come to work in Hollywood, further contributing to a cross-fertilization of visual style in the 1970s and 1980s.[3]

A second factor was a relaxation of union control over Hollywood cinematographers. As David Cook notes, for the first time since the 1920s the monopoly of the Hollywood cinematographers' union Local 659 was broken, lowering the rigid barriers to entry into the profession.[4] Local 659, the most conservative of all Hollywood unions, had restricted the number of persons who could serve as directors of photography to two hundred of its most senior members. By the mid-1960s, nearly all two hundred of these DPs were over the age of sixty, and younger cameramen were denied any opportunity of rising through the ranks to become cinematographers on Hollywood productions. In the late 1960s and early 1970s, cinematographers like Hall, Wexler, Kovács, and Zsigmond had to overcome an archaic and highly restrictive set of union rules in order to become DPs, an obstacle that later cinematographers would no longer face.

Two other changes in the late 1960s were an increase in location shooting and advances in technology—such as film stocks, cameras, and lenses—that allowed cinematographers to shoot more visually accomplished films on smaller budgets or under less optimal lighting conditions. Since the majority of the younger cinematographers had received their training outside the system of studio apprenticeship that had been the norm for cameramen of earlier generations, they were accustomed to shooting on smaller budgets, whether for television or on low-budget independent films such as those produced by Roger Corman's American International Pictures (AIP).

One of the results of these demographic changes was that by the late 1960s and early 1970s a number of cinematographers had become disenchanted with the glossy, highly saturated look that characterized Hollywood color filmmaking of the period. As Barry Salt notes, a major trend in American film photography of the 1970s was "the destruction of the ever-higher image definition and color reproduction made possible by the improvements in film stocks and lenses."[5] Conrad Hall recalled working in the late 1960s and early 1970s to desaturate the color in his films:

> I was struggling with the primariness of color. I didn't like blue to be strong blue [and] I didn't like pure green or those vivid kinds of colors. I

> didn't see light that way and there's always atmosphere between color and me in the form of haze, smog, fog, dust. There's a muting of color that goes on in life. There was none of that in [the printing of] colors in film. And so I objected to that. I couldn't stand that kind of primary color and I tried to change it.[6]

David Cook references several changes in the technologies of cinema that allowed cinematographers to experiment more freely with visual style: the introduction of faster lenses that could register images at very low levels of light, an increased use of diffusion, and an increase in the frequency of "pushing," or overdeveloping, film in the lab.[7] Indeed, color film stocks had become much faster since the 1950s, as had lenses. Starting with the introduction of the Eastman Kodak 5250 color negative (rated 50 ASA) in 1959, and continuing with the 5251 (still 50 ASA but with better definition and color rendition) in 1962 and the 5254 (rated 100 ASA and with even sharper image and better color rendition) in 1968, film stocks had become dramatically faster.[8] These faster and less grainy color stocks significantly changed the approach of American cinematographers, who now sought a more nuanced or understated approach to color.

Further, the introduction of faster lenses that afforded better resolution at lower light levels, along with significant improvements in zoom lenses and the introduction of new cameras and camera systems, had an important impact on film style in the 1970s. Two new high-resolution, high-speed zoom lenses became available in the early 1970s: the Taylor-Hobson Cooke Varotal, with a 5-to-1 zoom range (20mm to 100mm), and the Canon long-range zoom, with a 10-to-1 range (125mm to 1250mm).[9] Some of the most important new cameras were the lightweight 16mm Éclair ACL from France, the extremely lightweight 35mm Arriflex 35BL from Germany, the 35mm Panaflex from Panavision, and the Steadicam. The Panaflex, which became the industry standard by the end of the decade, was a relatively lightweight 35mm camera that could be used either for handheld work or mounted on a tripod. The Steadicam, introduced in 1975, was a floating camera mount that attached to the operator's chest and waist by means of a harness, allowing greater fluidity of movement than traditional handheld cameras. Fitted with a video viewfinder, the Steadicam liberated the operator from having to keep an eye attached to the camera, thus making it possible to execute smooth shots going up and down stairs, running through narrow passageways, or working in tight interior locations.

The experimentation made possible by the new technologies of the 1960s and 1970s took a number of different forms. Cinematographers could, for example, desaturate color or add a more distinctive look to their films by underexposing or overexposing the negative, or by preflashing or postflashing the film. For Sidney Lumet's *The Deadly Affair* (1967), cinematographer Freddie Young used preflashing (exposing the unexposed negative to a controlled white light before shooting) in order to desaturate the colors. For George Roy Hill's *Butch Cassidy and the Sundance Kid* (1969), Conrad Hall achieved desaturation by overexposing the negative by two stops during shooting and then correcting for the overexposure in the lab: this allowed him to remove the overly "picturesque" effect of the blue desert sky, while maintaining nearly all the clarity of the image.[10] In Francis Ford Coppola's *You're a Big Boy Now* (1967), cinematographer Andrew Laszlo took the opposite approach, underexposing or "pushing" the negative by three stops in order to shoot the interior of a big department store using only available lighting. And on *The Godfather* (1972), Coppola and Gordon Willis shot with extremely low levels of light compared with what had conventionally been used in color films. By pushing the negative two stops and then adjusting by only one stop in the lab, Willis was able to create darkly lit interior scenes that were composed of rich browns and blacks, almost drained of bright colors, and suffused with an amber glow.

In this chapter, I examine three films that took advantage of such advances in technology to experiment with radically different approaches to visual style. Rather than examine a multifilm collaboration between a director and a cinematographer as I have in the previous chapters, I analyze one film from each of three key partnerships. Although each of these three films can be the basis of a revealing case study of collaboration between a director with a claim to auteurist credentials and an exceptionally talented cinematographer, each also marks an important moment in the development of cinematographic technology and its application to cinematic style. In *McCabe and Mrs. Miller,* Robert Altman and Vilmos Zsigmond created a new stylistic vocabulary through a process that—though relatively straightforward in technical terms—lay so far outside the stylistic choices of commercial filmmaking at the time that they were obliged to keep it a secret from the studio. In both *JFK* and *Saving Private Ryan,* the manipulation of the filmic medium by a wide array of technical and stylistic means is further intensified. In *JFK,* this intensified visual presentation is the result of a combination of rapid editing techniques and the use of different film formats within the same sequence. In *Saving Private Ryan,* the use of technological innovation as a source of stylistic expression is even more pronounced, as the film's combination of a wide range of camera-based effects pulls the viewer into the action depicted on the screen.

FLASHING IN THE FOG: ROBERT ALTMAN, VILMOS ZSIGMOND, AND *MCCABE AND MRS. MILLER*

McCabe and Mrs. Miller (1971) emerged during a period of intensely innovative filmmaking in the United States. The year 1971 alone saw the release of a number of defining films of the New Hollywood, including *Harold and Maude* (Hal Ashby, cin. John Alonzo), *The Last Picture Show* (Peter Bogdanovich, cin. Robert Surtees), *Carnal Knowledge* (Mike Nichols, cin. Giuseppe Rotunno), *Klute* (Alan Pakula, cin. Gordon Willis), *Straw Dogs* (Sam Peckinpah, cin. John Coquillon), and *The French Connection* (William Friedkin, cin. Owen Roizman). The move toward self-conscious experimentation and rule-breaking during this period can clearly be seen in *McCabe and Mrs. Miller,* a brilliantly revisionary Western that showcases the contributions of both Altman as director and Zsigmond as cinematographer.

Born in 1930 and trained in cinematography at the Academy for Theater and Film Art in Budapest, Vilmos Zsigmond began working as a cameraman in the Hungarian state-run film studio in 1955. During the Hungarian Uprising of 1956, Zsigmond and his close friend and fellow cinematographer László Kovács hid an Arriflex camera in a shopping bag and recorded footage of the event, capturing shots of civilians attacking tanks with homemade weapons. Zsigmond and Kovács were able to escape to Austria, and from there to travel to the United States as political refugees. After spending time in a refugee camp in New Jersey, Zsigmond moved to Los Angeles, where he hoped to find work in the film industry. Unable to find film work, he worked as a lab technician and still photographer for several years. In the early 1960s, he began shooting low-budget films, many of them intended for the drive-in circuit. In low-budget films such as *The Sadist* (James Landis, 1963), *Summer Children* (James Bruner, 1965), and *The Name of the Game Is Kill* (Gunnar Hellstrom, 1968), Zsigmond honed the skills that would later make him one of the most technically accomplished and aesthetically innovative cinematographers in Hollywood.

Zsigmond's first opportunity to serve as DP on a major Hollywood production came when Peter Fonda hired him to shoot his directorial debut, *The Hired Man.* As soon as principal photography was completed on that film, Zsigmond began preparations to shoot *McCabe and Mrs. Miller* with Robert Altman. Set in the Pacific Northwest at the turn of the century, *McCabe* tells the story of a gambler who arrives in small northwest mining town and soon establishes a dominant position in the town's hierarchy. McCabe (Warren Beatty) builds a makeshift brothel, consisting of three prostitutes purchased from a pimp in a nearby town. Soon, however, an attractive madam named Constance Miller (Julie Christie) convinces McCabe that she can do a better job of managing the brothel than he can. The two become business partners, opening a high-class establishment that generates significant income. As the town becomes more prosperous, two agents from the local mining company attempt to buy out McCabe's business as well as the surrounding mines. McCabe refuses to sell at their offering price, and the two agents leave town before he can renegotiate. Three bounty killers, led by an enormous Englishman named Butler, are dispatched by the mining company to make an example of McCabe. Though McCabe initially tries to appease the gunmen, it becomes clear that a lethal confrontation is inevitable. In the final shootout, McCabe manages to kill two of the gunmen before Butler mortally wounds him. While the townspeople put out a fire that has broken out in the church, McCabe dies alone in the snow.

In his desire to provide the film with a feeling of visual authenticity, Altman sought to capture the look of antique, somewhat yellowed turn-of-the-century photographs. Zsigmond described the effect Altman sought as one of "looking through lots of haze to give you the feeling that the things you were seeing were really old and that they didn't exist anymore . . . like looking at old photos, except that these are moving pictures, not photographs."[11] Zsigmond claimed that another stylistic reference for the visual style of the film was the paintings of Andrew Wyeth, with their use of muted grays and browns.

Zsigmond told Altman that the most effective method for achieving such a look would be to flash the film, thus creating very desaturated colors, brownish or yellowish tones, and a somewhat grainy texture:

> We . . . wanted to have an old, antique look for the movie and, in those days, we didn't have much of an example of this style, so my idea was to "flash" the film. It was not my invention, as I think Freddie Young was the first to do it, but it worked perfectly for what we were trying to do. . . . [I]n those days everything had the Technicolor look in Hollywood, which meant very bright, very saturated colors, and we wanted this movie to look very old, like a faded color photograph. So we decided to shoot all the exteriors with a bluish look, and the interiors with a warm look. It was natural to do that, because when the film went from outdoor to indoor, the lights—which were mostly candles and lanterns—looked much warmer. And the overcast skies and rain in Vancouver . . . really helped us create a special look for that movie.[12]

Altman and Zsigmond tested flashing levels ranging from 10 to 25 percent before deciding on an ideal level of 15 percent, which they used for most scenes of the film.[13] They also used a heavy fog filter to accentuate even further the antique look of the film.[14] Since no lab in Los Angeles

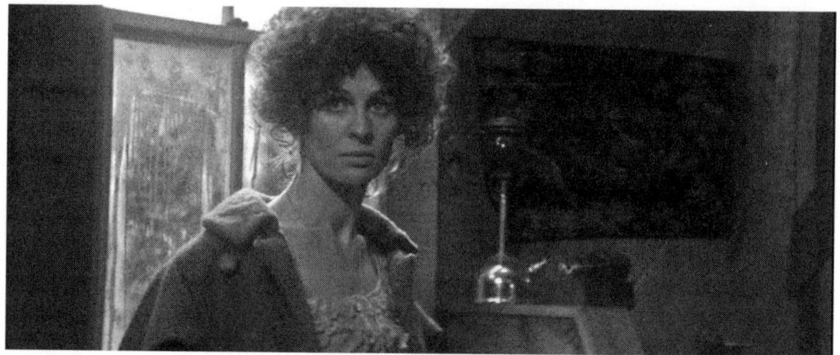

Figure 33. A luminous shot of Mrs. Miller (Julie Christie): Vilmos Zsigmond flashed the film to create the slightly faded look of an antique photograph. (*McCabe and Mrs. Miller,* Warner Bros., 1971)

would agree to flash the film and risk gaining a reputation for producing grainy, desaturated footage, Altman and Zsigmond had to find a lab in Vancouver to do the work. As Zsigmond recalled, they were able to find a small lab that was willing to develop the entire 300,000 feet of film.[15] When Warner Bros. executives complained about the grainy and foggy look of the footage—one executive even telling Altman that Zsigmond was incompetent and should be fired from the film—Altman blamed the quality of the footage on the work of the lab in Vancouver and promised to have the film developed by a different lab in Hollywood. This ploy bought him enough time to complete the film, while continuing to achieve the look he wanted.

In addition to flashing the film, Altman and Zsigmond experimented extensively with camera movement, including dramatic zooms as well as dolly shots. In *M*A*S*H,* Altman had established his predilection for the zoom, which was to become a stylistic signature of his 1970s films. In *McCabe and Mrs. Miller,* the use of zooms is particularly effective in creating a very unusual filmic space. As John Belton and Lyle Tector suggest, Zsigmond's zooms define transitions in both time and space while creating the sense of a "flat, dimensionless space," particularly in interiors, where the use of the zoom increases the "claustrophobic nature of the film."[16] Zooms also allow the camera to make small adjustments in the framing of shots without having to change the setup. By using this technique, Zsigmond was able to maintain focus in extreme long shots that situate characters within their physical environment.

The use of zooms was a new addition to Zsigmond's arsenal of photographic techniques. Operating the camera himself, Zsigmond quickly became accustomed to doing the unusual camera moves Altman demanded. David Cook observes that Altman's preference for a "fast, flexible pan-and-zoom style went hand in hand with his use of actor improvisation and ensemble playing, which in turn placed considerable creative responsibility on his cinematographers."[17] Zsigmond, as skilled an operator as he was a cinematographer, found that as the shooting progressed, Altman gave him increasing freedom to compose the shots himself: "He showed me a couple of times, the very first week I was there . . . what he wanted. After the week was over, he let me do it. He realized that I had learned . . . what it should look like so far as composition goes, as far as the camera moves go, and then from that point [on] he hardly ever even looked into the camera."[18]

In his book about the film, Robert Self noted the "gracefulness and lyricism" of Zsigmond's lighting and camerawork.[19] In fact, Zsigmond's cinematography is in large part responsible for the unique visual style of *McCabe.* The style of the film depends heavily on the contrasting of extremes: sharply focused shots juxtaposed with grainy, underlit shots; medium shots alternating with extreme long shots; and the flashed yellows of the first three-quarters of the film changing to the unflashed snowy shots of the film's final section. Very early in the film, we see a dramatic example of how Zsigmond's camerawork informs Altman's visual style: Zsigmond zooms in for a close-up of McCabe's face, thereby presenting the viewer with the image of a man seemingly in control of his situation. The effect of the close-up is immediately undermined, however, by a cut to a telephoto shot of the footbridge outside and the feet of a figure walking away from the camera. The figure on the footbridge turns out to be the minister of the town, the very person who will later participate in McCabe's murder by denying him sanctuary in the church.

The snow that largely defines the look of the final section of the film was in fact not a planned part of the design but a fortunate accident. When it began snowing toward the end of shooting, some members of the cast and crew, including Warren Beatty, argued for delaying the production. Altman, however, saw the snow as an opportunity to create an entirely new emotional effect in the final scenes. Since the film had been shot in sequence, the snow seemed a natural development within the film's diegesis. The snow also provided the filmmakers with such magical images that Zsigmond decided not to flash those scenes: "In the beginning [of the film], we were flashing heavily to create the antique mood of the film, but in the end, we pulled back the flashing and diffusion to make it look more real and dramatic as McCabe dies."[20] By shooting McCabe's death in the snow without diffusion and not flashing the film, Altman and Zsigmond allowed the scene to have a greater visual and dramatic impact.

McCabe is not only a radical departure from the traditional Western in terms of its setting, themes, and characters, but it constitutes an equally radical break with tradition in terms of its visual design and mise-en-scène. The town of Presbyterian Church is not the nineteenth-century boomtown of the traditional Hollywood Western, but a soggy mining outpost lacking all pretension to either the epic grandeur of the Western landscape or the clear moral codes on which the plots of Westerns like those of Ford and Hawks are based. In creating the distinctive look of Presbyterian Church, Altman, Zsigmond, and production designer Leon Ericksen departed from nearly every conventional image of the Hollywood Western: the setting is a wooded, rainy town in a nondescript season that appears to be late fall or early winter; the chief mode of transport is a steam tractor rather than a stagecoach; and the interior spaces are a monochrome brown with little decoration. Sheehan's Saloon, the singularly unglamorous bar where the opening scenes occur, is particularly disorienting to viewers accustomed to the stereotypical saloon of the classic Western. Zsigmond's lighting creates the sense of a dimly lit and grungy establishment lacking almost all the ambience of the iconic Western saloon, thus establishing, in the film's early scenes, its departure from the visual style of previous Westerns.

The visual style of *McCabe* was part of Altman's overall project of transforming "a very standard Western story" into a more realistic film that attempts to "destroy all the myths of heroism."[21] To a large extent the film succeeds in its objective. Whether we choose to call it a revisionist Western, an anti-Western, or a genre-commentary Western, *McCabe* is a film that stands in diametric opposition to classic Hollywood Westerns such as those made by Ford, Hawks, and other directors of the studio era. The transformation of the Western genre in *McCabe* is as much the result of Zsigmond's cinematography as it is of Altman's direction.[22]

VISUAL INTENSITY AND HISTORICAL REVISIONISM: OLIVER STONE, ROBERT RICHARDSON, AND *JFK*

JFK (1991) is a product of the director-cinematographer collaboration that may have had the most defining impact on American filmmaking in the 1990s: that of Oliver Stone and Robert Richardson. The first of a trilogy of 1990s films directed by Stone and photographed by Richardson that use radical techniques of both cinematography and editing to create a strikingly new visual style, *JFK* is a collage-like visual spectacle that follows the attempts of a New Orleans district attorney to get to the facts underlying the Kennedy assassination.

One of the preeminent cinematographers in American cinema of the past thirty years, Richardson has been the most highly awarded DP of his generation.[23] Educated at the Rhode Island School of Design and the American Film Institute—where he apprenticed with both Sven Nyqvist and Nestor Almendros—Richardson spent seven years shooting documentaries before breaking into feature films. After shooting the documentary *Crossfire* in El Salvador, Richardson was hired by Stone to shoot his fiction film *Salvador* (1985). Since then, Richardson has built his career largely on the basis of successful long-term collaborations with directors such as Stone, Martin Scorsese, Quentin Tarantino, and John Sayles.[24]

The eleven films Stone and Richardson made together between 1985 and 1998 place their collaboration in a tradition of important long-term collaborations between American directors and cinematographers that includes those of D.W. Griffith and Billy Bitzer in the silent era, Frank Capra and Joseph Walker in the 1930s, Douglas Sirk and Russell Metty in the 1950s, and Alfred Hitchcock and Robert Burks in the 1950s and '60s. In the trajectory from *Salvador* to *JFK* and beyond, we can trace both the growth of Stone into a more assured and ambitious filmmaker and the parallel development of Richardson into an innovative cinematographer capable of fashioning a highly individuated visual style.

The visual style of *JFK,* as Robert Rosenstone has remarked, is a "quantum leap" beyond that of Stone's previous films, initiating an entirely new visual vocabulary for Stone and Richardson.[25] Though the stylistic idiom Stone and Richardson developed for *JFK* finds even more extreme expression in their next film, *Natural Born Killers,* I will focus my discussion in this chapter on *JFK,* both because it was the first film to exploit the techniques that would come to be associated with Stone's signature brand of filmmaking and because it remains one of the most visually powerful films of the late twentieth century.[26] As Robert Kolker notes, *JFK* is the first film in which Stone "breaks radically with conventional linear narrative constructions," making "history, culture, and their formation part of the narrative construction itself."[27] The radically innovative construction of *JFK* is not simply a stylistic flourish intended to impress audiences: instead, it is a visual strategy aimed at capturing the fragmentary nature of our collective memory of historical events. Stone and Richardson convey—in a way that would not have been possible using a more conventional filmmaking style—the complex interplay of historical events, the media's presentation of those events, and the memories of those involved.

Stone's professed goal in making *JFK* was to create "an alternate myth" of the Kennedy assassination, one that would challenge the "official" version as presented in the infamous report by the Warren Commission. According to Stone, the film was not intended to solve the mystery of Kennedy's death, but to serve as a reminder of "how much our nation and our world lost when President Kennedy died" and of "what might have happened and why." Stone was severely criticized after the film's release for presenting a fictionalized narrative that questioned the Warren Commission's version of events and proposed that the assassination was part of a conspiracy.[28] The film's narrative follows the quest by its protagonist, New Orleans district attorney Jim Garrison (Kevin Costner), to understand the circumstances of the assassination: in the course of the film, Garrison comes to believe that the assassination could not have been carried out by a single individual and that the conspiracy to kill the president and its subsequent cover-up reached the highest levels of the federal government.

In order to create an effect of complex historical collage, Stone and Richardson combine an extraordinarily wide variety of film formats and shooting styles, resulting in a film of astonishing visual complexity. Through the use of highly innovative techniques, the film presents the viewer with a constantly changing flow of visual information. This visual approach was a significant departure from the style of Stone's previous films, and it was extremely effective in giving *JFK* an enormously engaging visual energy that helped to ensure its commercial success. The collage-like style of the film can also be attributed in part to the work of editor Hank Corwin. Corwin, who had worked with Richardson on television commercials, was brought onto the project by Richardson, who was convinced that Corwin would bring a more aggressively experimental approach to the editing of the film. Though not officially credited as an editor, Corwin was responsible for cutting many of the sequences involving multiple changes in format.[29] The techniques used in *JFK* would be pushed even further in Stone's next film, *Natural Born Killers,* a contemporary crime film in which the style was intended to reflect the "hallucinogenic quality that is in the killers' minds" while also conveying "a sense of the schizophrenic madness of the [twentieth] century."[30]

Shooting and assembling the footage for *JFK* was an extremely complex undertaking, involving at least eight different cameras, fourteen film formats, two thousand optical effects (mostly blowups from 8mm and 16mm formats to 35mm intermediate), and a total of over 2,800 shots.[31] The Dealey Plaza sequence alone required two Panaflex 35mm cameras, five 16mm cameras (integrated into the setting as equipment for news crews), and a Super-8 camera. The film stocks used by Richardson range from extremely grainy 8mm Kodachrome to a range of black-and-white stocks to state-of-the-art 35mm color stocks, all of which are supplemented by still photographs, diagrams, and other visual materials to create a constantly changing visual presentation.

The shifts between formats are used in two principal ways. For the sequences involving the Kennedy assassination and the subsequent shooting of Lee Harvey Oswald by nightclub owner Jack Ruby, the rapid montage of differently formatted images provides what Richardson described as a "strong documentary feel." The "concrete foundation of factual reality" that is established in these sequences provided Stone and Richardson with a visual scaffolding on which they were able to build the narrative that follows.[32] For the film's opening sequence, Richardson duplicated many of the original images taken from news footage and home movies (including the famous Zapruder film), and then enhanced them in 8mm, 16mm, and 35mm formats that were later edited into the montage. For the sequence involving the shooting of Oswald, Richardson recaptured the event on both 16mm black-and-white news film and video and then integrated that material with actual news footage.

The frequent shifts between formats also signal transitions from the present moment of the film's diegesis to the memories of different characters. For example, when Jack Martin (Jack Lemmon) is being questioned at the racetrack by Garrison and his assistant, he flashes back to a scene shown earlier in the film in which he is badly beaten by Guy Banister (Ed Asner). Here, as in other such scenes, the intercutting between the various formats was intended to have a jarring effect on the viewer. As Garrison questions Martin, the film cuts from an extreme close-up of his eyes to a slow-motion memory sequence of him being pistol-whipped by Bannister. Seconds later, we flash back once again to another memory, this time of an undercover military operation run out of Bannister's office. In this sequence, the color is highly desaturated, as if these memories are somewhat distanced in Martin's mind. The third flashback, involving a training camp located in the backwoods of Louisiana, is shot in grainy black and white, perhaps suggesting that these events are even more deeply buried in Martin's memory. The net effect of these multiple format shifts is one of profound disorientation. Like the characters in the film, the viewer is left with only with bits and pieces of the story, fragments from which a more accurate account of events can never be reliably composed.

Stone's films have shown a consistent preoccupation with different forms of media and with the ambiguous and at times dangerous intersection of the media with contemporary society. *Salvador* (1986) tells the story of a photojournalist who becomes enmeshed in the war in El Salvador; *Talk Radio* (1988) explores the complicated relationship between the entertainment media and American society through the depiction of a provocative late-night radio host; and *Natural Born Killers* (1994) represents the United States as a media-crazed nation whose thirst for violence is personified in the form of an amoral and self-obsessed journalist. The narrative of *JFK* concerns one of the most important media events of the American twentieth century: the assassination of a young, popular, and charismatic president. It also references the media's crucially important role in the aftermath of that assassination. In one scene early in the film, Stone re-creates a television news conference that was held at the Dallas Police Headquarters on the day after the assassination and shortly following the arrest of Lee Harvey Oswald. In the re-created footage, Oswald, played by Gary Oldman, makes the famous statement denying having shot Kennedy and referring to himself as a "patsy." The scene is witnessed through the eyes of Garrison and his family, who watch it on their black-and-white television screen. In this brief scene, Stone and Richardson weave together the televised spectacle of traumatic historical events that are being simultaneously viewed by the entire nation in stark black-and-white, and the domestic sphere of the Garrison household, which is softly lit and decorated in light pastel colors. The harmony of this domestic space is invaded—in a very material sense—by traumatic historical events that will soon engulf Garrison, strain his relations with his wife, and put his family at risk.

Two stylistic changes mark the movement from the earlier sections of the film to the later scenes. The first and most obvious change is the shift from the more collage-like, quasi-documentary approach of the opening sections to the more conventional stylistic continuity of the later sequences. The first ten minutes of the film, including the credit sequence and the reenactment of the Kennedy assassination, are edited at an extremely fast pace, with an average shot length of approximately 2.5 seconds. Here, the viewer is assaulted by a range of images depicting various events of the late 1950s and early 1960s. By twenty minutes into the film, however, the pace has slowed considerably—to an ASL of about six seconds—and the editing style reaches an equilibrium that remains fairly consistent throughout the remainder of the running time.

The second change—which may be less apparent to the average viewer—is a shift in the style of the cinematography. The opening sequences, involving the Kennedy and Oswald assassinations, were filmed with practically no diffusion in order to provide a sense of stark reality. The later sections, involving Garrison's continuing investigation, his family life, and the trial of Clay Shaw with which the film ends, were shot with substantial amounts of diffusion, creating a generally softer look. This change in style can be explained at least in part by the desire to make Garrison a more sympathetic character as the film comes increasingly to focus on his life and work. Stone was harshly criticized for making the fictional character of Jim Garrison more sympathetic than the real-life Garrison. In fact, Stone's depiction of Garrison is no more inaccurate than the rendering of real-life figures as fictional characters in any number of Hollywood films. Stone defended his characterization of Garrison as "a Capra everyman" who "comes to realize that a small-town whodunit has global repercussions," and Richardson lit Costner in such a way as to depict Garrison as "a flawed man, determined to do the right thing."[33] For example, the lighting of Garrison's home is softer with warmer hues, while the lighting of his office—where he is often seen in a conflictual relationship with members of his staff—is characterized by hard-edged light and more contrast.

As Robert Kolker notes, the scenes involving Garrison and his wife (played by Sissy Spacek) are the film's weakest, lacking the "visual [and] structural energy" that propels the rest of the movie. Indeed, these scenes soon devolve into "conventional family melodramatics," and the absence of the rapid editing techniques and format changes used in other parts of the film also makes them less compelling on a visual level.[34] On the other hand, the film's most effective scenes are those involving Garrison's interviews with various individuals who are in some way linked to the Kennedy assassination. These scenes are further helped by Stone's casting well-known and highly accomplished actors in a number of supporting roles, including Joe Pesci as David Ferrie, John Candy as Dean Andrews, Tommy Lee Jones as Clay Shaw, Jack Lemmon as Jack Martin, Kevin Bacon as Willie O'Keefe, and Donald Sutherland as the ex-military informant identified simply as "X."

The sequence in which Garrison meets with X in Washington, DC, is the narrative high point of the film. A pivotal scene in which Stone sought to "[educate] the audience to a higher level of concept [and] of motive" by revealing much of the background of the Kennedy assassination and its historical context, it combines a perfectly calibrated performance by Sutherland with effective mise-en-scène, elegant cinematography, and precise editing.[35] If *JFK* is indeed a "myth," as Stone would have it, then the city of Washington appears here as the film's most obvious mythic landscape. A visual pastiche of highly composed panoramic shots of the National Mall seen from different angles, the sequence is punctuated by views of its various monuments and by extended vistas over large open spaces. These

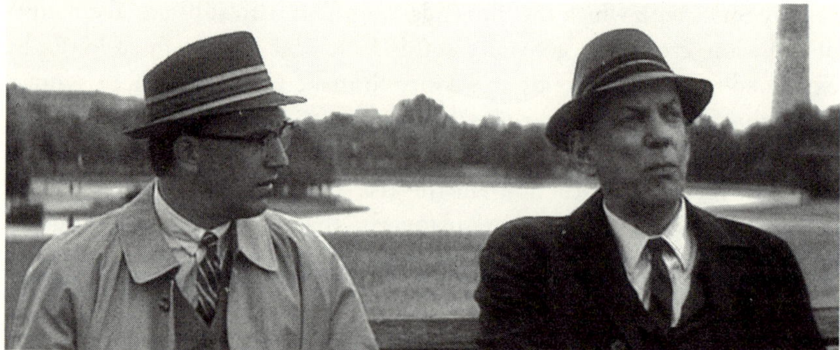

Figure 34. A resonant image: Jim Garrison (Kevin Costner) and "X" (Donald Sutherland) with the "paranoid space" of the nation's capital behind them. (*JFK*, Warner Bros., 1991)

spaces can be seen as a reminder of the unrealized potential of the United States as the world's greatest democracy, or, as Kolker suggests, as the "paranoid space" that Garrison is attempting to fill with his as-yet-incomplete but increasingly cogent view of historical events.[36]

Shot on location at the Lincoln Memorial and other parts of the Mall, the seventeen-minute sequence is almost entirely a monologue by Sutherland, with occasional interjections by Costner. As written in the screenplay, the scene was to have been constructed as a series of flashbacks, with voiceover commentary by X. As it appears in the film, however, the scene is different from that in the published screenplay: instead of relying on the well-worn technique of flashbacks accompanied by voiceover, Stone and Richardson make full use of the technique of intercutting Stone has exploited throughout the film. As Norman Mailer suggested, a scene in which a mysterious figure in a raincoat provides a detailed theory of the reasons for a conspiracy to kill Kennedy could easily have been "one of the more embarrassing moments in recent film history."[37] Instead, the scene remains a high point of 1990s filmmaking, one in which the cinematography and editing add a propulsive energy to Sutherland's performance. Whether or not we accept the theory of a complex and far-reaching conspiracy to kill an American president, we are drawn in by the scene's extraordinary technique, and we are subject to its considerable force of rhetorical persuasion.

The visual style of *JFK* was a striking departure from that of other films being made by Hollywood in the 1980s, and it helped to inaugurate the more kinetic style of filmmaking that would characterize American films of the 1990s. Rather than attempting to achieve a consistency of visual approach across its many scenes and locations, *JFK* deliberately exploits the differences in color and texture that are created by the different film formats. This approach was unsettling to those accustomed to a more classical form of visual continuity, but it was also highly effective in sustaining the film's sense of heightened anticipation throughout what might otherwise have been a fairly dry series of interviews and investigative procedures. An early example of the style that David Bordwell would identify as "intensified continuity," *JFK* not only draws the viewer into its unique visual architecture, but also reflects Stone's concern with the reception of visual information and with the need for each individual within an increasingly media-driven society to filter the complex array of visual and verbal information with which he or she is continually assaulted.[38]

HYPERREALISM IN THE COMBAT FILM: STEVEN SPIELBERG, JANUSZ KAMINSKI, AND *SAVING PRIVATE RYAN*

Saving Private Ryan was the fourth feature film on which Steven Spielberg collaborated with the Polish-born cinematographer Janusz Kaminski. Born in 1959 in Ziebice, Poland, Kaminski emigrated from Poland and moved to the United States when martial law was imposed in 1981. After earning a degree in film from Columbia College in Chicago, Kaminski moved to Los Angeles, where he earned an MFA in cinematography. Kaminski began working as a gaffer on B-movie features produced by Roger Corman and was promoted to second-unit cinematographer on Thierry Notz's *Watchers 2* and to director of photography on Wayne Coe's *Grim Prairie Tales.* Kaminski first worked with Spielberg in 1991, when the director hired him as cinematographer for a television pilot, *Class of '61*. On Kaminski's first feature with Spielberg—the black-and-white historical drama *Schindler's List*—he not only established his credentials as one of the most talented cinematographers in the industry, but became one of the youngest DPs to win an Academy Award for best cinematography. Kaminski has continued to work closely with Spielberg: the fourteen films he has shot with Spielberg are by far the most any cinematographer has photographed for the director, and their collaboration is one of the most important director-cinematographer collaborations in current American cinema.

Saving Private Ryan was a watershed for Spielberg and Kaminski in several respects. First of all, it was made in a style that was—at least compared with the tightly crafted style of Spielberg's earlier films—relatively unpolished, especially in the combat sequences. As part of this move toward roughness and spontaneity, Spielberg decided to abandon his usual practice of storyboarding, allowing the scenes of the film to evolve in a more organic way. He also decided—in order to maintain the illusion of the film's events occurring in real time and thus add a further sense of realism—to shoot the movie in strict continuity. Finally, in order to create a more naturalistic feeling during the battle scenes, Spielberg allowed much of the action in those two sequences to be improvised:

> I had a very strong screenplay and the actors and I were certainly following that as a blueprint. But in terms of my approach to the combat sequences, I was improvising all of them. I just went to war and did things the way I thought a combat cameraman would have [done]. I had a very good advisor for the battle scenes—retired Marine Captain Dale Dye. He served three tours of duty under fire in Vietnam, and he was wounded several times. In order to capture the realism of combat, I relied on Dale, as well as several World War II combat veterans who also served as consultants.[39]

Spielberg's contention that he filmed the combat sequences "the way . . . a combat cameraman would have" is in fact no more accurate than Hitchcock's contention that he shot *The Wrong Man* in a "documentary style." The film was shot using an array of highly sophisticated technical tools that would not have been available to combat cameramen in World War II, or for that matter to cinematographers operating in any war zone. It would be more accurate to say that the stylistic choices made for the film involved attempts to use advanced techniques of filmmaking to differentiate the look of the combat scenes from those of more conventionally made Hollywood productions in a way that *suggests* the reality of combat footage.

There is no doubt that *Saving Private Ryan* presents the viewer with a powerful visual spectacle, especially in the two long and intense combat sequences that occur at the beginning and the end of the film. Kaminski explained that the goal in the first combat sequence was "to create the illusion that there were several combat cameramen landing with the troops at Normandy." The means of doing that, however, involved what Kaminski admitted were "in-camera tricks and other technological means."[40]

Saving Private Ryan is a film that relies heavily on its ostensible goal of presenting the experience of World War II combat in as much visceral detail as possible. In comments to the media, Spielberg claimed that he was "trying to show something the war film really hadn't dared to show," and to shock viewers who had become "desensitized to mindless cinematic violence." Spielberg uses the rhetoric of rule-breaking in discussing his re-

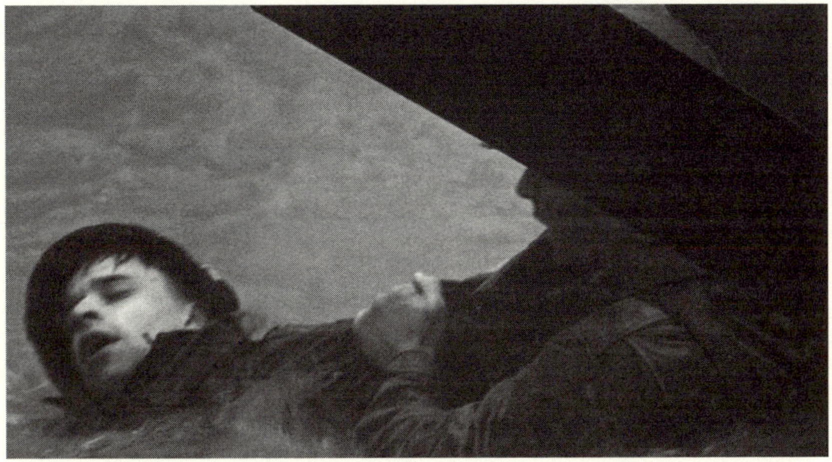

Figure 35. The look of authentic combat footage: Steven Spielberg and Janusz Kaminski re-create the Normandy landing. (*Saving Private Ryan,* DreamWorks/Paramount, 1998)

creation of the Omaha Beach landing, suggesting that he would present the battle in the way veterans experienced it rather than in the way previous Hollywood filmmakers had imagined it. Further, he appealed to standards of realism and authenticity, claiming that he had situated the viewer within "the physical experience of being inside the combat zone."[41]

Spielberg's sense of how viewers would receive the film was quite accurate. *Saving Private Ryan* created a stronger reaction among its viewers than any American war film in recent memory, as many viewers felt assaulted by the violence of the film's images. It was reported that a number of combat veterans left theaters rather than sit through the opening sequence and that there was an increase in visits to psychological counselors relating to post-traumatic stress disorder following the release of the film.[42] In her book on WWII combat films, Jeanine Basinger commented on the way in which "Spielberg's mastery of sound, editing, camera movement, visual storytelling, narrative flow, performance, and color combine to assault a viewer, to place each and every member of the audience directly into the combat experience." The opening Omaha Beach sequence—which shows "blood, vomit, dead fish, dismembered arms and legs, wounds spurting fountains of blood [and] torsos disintegrating while being dragged to safety"—is a cinematic "nightmare" that shocked audiences into silence.[43]

Basinger's contention that the film places members of the audience "directly into the combat experience" is at least somewhat debatable.

Though Spielberg and Kaminski clearly succeed in re-creating the impact (if not the actual style) of documentary footage shot by combat cameramen, their aesthetic has more to do with spectacle than with the lived reality of combatants. *Saving Private Ryan* established a new benchmark for the portrayal of violence in the war film, a standard that made possible the level of explicit violence in subsequent combat films such as Terrence Malick's *The Thin Red Line* (1999) and Ridley Scott's *Black Hawk Down* (2002).[44] Spielberg presented far more violence in *Saving Private Ryan* than he had in any of his previous films, even at the risk of having the film assigned the more restrictive NC-17 rating.[45] The apparent authenticity and realistic-looking violence of the battle sequences—which were staged with the help of military advisor Dale Dye—clearly establish them as the two dramatic high points of the film. Further, the sheer length of the sequences suggests a decision to use the passage of screen time to emphasize the intensity of combat in a way few previous films had done.

On the other hand, *Saving Private Ryan* seems in many respects to be less concerned with strict reality than with spectacularity and dramatic impact. Spielberg has admitted that in a number of cases he decided to forego strict historical accuracy for the purpose of achieving maximum dramatic effect. Robert Kolker concurs, noting that the film is ultimately less concerned with presenting a realistic depiction of World War II than with reworking the classical war film narrative: "[T]he film attempts to turn the tables on the war genre by allowing a fairly thorough and brutal destruction of the men involved, forcing the audience, through a variety of technical means . . . to share the anxiety of the dying while [being] awestruck by its spectacle."[46]

In this respect, Spielberg's film can be said to bear less of a family resemblance to the conventional Hollywood war film than to the combat films of the late 1990s and early 2000s that present military conflict in stylistically experimental ways and that seek, through the use of various filmic techniques, to destabilize and radically intensify our experience of combat. I would include in this category films such as *The Thin Red Line* and *Black Hawk Down*. *Black Hawk Down*, perhaps the most graphically "realist" of this group of films, presents uninterrupted combat for nearly its entire running time. In *Saving Private Ryan*, by contrast, the extreme violence is limited to two lengthy sequences.

Kaminski used a number of different methods to introduce a sense of authenticity into the combat sequences of *Saving Private Ryan*. One of these techniques was the manipulation of the camera lenses in order to render them as similar as possible to those that would have been used by combat cameramen of the 1940s:

> Obviously [the lenses of 1940s cameras] were inferior compared with what we have today, so I had Panavision strip the protective coatings off a set of older Ultraspeeds. Interestingly, when we analyzed the lenses, the focus and sharpness didn't change very much, though there was some deterioration; what really changed was the contrast and color rendering. The contrast became much flatter. Without the coatings, the light enters the lens and then bounces all around, so the image becomes kind of foggy but still sharp. Also, it's much easier to get flares, which automatically diffuses the light and the colors to a degree and lends a little haze to the image. If I had two cameras running on a scene, I'd mismatch the lenses on purpose, using one with coated Ultraspeeds and one without coatings. That gave us a certain lack of continuity in picture quality, which suggested the feeling of things being disjointed.[47]

Though Spielberg and Kaminski had originally intended to shoot *Saving Private Ryan* in black and white as they had done with *Schindler's List,* they ultimately abandoned this idea in favor of a desaturated color that would approximate the look of color footage director George Stevens had shot with a 16mm camera during the invasion of France. Kaminski post-flashed the film to desaturate the colors and then used the ENR process to add contrast and deepen the blacks.[48] He also relied heavily on handheld shots (Kaminski estimated that the film was about 90 percent handheld), shooting with both Steadicam and conventional handheld cameras. Since multiple cameras were required for the beach landing sequence, the shooting was performed by a number of operators, including Kaminski's principal operator Mitch Dubin. Shooting the film in this way was extremely demanding, especially since much of the action had to be shot from closer to ground level rather than from the more conventional shoulder height. "When the soldiers were running," Kaminski explained, "they were really running low. We wanted to be very close to them, so Mitch [Dubin] and Chris [Haarhoff] would often have to operate while looking at a little monitor as they ran."

Three additional techniques were used by Kaminski in his effort to enhance the feeling of combat realism. The first of these was the Clairmont Camera Image Shaker, a device that can be mounted on a handheld camera in order to increase the amount of shakiness in the image. A technology that can reproduce the more primitive conditions faced by cameramen of an earlier era, the Image Shaker is a kind of anti-Steadicam: it can be programmed to create both vertical and horizontal vibration, thus simulating the effect of a bomb exploding or a tank rolling past. The second technique was one that had been used by Douglas Milsome, the cinematographer on Kubrick's *Full Metal Jacket.* A device was added to the camera that creates an intentionally mistimed shutter. This mistiming, if done under the right conditions, results in a streaking effect from the top to the bottom of the frame. Kaminski described its strengths and drawbacks:

> It's a very interesting effect, but it's also scary because there's no way back once you shoot with it. It looked great when there were highlights on the soldiers' helmets or epaulets, because they streaked just a little bit. The amount of streaking depended on the lighting contrast. If it was really sunny, for instance, the streaking became too much. However, if it was overcast with some little highlights, it looked really beautiful.[49]

The third technique Kaminski adopted was the substitution of either a 45-degree or 90-degree shutter for the conventional 180-degree shutter. The 90-degree and 45-degree shutters render the visual image more intermittent, yet also sharper. The effect on the viewer is something akin to stop-motion animation, in which the eye is able to detect a kind of "jerkiness" in the image. Kaminski explained that the strobe-like effect of the 45-degree shutter creates a sense of visual tension, while the more highly defined image makes it especially effective for filming explosions: "When the sand is blasted into the air, you can see every particle, almost every grain, coming down. That idea was born out of our tests, and it created a definite sense of reality and urgency."[50] Barry Salt notes that although the 90- or 45-degree shutter "possibly creates something like a sense of urgency," it has little to do with reality, since the cameras used to shoot footage in World War II all had conventional 180-degree shutters.[51] Nevertheless, the 45-degree shutter became a popular technique in action and war films of the late 1990s and early 2000s: since its use in *Saving Private Ryan* the effect has been incorporated into a number of films, including *Three Kings* (1999), *The Dark Prince* (2000), *The Patriot* (2000), *Gladiator* (2000), and *Black Hawk Down* (2002). In fact, the 45-degree shutter largely came to replace slow-motion in the early years of the twenty-first century as the technique of choice for filmmakers seeking to increase the sense of brutality or viscerality in combat scenes.[52]

All of these techniques allowed for the production of images that feel less tightly controlled and more spontaneous than those of earlier war films. Even if the techniques are not entirely new, the combination of different techniques—each of them at least somewhat unusual within production methods of the 1990s—provides the viewer with a satisfyingly exciting visual spectacle.[53] In *Saving Private Ryan,* Spielberg and Kaminski combine both aesthetically oriented devices (for example, the use of the ENR process and the use of a mistimed shutter to create streaking effects) and mimetically oriented devices (the Image Shaker and the removal of protective coatings from camera lenses). In some cases, the effect is both aesthetically compelling and mimetically persuasive, as with the use of the 45-degree shutter.[54]

Saving Private Ryan also relied heavily on the use of special effects. For the beach-landing scene, Spielberg's special-effects crew prerigged the beach (Ireland's Ballinesker Beach, standing in for Omaha Beach) with squibs and mortars, while his stunt coordinator carefully planned and rehearsed the action. What appears on the screen to be total chaos was in fact highly choreographed movement. As Kaminski explained, "The physical and technical challenges of just getting the shots were daunting. Steven wanted to block huge day exterior scenes with hundreds of extras and do them in just one or two takes with two or three cameras. . . . If you have a huge field that takes a day and a half to pre-rig with squibs and explosives, you only have one take."[55]

Kaminski's comments would seem to refute Spielberg's contention that the film was shot "as a combat cameraman would have [shot it]." What appears instead is a careful balance between the meticulous planning of each sequence (along with a highly self-conscious use of both technology and filmic technique) and a sense of spontaneity or urgency created by the necessity of getting the scenes in relatively few takes. There is no doubt some irony, as Stephen Prince has observed, in the battle scenes of *Saving Private Ryan* being produced through the use of "an elaborately artificial audiovisual design" that provides an "explicit aesthetic frame" through which we experience the putatively "realistic" violence.[56]

Saving Private Ryan represents at once an extremely successful example of commercial Hollywood filmmaking and a technically sophisticated demonstration of the art of cinematography at the dawn of the digital age. Though neither as stylistically original as *McCabe and Mrs. Miller* nor as formally radical as *JFK*, it is nonetheless a film that exploits cutting-edge techniques of cinematography in the creation of a highly compelling visual spectacle. At the same time, the wide array of new technologies used in the production helped Spielberg to create a more authentically "realistic" sense of the look and feel of combat during World War II.

• • •

Although the three films discussed in this chapter by no means represent all the technical possibilities exploited by American filmmakers during the last three decades of the twentieth century, they do serve as cogent examples of a trend toward the increasingly self-conscious and intensified use of visual technologies to produce cinematographic effects. On one level, these effects were deployed in the service of the more aesthetically satisfying or stylistically compelling visual imagery that was required in order to attract the attention of viewers in an age of increasingly sophisticated visual presentation. Cinematographers of the 1980s and 1990s, even more than their 1960s and 1970s counterparts, suggests Paul Ramaeker, sought to develop "a hyperbolic, eclectic, often allusion-laced, frequently authorially driven visual style, a style that goes above and beyond narrative function as an aesthetic goal."[57] On another level, however, new technologies allowed cinematographers to work toward what they saw as a greater sense of realism, authenticity, or historical referentiality. These dual objectives—the drive toward ever more highly stylized visual imagery and the desire for an increased sense of authenticity—can be seen as guiding forces in the stylistic decisions made by many American directors and cinematographers in the late twentieth century. The 1990s were, in a sense, a predigital golden age for American cinematography, in which "star" cinematographers such as Zsigmond, Storaro, Willis, Richardson, and Kaminski achieved a quasi-auteur status that brought a new awareness to their work and made them, in some cases, nearly as celebrated as the directors with whom they worked. As I will argue in the last chapter, the increasing importance of digital techniques in the early twenty-first century are once again problematizing the hard-won status, authority, and visibility of cinematographers, forcing them to reexamine their role in the filmmaking process.

6 Cinematography, Craft, and Collaboration in the Digital Age

> Cinema traditionally involved arranging physical reality to be filmed though the use of sets, models, art direction, cinematography, etc. Occasional manipulation of recorded film (for instance, through optical printing) was negligible compared to the extensive manipulation of reality in front of a camera. In digital filmmaking, shot footage is no longer the final point but just raw material to be manipulated in a computer where the real construction of a scene will take place. In short, the production becomes just the first stage of postproduction.
>
> **Lev Manovich**

In the final decade of the twentieth century, film still represented the medium of choice for the vast majority of American directors, who still used conventional film cameras and celluloid film stocks to capture the images from which their movies were made. While computers had begun to play an important role in the production and postproduction of films, and digital capture was beginning to be explored as a viable option for films requiring extensive special effects, directors and cinematographers continued to rely on film as the basis for their productions.

Today, fifteen years into the next century, the landscape of Hollywood production looks very different. The majority of feature films produced in the United States are now made using digital capture rather than celluloid, and nearly all feature films rely on digital processes in postproduction.[1] The increase in the use of digital technologies in motion picture production has been accompanied by an equally significant change in the way in that visual media are consumed. We now have a wide range of options for viewing films, including DVDs, online streaming, and computer downloading, in addition to the more traditional options of theatrical and television viewing. As Thomas Schatz notes, the DVD—first introduced in 1997—was the earliest form of "digital delivery technology," predating digital film production and introducing digitalized films for the first time into millions of households.[2]

In several respects, 2012 was the tipping point in the shift from analog to digital filmmaking. It was the first year in which at least half the films produced in Hollywood were shot completely or primarily in digital format; it was the year in which both Panavision and Arriflex—the two companies producing most of the film-based motion picture cameras used in feature filmmaking—ceased production of their 35mm cameras; and it was the year in which Fuji Film—the second largest producer of motion-picture film after Eastman Kodak—announced that it would stop production of celluloid film for movie cameras. Kodak is now the only remaining source of celluloid film, and it remains to be seen how much longer the company will continue to produce celluloid, given the dramatic changes in the economics of the industry.[3]

Now that nearly all feature films undergo some form of digital manipulation—digital capture, digital effects, or digital correction of the film in postproduction—it is important to acknowledge this shift and its impact on cinematography. The shift to digital filmmaking has been so rapid that it has been difficult for film scholars and historians to keep pace. This fact has presented me with a dilemma. On the one hand, a book on collaborations between directors and cinematographers is at least somewhat incomplete without a discussion of digital filmmaking. On the other hand, because the digital technologies used by filmmakers are so new, so varied, and so complex, it is impossible to do justice to the myriad ways in which the digital era has affected the work of cinematographers and their relationships with directors. I have therefore limited my analysis of digital technologies to a single chapter, where my observations can remain more speculative and exploratory.[4]

• • •

If we define filmmaking as a photochemical process involving a strip of celluloid film that is run through a camera, developed in a photochemical lab, and then projected onto a movie screen through a celluloid-based projector, then we must conclude that digital cinema is an almost entirely different medium from film-based cinema. While traditional filmmaking works with the materiality of film, light, and color, digital techniques lack such material support. Digital filmmaking is no longer subject to conditions such as the speed or graininess of film stocks; instead, it relies on the functionality of computer hardware and software to produce visual images that can be programmed to resemble the images of film-based cinema—or to look altogether different. As Lev Manovich first observed nearly two decades ago, the shift from analog to digital filmmaking inevitably moves the emphasis of filmmaking from production to postproduction.[5]

Given the significance of these changes for the aesthetics of film as well as for the workflow involved in the creation of feature films, it is clear that the shift to digital filmmaking has important implications for the role of the cinematographer. A good deal of the work traditionally performed by the cinematographer will—as the emphasis changes from production to postproduction—increasingly be done by, or at the very least in consultation with, an array of digital colorists, digital compositors, and visual effects supervisors.[6] And while it is perhaps too early to say how this change will affect the collaboration of cinematographers with directors, it seems reasonable to assume that there will be at least some diminution of the privileged role cinematographers have enjoyed on film sets and a dilution of the aesthetic control cinematographers have exercised over the visual style of films.

The first aspect of digital filmmaking to come into widespread use was digitally produced visual effects. Starting in the early 1980s, George Lucas's company, Industrial Light and Magic (ILM), began producing computer-based special effects, more commonly known as computer-generated imagery (CGI). ILM created the first computer-generated visual effects sequence in 1982, for *Star Trek II: The Wrath of Khan*. This was followed by other major breakthroughs, such as the creation of digital morphing in *Willow* (1988) and a digitally generated 3-D creature in *The Abyss* (1989). By the mid-1990s, the use of CGI had become an industry norm, used in films as diverse as *Jurassic Park* (1993), *Forrest Gump* (1994), and *The Age of Innocence* (1995).

The two primary technologies that followed on the heels of CGI are digital cinematography—or what is often referred to as "digital capture" in order to differentiate it from other processes in the digital workflow—and digital postproduction, especially the use of the digital intermediate process for color grading and image enhancement. Since both of these areas of filmmaking have had a direct and significant impact on the collaborative relationship of the cinematographer with the director, and both have sparked significant controversy within the industry, I will attempt to draw out some strands of the discussion as it has evolved so far.

The first digital technique in which the cinematographer played a major role was the use of digital technology to adjust or alter the appearance of the negative in postproduction. The practice, generally referred to as "digital intermediate" (or simply DI), is one in which a digital process replaces analog processes such as photochemical color timing, flashing, and bleach bypass. In the DI process, the original footage is scanned from the camera negative into a computer in order to create a DI. This digital intermediate can then be manipulated in any number of ways before being scanned back onto film.[7]

Digital intermediate has been an increasingly valuable tool since the late 1990s, providing directors and cinematographers with a range of options that were not previously available. Stephen Prince explains that whereas traditional cinematography involved the creation of images according to decisions made primarily during production—leaving only a "minimal ability" to adjust and correct those images in postproduction—digital intermediate has made it possible for directors and cinematographers to alter colors and other image elements in postproduction in a far more comprehensive way.[8] Filmmakers can now add or subtract color at will, desaturating or supersaturating colors in a way that would have been impossible before DI. They can also adjust for highlights, shadows, and lighting conditions, and alter specific images or parts of the frame. Aylish Wood has analyzed the use of digital intermediate in Robert Rodriguez's 2005 film *Sin City,* in which DI is used at the "micro-level" to adjust individual objects within the frame rather than only at the macro-level of color correction or enhancement. Wood notes that DI makes it possible to deploy effects at an extremely specific level: "A character's tie or glasses, or the patches of bandages covering a wounded body, can be picked out separately from all other elements of the image."[9]

The implications of this technology for the work of the cinematographer are very significant indeed. On the one hand, digital intermediate liberates cinematographers and their crews from having to produce a perfectly photographed film during shooting. Vilmos Zsigmond notes that since much of the work can now be done after the camera negative has been completed, "we sometimes can let certain things go on set if we don't have enough time to fine-tune the lighting, or if we don't have the right weather."[10] This freedom, however, is something of a double-edged sword for cinematographers: while it gives greater latitude in terms of weather and other shooting conditions, it also takes away at least some of the control the cinematographer has traditionally exercised over the film's visual style. Aspects of the cinematographer's craft such as the choice of lighting and of cameras, lenses, and filters will continue to be important in the production of digitally made films, but they will matter somewhat less than they did in the production of celluloid films. Directors, on the other hand, have the ability to exercise a relatively greater degree of control over the final look of their films, since they are less dependent on the knowledge and expertise of their cinematographers in acquiring footage on the set or location. If a director wants a particular shade of green for a car, or a particular red for the actress's dress, it is no longer necessary to light them in a particular way, since the colors can easily be adjusted in postproduction. This new ability to make changes in postproduction may please directors who seek greater control over the look of their films, but it detracts from the collaborative relationship of the director with his crew, including the cinematographer.

The earliest use of the digital intermediate process in feature films occurred just as the twentieth century was coming to a close. In *Pleasantville* (1998), director Gary Ross and cinematographer John Lindley made the manipulation of color a crucial element in the film's plot. Two 1990s teenagers travel back in time to the 1950s, where they find themselves in the black-and-white world of a 1950s sitcom. As their viewpoint begins to permeate that of the retro world they have entered, color is selectively introduced. Though a clever premise, the film is essentially one sustained visual effect, in which color gradually seeps into the film's black-and-white diegesis.

In *O Brother, Where Art Thou?* (2000), Joel and Ethan Coen and their cinematographer Roger Deakins used the digital intermediate process in a more nuanced way. Instead of using the DI process as a visual effect, Deakins used it to manipulate the film's color palette in postproduction, thus becoming the first cinematographer to use digital technology to do what had previously been accomplished by the analog technique of photochemical color timing. Before shooting the film—which is set in the Deep South during the 1930s—the Coens had told Deakins that they wanted a Dust Bowl–era look, with a palette of primarily warm browns and earth tones. Deakins pointed out that since *O Brother* was scheduled to be shot on location in Mississippi during the summer months—when the landscape was dominated by lush greens—it would be impossible to achieve this look through traditional color timing, and even techniques such as bleach bypass would not be sufficient to achieve the desired look. An advantage of digital grading over such analog techniques is that it allows the filmmakers to desaturate some parts of the color spectrum, such as the greens, without having to desaturate all the other colors at the same time. In *O Brother,* Deakins was able to retain the bright red cans of Dapper Dan Pomade used by the film's protagonist Ulysses Everett McGill (George Clooney), while turning the bright green Mississippi fields into highly desaturated greenish-browns.

The use of digital intermediate represented a turning point in the creation of visual style. For the first time since the creation of the earliest motion pictures, filmmakers were able to work outside the limits imposed by their physical tools. Any stylization of the visual image that could not be created through film stock, camera, lenses, and lighting could be achieved through digital manipulation. Almost exactly a century after cameramen like Billy Bitzer began experimenting with hand-cranked cameras and primitive, orthochromatic film stock, filmmakers were working in a cinematic medium that did not require celluloid film and photochemical development to produce images.

If the Coens' use of digital intermediate was a major breakthrough in feature filmmaking, an even more sophisticated use of the process can be seen in Martin Scorsese's 2004 film *The Aviator.* Scorsese and his cinematographer Robert Richardson used digital color techniques not simply as a means of achieving a particular color palette but as a self-conscious allusion to the history of color cinematography. Scorsese decided that for his biopic based on the life of the eccentric billionaire Howard Hughes, he would evoke both two-color and three-color Technicolor as a stylistic reference. Scorsese and Richardson used digital intermediate to create a simulation of the two-color Technicolor palette for approximately the first third of the film and a three-color Technicolor palette for the remainder.[11]

The creation of the digital Technicolor look involved a complex collaboration between Scorsese, Richardson, visual effects supervisor Rob Legato, and Technicolor digital colorists Steve Arkle and Stephen Nakamura. First, Legato created versions of two- and three-color Technicolor by manipulating photographs on his laptop computer. The colors in those photographs were used as a model for treating the high-definition video dailies that Scorsese screened during production. Josh Pines, the vice president of research and development at Technicolor Digital Imaging, then developed intermediate filters called "lookup tables" (LUTs), which allowed him to imitate the look of either two-color and three-color Technicolor for every scene of the film. Once the LUTs had been prepared, Richardson and Nakamura were able to view the footage through the LUTs and adjust colors, shadows, and other details from shot to shot. All of this information was then "baked in" to a final negative from which release prints were produced.

LUTs were an important technical advance in the practice of digital color grading. Rather than relying on intensive shot-by-shot intervention by the cinematographer and colorists, filmmakers could now use color tables to apply an overall look to a film. From the baseline look created by the LUTs, Richardson was able to manipulate scenes and sequences with far more precision than he would have had using photochemical color timing.[12] The years of Hughes's life from 1927 to 1936 are rendered through colors available on the more limited spectrum of the two-color LUTs, while the section of the film that takes place from 1937 to 1947 utilizes the more vibrant and tonally rich palette of the three-color LUTs. The two-color LUTs eliminate the pure greens and blues and translate them as various shades of turquoise and aquamarine, while the three-color LUTs create vibrant, supersaturated greens, strong blues, and bright reds, along with an overall saturation along the entire color spectrum.

The self-conscious artifice of digital color in *The Aviator* alerts the viewer (in a much more overt way than it does in *O Brother Where Art Thou*) to the fact that color is an active choice made by the filmmakers, a stylistic element that represents a self-conscious manipulation of the image. While viewers of the Coens' film would never be aware that Deakins had changed the colors of the landscape through digital intermediate, viewers of *The Aviator* are very likely aware that the color palette has been manipulated for stylistic purposes, even if they are not aware of the exact historical references being made.

Although each of *The Aviator*'s two looks departs from the color palette of other films, only the two-color section of the film identifies itself as an obvious break with "natural" color. Sky and foliage are particularly sensitive to treatment by digital intermediate, and they become important indicators for viewers of whether we are in two-color or three-color Technicolor. In an early scene, Hughes (Leonardo DiCaprio) courts Katherine Hepburn (Cate Blanchett) on a golf course featuring blue-green grass and an aquamarine sky. Later, a cluster of beautifully colored scenes highlights the transition to three-color Technicolor: here the work of production designer Dante Ferretti complements both Richardson's cinematography and the work done in postproduction. Ferretti's design for the office of Pan Am executive Juan Trippe (Alec Baldwin), the first interior set we see in the three-color portion of the film, features midnight-blue walls painted with murals of maps featuring green accents. In another visually striking scene, Hughes is seen in a bathroom decorated with disturbingly bright greens. The climax of this introduction to three-color style comes as Hughes and Hepburn drive to her Connecticut estate. In a shot that includes the film's strongest three-color Technicolor moment, grass and foliage are now a powerfully saturated bright green, while sky and ocean are rendered in deep, pure blues.

In deliberately foregrounding his use of the digital intermediate technology, I would argue, Scorsese participates in what David Bordwell has termed the "intensified continuity" of contemporary visual style.[13] While still embracing the goals of narrative-centered continuity, contemporary filmmakers like Scorsese are able to manipulate technologies such as digital intermediate to intensify the role of style itself. Bordwell's analysis is insightful, but I would argue that with the greatly increased use of DI since 2000, we need to include it as an important tactic in contemporary filmmakers' quest for an intensified visual style. The exaggerated or highly stylized use of color made possible through digital intermediate has been responsible for an increase in the number of films foregrounding color as a stylistic element.[14]

One can argue that digital intermediate does not really signal the shift to digital filmmaking, since the technique relies on the photochemical image shot by the cinematographer. However, it is more accurate to view digital intermediate within a continuum of digital techniques that includes digital capture, digital visual effects, and digital postproduction. The technique has raised red flags among some cinematographers. According to John Bailey, prints produced by a digital finish lack the beauty and clarity of prints produced using the traditional photochemical process. Further, the use of digital intermediate erodes the creative function of the cinematographer: once directors, studio executives, and stars are able to enter digital color suites and offer their creative input, the role of the cinematographer will be diminished to that of a relatively insignificant technician. By utilizing digital intermediate, Bailey writes, "we cinematographers may have unwittingly begun to write our own epitaph on the subject of image control." If a director or studio executive is able to relight and recolorize the film in postproduction, "Why do we need a cinematographer at all?"[15]

Other cinematographers have taken issue with Bailey's position. Roger Deakins, for example, in a piece written in response to Bailey's, declared that even though a Super 35mm image scanned and finished digitally would arguably not match the resolution of an anamorphic image produced through today's photochemical means, it would be far superior to a release print produced photochemically in the 1960s or 1970s. In other words, there is a necessary time lag before new technologies reach their full potential: just as the production of sound films went through a period of awkwardness in the late 1920s and early 1930s, and Technicolor did not achieve its full potential for several years after its introduction, digital intermediate should not be expected to reach the level of photochemical finishing within a few short years.[16] We have already seen an evolution from 2K scans in the early years of digital intermediate to 4K scans, and the possibility of 8K scans exists.[17]

• • •

As important as the use of digital postproduction techniques have been in American filmmaking of the past ten years, an even more controversial shift has been in the area of digital capture. This process involves not simply the transfer of a filmic negative to digital format so that it can be adjusted in postproduction, but an entirely digital workflow in which no actual film is ever used. Over the past decade, there has been both an enormous increase in the number of films shot using digital capture and a significant improvement in the quality of the images captured digitally. But although the quality of digital cameras has improved substantially, a number of filmmakers—including Steven Spielberg, Quentin Tarantino, and Christopher Nolan—have remained outspokenly opposed to the idea of shooting their movies in digital format. Spielberg has stated that he will continue to shoot his movies on film as long as it is physically possible to do so, and Tarantino has gone as far as suggesting that the pressure to make and exhibit films digitally may drive him to an early retirement. "I can't stand all this digital stuff," Tarantino proclaimed at a November 2012 roundtable, adding that shooting films in digital format is nothing more than presenting "TV in public."[18]

Christopher Nolan's comments on the subject of digital filmmaking are particularly interesting and worth quoting at some length:

> For the last ten years, I've felt increasing pressure to stop shooting film and start shooting video, but I've never understood why. It's cheaper to work on film, it's far better looking, it's the technology that's been known and understood for a hundred years, and it's extremely reliable. I think, truthfully, it boils down to the economic interest of manufacturers and [an] industry that makes more money through change rather than through maintaining the status quo. We save a lot of money shooting on film and projecting film and not doing digital intermediates. In fact, I've never done a digital intermediate. Photochemically, you can time film with a good timer in three or four passes, which takes about twelve to fourteen hours as opposed to seven or eight weeks in a DI suite. That's the way everyone was doing it ten years ago, and I've just carried on making films in the way that works best and waiting until there's a good reason to change. But I haven't seen that reason yet. . . . When I look at a digitally acquired and projected image, it looks inferior against an original negative anamorphic print or an IMAX one.[19]

Wally Pfister, the cinematographer who has collaborated with Nolan on several of his films, identifies a number of problems with the industry's shift to digital capture. Not only is digital capture less reliable than film—especially for shots involving stunts, high-speed filming, or extreme light conditions—but it also lacks the characteristic qualities that have always marked film as an enduringly successful visual medium. "Film has this organic softness," says Pfister, "plus the contrast to be able to handle the subtleties of scenes that are lit with candlelight or firelight."[20]

On the other side of the analog-digital debate are directors such as Michael Mann and David Fincher, both of whom have enthusiastically embraced digital filmmaking. Mann has shot four films digitally, working with cinematographer Dion Beebe on *Collateral* (2004) and *Miami Vice* (2006), with Dante Spinotti on *Public Enemies* (2009), and with Stuart Dryburgh on *Blackhat* (2015).[21] Fincher has also made four films in digital format: *Zodiac* (2007) with Harris Savides, and *The Social Network* (2010), *The Girl with the Dragon Tattoo* (2011), and *Gone Girl* (2014) with Jeff Cronenweth. Fincher's *Zodiac* was the first feature film to be shot entirely in digital data mode, without the use of any film or tape.[22]

Ultimately, the question of whether film or digital is a better format in which to make motion pictures is not one that can be answered in any meaningful way. As is clear in the 2012 documentary *Side by Side*—which explores differences between celluloid and digital filmmaking—there is a wide range of responses within the film industry to the growth of digital cinema, ranging from full acceptance to adamant rejection.[23] That will no doubt be the case for some time to come.

In an ideal world, filmmakers would have the ability to choose whether to shoot their films on celluloid or in digital format. Unfortunately, however, that choice has in many cases been taken out of the hands of directors and cinematographers. Even Martin Scorsese, one of the most celebrated directors in the industry, has had to adjust to a new reality of film production in which digital is often seen as more cost-efficient than shooting on film. In the summer of 2012, Scorsese made the announcement that he would "abandon shooting movies on film and turn to digital." Scorsese's long-time editor, Thelma Shoonmaker, added that Scorsese had "lost the battle" over shooting his movies on film when he asked to shoot *The Wolf of Wall Street* (2013) on film but was told that he had to shoot it digitally.[24] After a set of preproduction tests in which Scorsese still felt the celluloid footage looked better than that shot on digital, he and cinematographer Rodrigo Prieto were able to convince the film's producers to let them shoot in a combination of digital and 35mm film formats. This "hybrid" approach, an option increasingly adopted by filmmakers, entailed shooting most of the movie's footage on film and using a digital camera for night scenes, visual effects, and scenes involving changes in shutter speed.[25]

Like the shift to digital intermediate, the shift from celluloid to digital capture may decrease the creative control of the image by the cinematographer. Prince cites the remarks of cinematographer Uta Briesewitz, who has shot both on film and digitally. According to her, one artifact of the change to digital is the use of a waveform monitor in place of a light meter. Ever since they first came into use in Hollywood, the ability to use a light meter like a fine-tuned instrument to determine correct exposure has made the cinematographer a kind of "alchemist" on the set. Though some cinematographers continue to use light meters on digital productions, it is no longer necessary to do so, since a video monitor records the amplitude of the visual signal and indicates where information is being lost due to highlights or shadows. As Briesewitz notes, "Anyone can [now] gather around the monitor and make an opinion known. That's a very different dynamic for a cinematographer."[26]

The use of monitors on the set has also eliminated the traditional practice of watching dailies, which had for decades provided a forum in which the director and cinematographer could view the day's footage together and consult about the evolving visual style. In the digital workflow, a more likely scenario is for the original camera files to be transcoded by a technical assistant, who produces the files that can be viewed and edited by members of the crew. In this transcoding process, and again in the editing, decisions made by the cinematographer can easily be undone.[27] Further, this workflow means that directors are more likely to go directly to editing once footage has been shot, depriving cinematographers of the opportunity to see how their footage has been manipulated until later in the process. By the time cinematographers are included in postproduction—for example, in the color timing process—the film may have already been altered in a number of ways.[28]

Even those cinematographers who have worked successfully with digital capture have expressed reservations about the use of the new technology. In shooting *Zodiac*, for example, Harris Savides was not entirely satisfied with the visual style he achieved with the Thomson Viper digital camera:

> The Viper [gives] the images an almost hyper-real quality that might work [well]. . . . However, I also tried to go against that look a bit because *Zodiac* is a period film, and the audience has some impression of what [the 1970s] looked like. . . . To my eyes, the Viper's digital images have a synthetic quality that is at odds with what we were trying to do. It's [already] hard to put the audience in a darkened theater and screen "reality" for them, because the whole thing is a falsehood. But if you have a synthetic image like the Viper's—which reminds me a bit of the vivid, colorful look of a cibachrome photo—you're taken right out of the story. I wanted to give the image a patina, to remove the newness. However, that vivid, hyper-real quality [of digital] may also work to bring a psychological tension to the surface, since we have these characters searching and trying to see something that's just beyond their vision. With the Viper, the audience will see more than they normally

> see in a movie—literally, the pores on people's faces and the hair on their heads—so it has a more immersive effect.[29]

Savides makes a number of cogent points here about the differences between the look of film and the look of digital, and about their respective effects on the audience. Digital capture creates a greater sense of "hyper-reality" than film, and as a result it has a potentially more "immersive" effect on the viewer. Although these qualities can potentially work to the advantage of the cinematographer, the "synthetic" quality of digital can also detract from a believable portrayal of lived reality, particularly in the case of films set in earlier eras. In my own viewing of both *Zodiac* (set in the 1970s) and *Public Enemies* (set in the 1930s), I found the look of digital to be a distraction from the period setting and a detriment both to the films' feeling of authenticity and to their overall aesthetic appeal. Savides poses a very important question: should a movie look like film or like something else? This question is, in fact, the crux of the matter as we begin to understand the significance of the change from film-based cinema to digital cinema. Heather Stewart, the program director of the British Film Institute, cautions that the differences between the visual presence of film and that of digital cannot simply be ignored:

> Film is an organic material: different stocks or color processes, each with their own special characteristics, can be transformed into a work of art. Film is imperfect, not evenly sensitive, with a curve that responds beautifully to light. Film has density and weight, something missing from digital images. . . . Compelling works of art can be digital. But the qualities are not those of film. Digital can be fatiguing to watch (sometimes nauseating), as dead as mutton when not in the hands of a skilled director of photography.[30]

The most ardent supporters of digital media suggest that digital capture is a more flexible medium than film, enabling the filmmaker to create more varied and compelling visual images. George Lucas, for example, notes the greater "malleability" of digital filmmaking, its potential to be "much more flexible, in terms of what you can do with the image, how you can change the image and work with the image."[31] That is no doubt true, but it is not a sufficient rationale for what appears to be an industry-wide shift to digital production. Further, it begs a number of important questions.

How does this greater malleability of the digitalized image affect the aesthetic or ontological status of the cinematic image? Is there a necessary tradeoff between the inherent beauty of the photographic image and the greater malleability of the digital image? Should digital cinema attempt to emulate the visual style of film, a style that developed in response to the specific capabilities and limitations of the filmic medium? Or should digital cinema be approached as an entirely different medium from film, a mode of cinema that has less in common with the film-based motion picture than it does with such digital artifacts as computer graphics and video games? Is the artistic rationale behind the creation of digitalized images the same as the artistic rationale for film-based cinema, or is it different? Or, to put it another way, do the qualities of the digital medium itself—its very malleability and lack of inherent physical structure—dictate a different set of stylistic choices on the part of directors and cinematographers? Will the different stylistic choices necessitated by digital cinema be accepted by audiences accustomed to the look of film? Are viewers who most often consume visual media on televisions, home computers, and handheld electronic devices even aware that the image they are watching on the movie screen is no longer that of film projected through light at twenty-four frames a second, but something closer to high-def video projected onto a gigantic television screen? What are the implications of digital technology for the storage, archiving, and restoration of films?[32] Is the distinction between film and television even a meaningful one in an age in which, as Noel Carroll has suggested, there is no longer an "essential difference" between TV and film, but only "contingent, technological differences of degree"?[33]

To answer any one of these questions with any degree of thoroughness would take another book. Instead, I will return to my primary topic: the collaboration between directors and cinematographers. I began the book with some questions about the nature of the director-cinematographer collaboration, and I will conclude with some final reflections on these same questions. If, as I have suggested, the collaboration of the director and the cinematographer represents an artistic partnership that takes place across the transom of technology, then this particular relationship may ultimately be less meaningful in the digital age than it has been throughout the 120-year history of film-based cinema. As Christopher Lucas has observed, the cinematographer's role has shifted from that of the "primary visual architect of the look of films"—who had "relatively unquestioned . . . authority" over matters of visual style—to a position of "more diluted authority shared among several members of a visual design team."[34] Although cinematographers remain highly valued members of the crew—skilled technicians who bring an intimate knowledge of the history of lighting and camerawork and an expert eye for color and composition—they are in danger of losing their privileged status as "painters of light" whose creative contribution to films is in many cases second only to that of the director.

The role of the cinematographer in the digital age will be a more malleable one, and the cinematographer's claim to "authorship of a film's look" more difficult to establish.[35] This will be true for at least two reasons. First, the nature of the filmmaking process requires a technical effort that is focused less on the cinematographic aspects of production and more on aspects of the digital workflow, including previsualization, computer-generated effects (CGI), and techniques such as digital intermediate in postproduction. Second, the far greater possibilities for adjusting, altering, or manipulating images through CGI and digital intermediate will inevitably mean a decrease in the precision of image capture. Although there will undoubtedly be films produced digitally that continue to exhibit the stylistic imprint of their cinematographers, it is likely that in the vast majority of digital films we will lose some of the particularity of the filmic image, that unique visual presence that results from what Martin Scorsese has elegantly described as "a passionate, physical relationship between celluloid and the artists and craftsmen and technicians who handle it."[36] Already, many films use a form of "digital suture" to blend live action with CG enhancements, creating convincingly photoreal environments and mise-en-scène and thus blurring the line between cinematography and other forms of image creation.

A case in point is James Cameron's phenomenally successful 2009 film *Avatar,* which combined live-action footage with computer-generated imagery. When Mauro Fiore, the film's cinematographer, was nominated for an Academy Award for best cinematography and then went on to win the Oscar, some in the industry questioned the decision. Concerns were raised about the extensive previsualization of the film's look, the control of the color palette, and the use of virtual sets and illumination. The film was, by Cameron's own estimate, about 60 percent computer generated and 40 percent live action, but since the goal was to create such a seamless interaction between the two that the audience would be unable to tell which was which, it is appropriate to ask questions about the role of the cinematographer. How could members of the Academy be expected to evaluate the quality of the film's cinematography if they could not tell whether a particular image or scene was photographed, digitally created, or some combination of the two? Would they still have voted to award the best cinematography Oscar to the film had they known that it was created primarily with CGI?[37] Similar concerns were raised about Claudio Miranda's best cinematography award for *The Life of Pi* (2012), which underwent a significant amount of digital manipulation. *Gravity* (2013), directed by Alfonso Cuaron and photographed by Emmanuel Lubetski, won the best cinematography award despite an even higher percentage of CGI than *Avatar.*[38]

It is difficult, at this early stage in the development of digital cinema, to know what the work of a truly brilliant digital cinematographer will look like. Perhaps there will be a Billy Bitzer, a Gregg Toland, or a John Alton of the digital age, but what his or her contribution to the art of cinematography will be is harder to predict. It is very possible that the function of the cinematographer will morph into something new and as yet unforeseen, as the working relationship between cinematographers and other film workers such as editors, special-effects technicians, and production designers is restructured to reflect the new realities of the digital age. For example, digital editing technology has given far greater control over a film's visual style to editors, who can now work with stylistic elements such as camera movement, framing, and color timing that were previously the province of the cinematographer.[39] At the same time, as more and more films are made using a combination of camera capture and digital effects, the relationship of the cinematographer and the special effects supervisor has changed. Finally, advances in digital previsualization software now enable filmmakers to experiment with cinema angles, composition, and movement on 3-D virtual sets before the film is shot. Since much previsualization is done before the cinematographer comes onto the set, decisions regarding composition and camerawork are sometimes made without the input of the DP.

This is not to say that the director-cinematographer collaboration as I have delineated it in the chapters of this book is a relic of the past, or that it is on the verge of going the way of hand-cranking or three-strip Technicolor. But it does need to be acknowledged that the terms of that collaboration have changed in both obvious and less obvious ways. In a world of digital production, the relationship of the director to the cinematographer—who was the sole provider of compelling visual images from which the final film would be created—is radically altered. These new technological realities necessitate new forms of collaboration, shifting the roles of workers within the film industry to an extent that has perhaps not been seen since the beginning of the sound era. As in the earliest days of cinema, when a more fluid and less hierarchical system of production allowed for highly inventive modes of artistic collaboration, the traditional roles assigned to those who participate in the making of films no longer apply. This fact in itself will put additional pressure on the notion of the director as singular auteur, leaving room for more informed conversations about the nature of collaboration and about the various aesthetic effects that collaborative work can produce.

Notes

INTRODUCTION

1. C. Paul Sellors, *Film Authorship: Auteurs and Other Myths* (London: Wallflower, 2010), 3, 6.

2. Alternatives to the director-as-auteur model have been proposed, though they remain the exception rather than the rule. John T. Caldwell's "industrial auteur theory" includes the contributions of both above-the-line personnel such as producers, directors, and cinematographers and below-the-line personnel such as editors, gaffers, and operators within a system of industrialized film production, while Jerome Christensen's "studio authorship thesis" proposes the Hollywood studio itself as the "author" of films during the studio era. John T. Caldwell, *Production Culture: Industrial Reflexivity and Critical Practice in Films and Television* (Durham, NC: Duke University Press, 2008); and Jerome Christensen, *America's Corporate Art: The Studio Authorship of Hollywood Motion Pictures* (Stanford, CA: Stanford University Press, 2012).

3. Thomas Schatz, *The Genius of the System: Hollywood Filmmaking in the Studio Era* (New York: Pantheon, 1988), 5.

4. Peter Wollen, "The Auteur Theory," in *Signs and Meaning in the Cinema* (Bloomington: Indiana University Press, 1972); reprinted in Barry Keith Grant ed., *Auteurs and Authorship: A Film Reader* (Malden, MA: Wiley-Blackwell, 2008), 64. In citing Wollen's argument, I am aware that this essay, first published over forty years ago, may no longer represent his current views. However, as the essay exemplifies a particularly strong statement of the most extreme version of the auteurist argument, I believe it is worth considering.

5. The published literature on cinematography includes biographical and autobiographical studies of individual DPs as well as collections of interviews with or essays on groups of cinematographers. The former category includes G.W. Bitzer, *Billy Bitzer: His Story* (New York: Farrar, Straus, and Giroux, 1973); Joseph Walker and Juanita Walker, *The Light on Her Face* (Los Angeles: ASC Press, 1993); Karl Brown, *Adventures with D.W. Griffith* (London: Secker and Warburg, 1973); Fred Balshofer and Arthur C. Miller, *One Reel a Week* (Berkeley: University of

California Press, 1967); Charles Clarke, *Highlights and Shadows: The Memoirs of a Hollywood Cameraman*, ed. Anthony Slide (Metuchen, NJ: Scarecrow Press, 1989); Todd Rainsberger, *James Wong Howe: Cinematographer* (New York: A.S. Barnes: 1982); and Alain Silver and James Wong Howe, *James Wong Howe: The Camera Eye: A Career Interview* (Santa Monica, CA: Pendragon Press, 2010). In the latter category are Charles Higham, *Hollywood Cameramen* (London: Thames and Hudson, 1971); Leonard Maltin, *The Art of the Cinematographer*, rev. ed. (Mineola, NY: Dover, 2012); Dennis Schaeffer and Larry Salvato, *Masters of Light: Conversations with Contemporary Cinematographers*, rev. ed. (Berkeley and Los Angeles: University of California Press, 2013); Vincent LoBrutto, *Principal Photography: Interviews with Feature Film Cinematographers* (Westport, CT: Praeger, 1999); Scott Eyman, *Five American Cinematographers* (Metuchen, NJ: Scarecrow Press, 1987), Peter Ettedgui, *Cinematography* (Woburn, MA: Butterworth-Heinemann, 1998); Alex Ballinger, *New Cinematographers* (New York: Harper, 2004); and Jon Fauer, ed., *Cinematographer Style: The Complete Interviews*, Vol. 1 (Hollywood: ASC Press, 2008).

6. Richard Dyer, "Introduction to Film Studies," in John Hill and Pamela Church Gibson, eds., *Oxford Guide to Film Studies* (Oxford and New York: Oxford University Press, 1998), 3.

7. Paul Ramaeker, "Notes on the Split-Field Diopter," *Film History* 19 (2007): 179.

8. Barry Salt, *Film Style and Technology: History and Analysis*, 3rd ed. (London: Starwood, 2009), 241.

9. Since the publication of James Lastra's *Sound Technology and the American Cinema: Perception, Representation, Modernity* (New York: Columbia University Press, 2000), there have been several books devoted to film sound. See, for example, Richard Abel and Rick Altman, eds., *The Sounds of Early Cinema* (Bloomington: Indiana University Press, 2001), Charles O'Brien, *Cinema's Conversion to Sound: Technology and Film Style in France and the U.S.* (Bloomington: Indiana University Press, 2005), and Tony Beck and Tony Grajeda, eds., *Lowering the Boom: Critical Studies in Film Sound* (Urbana: University of Illinois Press, 2008).

10. Patrick Keating, *Hollywood Lighting: From the Silent Era to Film Noir* (New York: Columbia University Press, 2010). Also see Patrick Keating, ed., *Cinematography* (New Brunswick: Rutgers University Press, 2014).

11. Charles Musser, "The Early Cinema of Edwin S. Porter," in Cynthia Lucia, Roy Grundman, and Art Simon, eds., *The Wiley-Blackwell History of American Film*, Vol. 1, *Origins to 1928* (Oxford: Wiley-Blackwell, 2012), 44.

12. Charles Musser, "Pre-Classical Modes of American Cinema: Its Changing Modes of Production," in Richard Abel, ed., *Silent Film* (New Brunswick: Rutgers University Press, 1996), 85–108.

13. Charlie Keil, *Early American Cinema in Transition: Story, Style, and Filmmaking, 1907–1913* (Madison: University of Wisconsin Press, 2001), 33.

14. David S. Hulfish, "Art in Moving Pictures," *Nickelodeon* 5 (May 1909): 139, quoted in Keil, *Early American Cinema*, 33.

15. "The Qualitative Picture," *Moving Picture World* 6.25 (June 1910): 1090, quoted in Keil, *Early American Cinema*, 33.

16. Keil, *Early American Cinema*, 149. The technological developments in lighting during the period included the widespread adoption of Cooper-Hewitt mercury vapor lamps, as well as the use of arc lamps for more specific effects. For a detailed discussion of developments in lighting during this period, see Salt, *Film Style and Technology*, 69–84.

17. Long-term collaborations between directors and cinematographers have played an important role in American cinema since its origins. Some of the most significant of these collaborations are those of Griffith and Bitzer (1908–1924), DeMille and Wyckoff (1914–1923), John Ford and George Schneiderman (1920–1935), Frank Capra and Joseph Walker (1930–1946), Michael Curtiz and Sol Polito (1936–1943), Alfred Hitchcock and Robert Burks (1951–1964), Robert Aldrich and Joseph Biroc (1954–1981), Sidney Lumet and Boris Kaufman (1957–1968), Jonathan Demme and Tak Fujimoto (1974–2004), Woody Allen and Gordon Willis (1977–1985), Brian De Palma and Stephen Burum (1984–2000), Spike Lee and Ernest Dickerson (1985–1992), Oliver Stone and Robert Richardson (1985–1998), the Coen brothers and Roger Deakins (1991–2010), and Steven Spielberg and Janusz Kaminski (1993-present).

18. David Bordwell, Janet Staiger, and Kristin Thompson, *The Classical Hollywood Cinema: Film Style and Mode of Production to 1960* (New York: Columbia University Press, 1985), 345.

19. Keating, *Hollywood Lighting*, 26.

20. John Arnold, "Art in Cinematography," *American Cinematographer* (April 1932): 25.

21. "Through the Editor's Finder," *American Cinematographer* 23.2 (1942): 65.

22. Rainsberger, *James Wong Howe: Cinematographer*, 160–61. For a discussion of studio house style and its implications for cinematography, see Chris Cagle, "Classical Hollywood, 1928–1946," in Patrick Keating, ed. *Cinematography*, 47–53. As Cagle rightly points out, house style is a complex entity, involving diverse elements such as cinematography, production design, costume and special effects departments, as well as directives from producers or studio heads. In addition, while most equipment was standardized across the film industry, there were certain differences between the equipment and processes used by individual studios, such that "studio-specific technical standards" often served as a "baseline" for a recognizable house style (49).

23. Todd McCarthy, "Through a Lens Darkly: The Life and Films of John Alton," introduction to *Painting with Light*, by John Alton, rev. ed. (Berkeley and Los Angeles: University of California Press, 2013), xxvi.

24. Keating, *Hollywood Lighting*, 282.

25. Garmes shot much of the opening portion of *Gone with the Wind,* but both Selznick and Technicolor supervisor Ray Rennahan disagreed with Garmes's muted color scheme, and he was replaced.

26. Don Fairservice, *Film Editing: History, Theory and Practice* (Manchester: Manchester University Press, 2001), 250–51.

27. There are a few notable exceptions to this trend toward more conservative cinematography. The horror genre of the early 1930s achieved highly expressive lighting effects that anticipated those of 1940s film noir, while also incorporating innovative uses of trick photography. Certain directors experimented with more stylized cinematography in their films of the 1930s. John Ford's *The Informer* (1935), photographed by Joseph August, is an unusual example of highly expressionistic cinematography in an American film of the mid-1930s.

28. Keating, *Hollywood Lighting,* 165–69.

29. Keating, *Hollywood Lighting,* 170–79. As Keating suggests, the studios' rules about glamour lighting were extremely rigid, especially when it came to the lighting of female stars. This emphasis on glamour lighting severely limited the possibilities for introducing innovative lighting effects, which might distract from a glamorous presentation of the star. During the 1930s, glamour lighting was not simply a "subordinate principle" of studio cinematography; it was the "dominant principle," with an importance equal to that of narrative clarity.

30. Karl Struss, "'Dramatic Cinematography," *Transactions of the Society of Motion Pictures Engineers* 34 (1928): 317.

31. Karl Struss, "Photographic Modernism and the Cinematographer," *American Cinematographer* (November 1934): 296.

32. Richard Koszarski, "The Cinematographer," in Barbara McCandless, Bonnie Yochelson, and Richard Koszarski, eds., *New York to Hollywood: The Photography of Karl Struss* (Fort Worth and Albuquerque: Amon Carter Museum and University of New Mexico Press, 1995), 190–91.

33. Although the film noir cycle ended in the late 1950s, the production of black-and-white films containing excellent cinematography continued into the 1960s. Films such as Martin Ritt's *Hud* (1962, cin. James Wong Howe), Elia Kazan's *America, America* (1963, cin. Haskell Wexler), Sidney Lumet's *The Pawnbroker* (1964, cin. Boris Kaufman), John Huston's *The Night of the Iguana* (1964, cin. Gabriel Figueroa), Mike Nichols's *Who's Afraid of Virginia Woolf* (1966, cin. Haskell Wexler), and Richard Brooks's *In Cold Blood* (1967, cin. Conrad Hall) indicate that black-and-white cinematography played a vital role in dramatic productions well into the decade. In the late 1960s, the production of black-and-white feature films almost completely disappeared, resulting in the elimination of the separate Academy Award for best black-and-white cinematography in 1967.

CHAPTER 1

Epigraph: Joseph Walker and Juanita Walker, *The Light on Her Face* (Hollywood: ASC Press, 1984).

1. David Cook, *A History of Narrative Film,* 4th ed. (New York: Norton, 2004), 51.

2. Charlie Keil, *Early American Cinema in Transition: Story, Style, and Filmmaking, 1907–1913* (Madison: University of Wisconsin Press, 2001), 3. Keil defines the transitional period as that "beginning with a simultaneous turn to narrative and adoption of the single-reel format and concluding with the advent of the feature film." For the purposes of this chapter, I have adopted Keil's dates of 1907 to 1913, both because they seem reasonably accurate for defining the period of transition between primitive and classical filmmaking and because they correspond almost exactly with the time frame of Griffith's collaboration with Bitzer at Biograph.

3. Charles Musser, "Pre-Classical American Cinema: Its Changing Modes of Film Production," in Richard Abel, ed. *Silent Film* (New Brunswick: Rutgers University Press, 1995), 86, 90. Musser proposes a simpler and I believe more accurate pattern for the development of the American film industry than the one proposed by Janet Staiger. For Musser, the fundamental transformation in U.S. film production was from a collaborative system based on partnerships of relative equals to a more hierarchical system that resembled the structure of modern corporations. Over time, this top-down system of production meant that power shifted from the cameraman to the director, and then from the director to the producer, though not in as orderly or as universal a way as Staiger's typology suggests.

4. Musser, "Pre-Classical American Cinema," 87–88.

5. *Film Index* (June 6, 1908), quoted in Musser, "Pre-Classical American Cinema," 88.

6. Unlike Griffith, who had no technical training and was forced to rely on a cameraman to photograph his films, Porter had a strong technical background and was thus able to photograph and edit his films as well as direct them. Porter eventually relinquished the duties of shooting the film to a cameraman, though it was not always easy for him to separate his directorial function from that of operating the camera. "It was a struggle for [Porter] to stay away from the camera," notes Fred Balshofer, since he "found it necessary to be able to perform all the duties that went into making a motion picture, including the developing and printing of the film." Fred Balshofer and Arthur C. Miller, *One Reel a Week* (Berkeley: University of California Press, 1967), 49.

7. Musser, "Pre-Classical American Cinema," 96–97.

8. Billy Bitzer, quoted in Seymour Stern, "11 East 14th Street," *Films in Review* 3.8 (1952): 405.

9. G.W. Bitzer, *Billy Bitzer: His Story* (New York: Farrar, Straus, and Giroux, 1973), 69.

10. The only concrete example that has been passed down of a disagreement between Griffith and Bitzer occurred during the making of *Pippa Passes* (1909). As the story goes, Bitzer stubbornly opposed Griffith's idea for the lighting of the picture, but when the lighting turned out to be highly effective, Bitzer was forced to admit his mistake. However, it is perhaps wiser to take such anecdotal accounts with a grain of salt, especially given the desire of some Griffith partisans, such as Linda Arvidson and Lillian Gish, to boost Griffith's reputation at

Bitzer's expense. Melvyn Stokes, *D.W. Griffith's* The Birth of a Nation*: A History of the Most Controversial Motion Picture of All Time* (New York: Oxford University Press, 2007), 305.

11. Richard Schickel, *D.W. Griffith: An American Life* (New York: Simon and Schuster, 1984), 105–6.

12. In the 1903 Biograph film *A Search for Evidence,* for example, Bitzer is credited as the cameraman, but there is no known director. Bitzer used a keyhole-shaped mask on the camera's lens to make the viewer a participant in a voyeuristic search through a succession of hotel rooms for a philandering husband. In the 1906 Biograph film *The Paymaster,* again photographed by Bitzer and with no known director, there is a scene in a windmill in which sunlight coming through the windows produces a strong chiaroscuro effect. David Robinson, *From Peep Show to Palace: The Birth of American Film* (New York: Columbia University Press, 1996), 124; Barry Salt, *Film Style and Technology: History and Analysis,* 3rd ed. (London: Starwood, 2009), 47.

13. Noel Burch calls the 1905 film *A Kentucky Feud,* photographed by Bitzer, "the high point in primitive cinema" and "one of the authentic masterpieces" of the early silent era. Burch, *Life to Those Shadows,* trans. Ben Brewster (Berkeley and Los Angeles: University of California Press, 1990), 128, 153.

14. "The Qualitative Picture," *Motion Picture World* (25 June 1910), quoted in Keil, *Early American Cinema,* 256.

15. In 1908, Bitzer shot a total of sixty-four films to Marvin's thirty-seven. This rate of production increased dramatically in 1909, when Bitzer shot an extraordinary 139 films—including nearly all of Griffith's—while Marvin is credited with fifty-five. In many cases, Marvin is credited as Bitzer's co-cameraman, though it is difficult to know whether he was working as Bitzer's equal or as a second or assistant cameraman. In 1910, as Griffith's one-reel films began to require a greater number of shots and more complicated camera setups, Bitzer still managed to shoot a remarkable eighty-five films, including nearly all of Griffith's.

16. Schickel, *D.W. Griffith,* 204–5. Although Griffith was prophetic in his prediction that he and Bitzer would collaborate on some of the most important American films ever made, he was less prescient about the possibility of Bitzer becoming wealthy or enjoying a comfortable retirement. Bitzer's career would go into a gradual decline beginning in the early 1920s and would be over by the end of the decade.

17. Karl Brown, interview with Barnet Bravermann (May 18, 1943); quoted in Robert Henderson, *D.W. Griffith: His Life and Work* (New York: Oxford University Press, 1972), 154. Curiously, Brown contradicts himself in the interview, claiming that "Griffith would have succeeded as well with [Sam] Landers, or Tony Gaudio, or Art Martinelli, or Lyman Broening as he did with Bitzer. The cameraman was then and is now a very minor factor in the success or failure of all but a microscopic minority of pictures produced" (quoted in Henderson, *D.W. Griffith,* 228). This comment is so out of keeping with everything else Brown says about Bitzer that I am tempted to dismiss it.

18. Karl Brown, *Adventures with D.W. Griffith* (New York: Farrar, Straus, and Giroux, 1973), 50–51. Arthur Miller also relates an anecdote in which cameraman Fred Balshofer referred to Bitzer as "the best cameraman in the business." Miller, a young assistant cameraman at the time, "couldn't believe that anyone was a better cameraman than Fred Balshofer. But, years, later, when I saw *Birth of a Nation, Way Down East,* and *Broken Blossoms,* I at last realized how great Bitzer was." Balshofer and Miller, *One Reel a Week,* 34.

19. Bitzer, *His Story,* 67. Stokes, *Griffith's* Birth of a Nation, 75.

20. Bitzer, His Story, 84.

21. The close-up had been used in films by other directors, including Edwin S. Porter in *The Great Train Robbery* (1903); the fade-out, or dissolve, had been used by Georges Méliès, among others; "distant views" (long shots) predated Griffith's use of them by several years; Porter had used crosscutting, or parallel editing, before Griffith, and the technique was employed with some frequency in films by Selig and Vitagraph while Griffith was at Biograph.

22. For example, the artificial firelight in Griffith's *The Drunkard's Reformation* (1909), long thought to be the first use of artificial lighting to create the effect of a source light, was preceded by four years in a scene from Edwin S. Porter's *The Seven Ages* (1905).

23. Salt, *Film Style and Technology,* 68.

24. In addition to the many books, dozens of book chapters, and hundreds of articles published on Griffith's life and career, we have Paolo Cherchi Usai's multivolume opus *The Griffith Project,* published by the British Film Institute between 1996 and 2008. The project, which contains commentaries on every film directed or produced by Griffith, is the largest publication ever to be devoted to the career of an individual filmmaker. By comparison, the amount of scholarship on Griffith's contemporaries, especially those active from 1908 to 1915, is extremely limited. Valuable resources on filmmakers other than Griffith from this period include Anthony Slide, *The Big V: A History of the Vitagraph Company* (Metuchen, NJ: Scarecrow Press, 1987); Eileen Bowser, *The Transformation of Cinema, 1907–1915* (New York: Scribner's, 1990); and Keil, *Early American Cinema.*

25. Vitagraph, for example, had between twelve and fourteen cameramen shooting its films in 1908, but we have no record of who they were. Slide, *The Big V,* 17.

26. This is not even to mention the films being made by Griffith's contemporaries in Europe, many of which were more advanced in their use of cinematic technique than Griffith's films. Noel Burch writes that Danish filmmakers were already "adept in the use of chiaroscuro [effects] obtained by means of daylight only" and were "ahead of everything being achieved in the normal run of things at Biograph." Bitzer and the other American cameramen "were a long way behind the Danes, the Italians, and even the French." Burch, *Life to Those Shadows,* 177–79. Charlie Keil points out that the French company Pathé "developed many if not all of the formal innovations American companies eventually adopted in 1910." Keil, *Early American Cinema,* 15.

27. Joyce Jesionowski, for example, points out that "although Griffith has a reputation for innovation . . . his Biograph films are notably conservative in respect to many of the technical capabilities of the camera that were already taken for granted in 1908." Jesionowski, *Thinking in Pictures: Dramatic Structure in D.W. Griffith's Biograph Films* (Berkeley: University of California Press, 1989), 17. The fact that Griffith generally avoided trick shots and special effects was probably related to his background in theatrical performance rather than cinema. Such specifically filmic effects as fade-outs, matte shots, and cut-ins were of limited interest to Griffith, who preferred to use film in ways that were analogous to either the theater or the novel. Even the close-up, which early commentators claimed was one of Griffith's primary innovations, was used relatively infrequently in Griffith's Biograph films compared to those of his contemporaries.

28. Brown, *Adventures with D.W. Griffith*, 25.

29. Bitzer, *His Story*, 7.

30. Charles Musser, *The Emergence of Cinema: The American Screen to 1907*, Vol. 1, *History of the American Cinema* (New York: Scribner's, 1990), 145–48.

31. Bitzer, *His Story*, 63–64.

32. Bitzer, *His Story*, 66.

33. Tom Gunning, "The Country Doctor," in Usai, *Griffith Project*, Vol. 2, *Films Produced in January–June 1909* (London: British Film Institute, 1999), 165–66.

34. In dating the Biograph films, I refer to shooting dates rather than release dates.

35. The cameramen who shot their first films between 1912 and 1916 include many who went on to highly successful careers as Hollywood cinematographers. The most prominent of these were Joseph August, Arthur Edeson, J. Roy Hunt, Arthur Miller, Victor Milner, Hal Mohr, Roy Overbaugh, Ernest Palmer, Charles Rosher, Harold Rosson, Joseph Ruttenberg, John Seitz, Walter Stradling, and Alvin Wyckoff.

36. Charlie Keil, "Transition through Tension: Stylistic Diversity in the Late Griffith Biographs," *Cinema Journal* 28.3 (1989): 24.

37. Keil, "Transition through Tension," 24.

38. Keil, "Transition through Tension," 25–26.

39. Russell Merritt, "*The Musketeers of Pig Alley*," in Usai, *Griffith Project*, Vol. 6, *Films Produced in 1912* (London: British Film Institute, 2002), 162.

40. Keil, "Transition through Tension," 30.

41. Gilbert Seldes, *The Seven Lively Arts* (New York: A.S. Barnes, 1962), 277.

42. Stokes devotes a good deal of his discussion in *Griffith's* Birth of a Nation to issues of race and racism in both Dixon's novel and Griffith's film.

43. Sergei Eisenstein, quoted in Stokes, *Griffith's* Birth of a Nation, 284.

44. Griffith and Frank Woods are credited for writing the scenario, though Griffith later claimed that the scenario was thrown away "at an early stage,"

and the actual shooting script continued to evolve "from day to day." Since there is no surviving script or screenplay, it is impossible to know the exact circumstances under which the film was made.

45. Iris Barry and Eileen Bowser, *D.W. Griffith* (New York: MOMA /Doubleday, 1965), 37.

46. Brown, *Adventures with D.W. Griffith,* 28–29, and Bitzer, "D.W. Griffith," in David W. Griffith Papers, 1897–1934, Manuscript Division, Library of Congress; both cited in Stokes, *Griffith's* Birth of a Nation, 90. Also see Anthony Slide, ed. *Before, In, and After Hollywood: The Autobiography of Joseph Henabery* (Lanham, MD: Scarecrow Press, 1997), 79–80.

47. Stokes, *Griffith's* Birth of a Nation, 94–95.

48. Miriam Cooper, *Dark Lady of the Silents: My Life in Early Hollywood* (Indianapolis: Bobbs-Merrill, 1973), 67.

49. Stokes, *Griffith's* Birth of a Nation, 95. Stokes identifies three scenes that were shot by the light of bonfires, including one of refugees fleeing from a burning Atlanta, and another of the battle of Petersburg at night.

50. More detailed information about the film's cinematography can be found in two articles from the 1960s: George J. Mitchell, "Billy Bitzer: Pioneer and Innovator," *American Cinematographer* (December 1964), and Herb Lightman, "The Film Artistry of D.W. Griffith and Billy Bitzer," *American Cinematographer* (January 1969).

51. Stokes, *Griffith's* Birth of a Nation, 176–77. In order to create a greater sense of realism, genuine Civil War–era muskets were purchased for use in the battle scenes, and prop supervisor Huck Wortman and his crew built highly realistic replicas of gun carriages and cannons. Though built of thin plywood, the weapons were painted with a black paint that contained graphite so that they would appear to be made of polished iron.

52. Bitzer, *His Story,* 108.

53. Brown, *Adventures with D.W. Griffith,* 74–75.

54. Bitzer, *His Story,* 109.

55. Brown, *Adventures with D.W. Griffith,* 18–19. See also the firsthand account in Bitzer, *His Story,* 105.

56. Accurate figures for the number of the film's viewers are not available, but a conservative estimate is that between 3 million and 5 million Americans saw the film between 1915 and 1917. Estimates run as high as 10 million. Given the wide range of these figures, the film's box office receipts are also difficult to estimate with any precision, but a domestic gross of at least $5 million in its initial release seems a reasonable guess. To put this in perspective, no previous American film had grossed more than $500,000.

57. According to Bitzer, at one point his investment in *Birth* was earning him $3,500 a week. Bitzer, *His Story,* 113.

58. Miriam Hansen, *Babel and Babylon: Spectatorship in American Silent Film* (Cambridge: Harvard University Press, 1989), 132. Hansen's discussion of *Intolerance* remains the best critical treatment to date. Despite its promising title, William M. Drew's *D.W. Griffith's* Intolerance*: Its Genesis and Vision*

(Jefferson, NC: McFarland, 1986) provides little information about the actual making of the film and virtually nothing about Bitzer's involvement. More informative are the discussions by Bitzer in *Billy Bitzer: His Story* and Karl Brown in *Adventures with D.W. Griffith.* For well-informed critical treatments of different aspects of the film, see the entries by Russell Merritt, Tom Gunning, and Charlie Keil in Usai, *Griffith Project,* Vol. 9, *Films Produced in 1916–18* (London: British Film Institute, 2004). Many film histories contain discussions of the film; two of the most useful are A.R. Fulton, *Motion Pictures: The Development of an Art from Silent Films to the Age of Television* (Norman: University of Oklahoma Press, 1960); and Lewis Jacobs, *The Rise of the American Film: A Critical History* (New York: Harcourt, Brace, 1939; repr., New York: Teachers College Press, 1967).

59. As Scott Simmon has argued, Griffith's goal was not simply to be the "grandest showman" of the American cinema but to be its "most prominent defender of film's legitimacy as art." Griffith was outraged by a 1915 Supreme Court decision, *Mutual Film Corporation v. Industrial Commission of Ohio,* which held that filmmaking was "a business pure and simple" and thus ineligible for First Amendment free-speech protection. Griffith was determined to prove that, on the contrary, film could rise to the level of great art and thus be deserving of the same protections as literature and the arts. Simmon, *The Films of D.W. Griffith* (New York: Cambridge University Press, 1993), 137.

60. Bitzer suggests that because of wartime restrictions on shipping, it would have been impossible to obtain a herd of elephants for use in the film. Bitzer, *His Story,* 130. Schickel, however, notes that Griffith was able to round up a herd of elephants, "despite a certain confusion when it was discovered that male and female elephants were not amenable to following directions when they were mixed." Schickel, *D.W. Griffith,* 320. At least one live elephant can be clearly seen in some of the Babylon scenes.

61. Schickel, *D.W. Griffith,* 310–11.

62. Griffith's desire to differentiate the visual styles of the four sections is clear in his decision to tint the original prints of the film with different colors: amber for the Modern Story, sepia for the French Story, blue for the Judean Story and gray-green for the Babylonian Story. Exterior scenes were tinted yellow, and battle scenes red. Drew, *Griffith's* Intolerance, 67.

63. Keil, "*Intolerance,*" in Usai, *Griffith Project,* Vol. 9, 58.

64. Fulton, *Motion Pictures,* 110.

65. Jacobs, *Rise of the American Film,* 198.

66. Jacobs, *Rise of the American Film,* 222.

67. Robert Sklar, *Movie-Made America* (New York: Random House, 1974), 61.

68. Bitzer, letter to Seymour Stern, reprinted in Fulton, *Motion Pictures,* 108–9.

69. Joseph Henabery, who served as an assistant director on the film, provides another account of making the unique shot, which required an unusually high degree of technical precision. "It was a tricky scene; nothing like it had

been done before. The forward movement of the camera tower had to be absolutely steady, as did the lowering of the camera platform. The camera had to be panned and tilted precisely during the movement down and forward. The action of the people in the scene had to be correct. We had to coordinate by rehearsals [and] then, to play safe, make several takes." Slide, *Autobiography of Joseph Henabery,* 331. Since a megaphone was not loud enough to be heard by the dancers and extras in the crowd below, Henabery had to get off the tower after each take, make corrections to the crowd action, and then get back on the tower for the next take. Though Karl Brown's account suggests that the shot was done in a single take, Henabery's account of doing several takes of the scene makes more sense given the complexity of the shot. Brown, *Adventures with D.W. Griffith,* 170.

70. Brown, *Adventures with D.W. Griffith,* 169–70. Russell Merritt argues that the famous forward and downward tracking shot of *Intolerance* was "guaranteed to make concentration impossible": "[T]he forward movement does not work to discover or pinpoint any particular detail [and] the effect of the track is not to draw us centripetally toward a central focal point, but rather to propel the set outward, setting elephants, columns, and architectural details in motion." Miriam Hansen notes that shots such as this and other less spectacular but nonetheless stylistically charged shots in *Intolerance* "invite the viewer to marvel at the sights displayed like a visitor to a world's fair or an archaeological site." Such shots, according to Hansen, draw attention to their own virtuosity as much as they "foreground the monumental dimensions of the set." Merritt, "On First Looking into Griffith's Babylon," *Wide Angle* 5.1 (1979); and Hansen, *Babel and Babylon,* 180.

71. Bitzer, "*Intolerance:* The Sun Play of the Ages," *The International Photographer* (October 1934): 24.

72. However, accounts of the film as a financial disaster of monumental proportions are surely exaggerated. Despite a negative cost of approximately half a million dollars (not two million, as has often been reported), the film probably at least broke even, and may have even turned a profit when both domestic and foreign receipts are included.

73. Alexander Woollcott, "Second Thoughts on First Nights," *New York Times* (10 September 1916); reprinted in George C. Pratt, *Spellbound in Darkness: A History of the Silent Film* (Greenwich, CT: New York Graphic Society, 1973), 216.

74. Julian Johnson, "The Shadow Stage," *Photoplay Magazine* 11.1 (December 1916); reprinted in Pratt, *Spellbound in Darkness,* 220.

75. There is no way to view the exact version of the film that would have been seen by its first audiences. When Griffith re-edited both the Modern and Babylonian stories for release as separate films in 1919, he made a number of changes. Lacking either a duplicate negative or inter-negative, Griffith made cuts on the original negative, making it impossible to reproduce a print corresponding to the original version. The film's original length has been estimated at between 13,500 and 13,700 feet, which indicates a running time of about

three and half hours. Though there have been several attempts at a reconstruction of the film, none is definitive, and each differs slightly from the others. The running times of currently available versions range from 176 minutes to 197 minutes. For a discussion of the complicated history of the film, see Russell Merritt, "D.W. Griffith's *Intolerance:* Reconstructing an Unattainable Text," *Film History* 4.4 (1990).

76. A typical assessment of Griffith's later career is that of David Cook in *A History of Narrative Film:* "Griffith continued to make interesting films . . . but most of his postwar features are either disappointingly conventional or hopelessly old-fashioned" (80).

77. In recent years, there has been an effort to resurrect Griffith's neglected films of the 1920s. Tom Gunning, for example, writes of the "pernicious—and difficult to dispel—myth" of Griffith's "long and inevitable decline." According to Gunning, claims for Griffith's decline are overstated, unjustly obscuring the continuing power of Griffith's films of the 1920s. Gunning, "The White Rose," in Usai, *Griffith Project,* Vol. 10, *Films Produced in 1919–46* (British Film Institute, 2006).

78. Bitzer sailed for Europe with actors Robert Harron and Dorothy Gish, intending to shoot location footage in both Britain and France. Apparently, however, Bitzer's Germanic name caused so much suspicion in England that when it was time for Griffith and his cast and crew to cross the channel to shoot footage in France, Bitzer's application for a visa was denied. Griffith hired a French cameraman, Alfred Machin, to take shots of a village that had been destroyed during the German advance on Paris. As it turned out, very little of Machin's footage was included in the final cut of the film. Most of the film was shot by Bitzer in England (in the villages of Sheer and Stanton Broadway and on Salisbury Plain) and in California, and only four or five shots taken by Machin were included. Russell Merritt, "The Making of *Hearts of the World,*" *Quarterly Review of Film Studies* 6.1 (1981): 63. Much of the leftover footage shot in England was used in Griffith's next two films, *The Great Love* and *The Greatest Thing in Life.*

79. Artcraft was a subsidiary of Adolph Zukor's Paramount–Famous Players–Lasky, founded in 1916 as a distributor for Mary Pickford's films. Griffith signed a contract with Zukor to direct six films and to oversee the production of several others.

80. This is not to suggest that other films directed by Griffith during this period are lacking in artistic value. *The Greatest Question,* for example, is notable for the quality of its cinematography, which *Variety* singled out for particular praise. *True Heart Susie,* though generally seen as a minor film in the Griffith canon, is highly regarded by some Griffith scholars, including Tom Gunning, who describes it as "a masterpiece . . . nearly incandescent in its confessional and emotional power." Gunning particularly admires Bitzer's close-ups of Gish in the film, which predate the more famous close-ups of *Broken Blossoms.* Gunning, "True Heart Susie," in Usai, *Griffith Project:* Vol. 10, 19–20.

81. According to Gish, the two head shots that Sartov had taken of her and that were later inserted into *The Greatest Thing in Life* were better than the ones Bitzer had gotten: "When they were shown on the screen at Clune's [Auditorium], the audience murmured 'ah' and then burst into applause." Lillian Gish, *The Movies, Mr. Griffith, and Me* (New York: Prentice Hall, 1969), 207–8.

82. Maury Kains, who worked as an assistant to Sartov, recalled that Sartov never learned hand-cranking, and "always used a motor in his Bell & Howell camera." George Mitchell, "*America:* 1924's Forgotten Classic," *American Cinematographer* (October 1990): 37.

83. Brown, *Adventures with D.W. Griffith,* 206.

84. Bitzer, *His Story,* 210.

85. Julian Johnson, "The Shadow Stage," *Photoplay Magazine* 16.3 (August 1919); reprinted in Pratt, *Spellbound in Darkness,* 251.

86. Balshofer and Miller, *One Reel a Week,* 150. A 1922 article in *American Cinematographer* credits the cinematographer John Leezer as being the first to use a soft-focus lens for motion-picture photography. Whether or not Leezer was the first to use soft-focus technique (in a now forgotten 1916 film entitled *The Marriage of Molly O*), the fact remains that it was *Broken Blossoms* that had the greatest stylistic impact of any film of the period on American cinematographic style. "John Leezer," *American Cinematographer* (February 1922).

87. Kristin Thompson, "Dream Street," in Usai, *Griffith Project,* Vol. 10, 113.

88. Schickel, *D.W. Griffith,* 435.

89. Bitzer, *His Story,* 236.

90. Bitzer, *His Story,* 227.

91. While Karl Brown suggests that alcohol may have played a role in Bitzer's growing problem with Griffith, Joseph Henabery asserts that Bitzer's problem with drink had not yet begun at the time of *The Birth of a Nation* and *Intolerance:* "[Brown] makes us feel that frequently Bitzer went to the 'bottle' for support. Maybe in his later years with D.W., he did drink too much. But when I was working for him, I was often standing close to Bitzer, and I never smelled liquor on him or saw him under the influence." Brown, *Adventures with D.W. Griffith;* Slide, *Autobiography of Joseph Henabery,* 336.

92. Brown, *Adventures with D.W. Griffith,* 207.

93. Gish, *The Movies, Mr. Griffith,* 243. As Gish correctly recalled, Sartov had been the sole cinematographer on *Dream Street,* making it the first Griffith film in over a decade on which Bitzer had not participated.

94. Bitzer, *His Story,* 236.

95. Jan-Christopher Horak, "Southern Landscapes of the Mind's Eye: Griffith's *The White Rose,*" in Marshall Deutelbaum, ed. *Image on the Art and Evolution of the Film: Photographs and Articles from the Magazine of the International Museum of Photography* (New York: Dover, 1979), 157–59. Horak identifies one deep-focus composition in particular in which the character of Bessie (Mae Marsh) is seen huddling in front of a window trying to protect her

baby from the driving rain while Joseph (Ivar Novello) is seen inside confessing his guilt to Marie (Carol Dempster). A toned and tinted 35mm print of the film was allowed to decay in the early 1960s, leaving only a poor-quality dupe negative. The only DVD version currently available is of very poor quality, making it nearly impossible to appreciate the beauty of Bitzer's images.

96. Mitchell, "*America:* 1924's Forgotten Classic," 37.

97. Bitzer is credited as assistant photographer on *Drums of Love* (1927) and as co-cinematographer on *The Battle of the Sexes* and *Lady of the Pavements*—both shot in 1928. Bitzer was not asked to participate in the making of Griffith's final two films: *Abraham Lincoln* (1930) and *The Struggle* (1931).

CHAPTER 2

Epigraphs: Walter Blanchard, "Aces of the Camera XIII: Gregg Toland, A.S.C.," *American Cinematographer* (January 1942); Gregg Toland, "The Motion Picture Cameraman," *International Photographer* (February 1941).

1. David Bordwell, Janet Staiger, and Kristin Thompson, *The Classical Hollywood Cinema: Film Style and Mode of Production to 1960* (New York: Columbia University Press, 1985), 347.

2. Wyler would have worked with Toland on more films if he had been allowed to do so. When Wyler directed *The Letter* (1940), for example, he asked Goldwyn to loan out Toland to Warner Brothers, where the film was being made. When his request was turned down, he shot the film with Warner Brothers staff cinematographer Tony Gaudio.

3. Andrew Sarris, *The Primal Screen: Essays on Film and Related Subjects* (New York: Simon and Schuster, 1973), 36.

4. The documentary film *Visions of Light* devotes an entire chapter to Toland's career and influence on later cinematographers. Arnold Glassman, Todd McCarthy, and Stuart Samuels, dirs., *Visions of Light* (American Film Institute and NHK, 1992). When a panel of cinematographers was asked in 2006 to name the greatest directors of photography in the history of American film, every member of the panel named Toland first.

5. Indeed, from a purely statistical perspective, Miller's career was more successful than Toland's. Miller photographed a total of 140 feature films compared with Toland's sixty, and he received seven Academy Award nominations, winning three times, compared with Toland's six nominations and one win. From 1940 to 1947, Miller was the most highly regarded DP in the industry, receiving Academy Award nominations in every year but one. It should be remembered, however, that during much of this time Toland was away on military duty and thus not in competition with him.

6. Toland died on September 28, 1948, from a blood clot in his heart.

7. Toland's regular crew included camera operator Bert Shipman, assistant cameraman Eddie Garvin, grip Ralph Hoge, and gaffer Bill McClellan.

8. Patrick Ogle, "Technological and Aesthetic Influences on the Development of Deep-Focus Cinematography in the United States," in Bill Nichols, ed., *Movies and Methods,* Vol. 2 (Berkeley and Los Angeles: University of California Press, 1985), 68.

9. Roger Wallace, "Gregg Toland—His Contributions to Cinema" (PhD dissertation, University of Michigan, 1976), 40–55.

10. Wallace, "Gregg Toland," 13–14.

11. Sarah Kozloff, *The Best Years of Our Lives* (London: BFI/Palgrave Macmillan, 2011), 66.

12. Leonard Maltin, *The Art of the Cinematographer,* rev. ed. (Mineola, NY: Dover, 2012), 34.

13. I would agree with Barry Salt that Toland's films of the period are marked by "a noticeable simplicity of lighting when compared with the usual lighting setups in similar scenes by other cameramen," generally using fewer lighting units and creating "a slightly unusual disposition of shadows." Salt, *Film Style and Technology: History and Analysis,* 3rd ed. (London: Starwood, 2009), 258. The cinematography of *The Wedding Night* anticipates the subtlety of lighting Toland would later achieve in films of the late 1930s and early 1940s such as *Wuthering Heights, The Long Voyage Home,* and *Citizen Kane.* As the film's mood becomes darker—moving toward its tragic ending—there is a shift toward lower-keyed, more dramatic lighting and a greater use of shadows.

14. For useful summaries of the changes in the technology of cameras and lighting during the transition to sound, see Donald Crafton, *The Talkies: American Cinema's Transition to Sound, 1926–1931* (Berkeley: University of California Press, 1999); and Patrick Keating, *Hollywood Lighting: From the Silent Era to Film Noir* (New York: Columbia University Press, 2010).

15. Keating, *Hollywood Lighting,* 109.

16. Joseph Walker and Juanita Walker, *The Light on Her Face* (Hollywood: ASC Press, 1984), 171.

17. Bert Glennon, "Cinematography and the Talkies," *American Cinematographer* (February 1930): 7.

18. Gregg Toland, "Realism in *Citizen Kane,*" *American Cinematographer* 22.2 (1941); reprinted in *American Cinematographer* 72.2 (1991).

19. It is important to keep in mind the precise meanings of the terms "depth of field," "staging in depth," and "deep focus." Depth of field, which refers to the range in which objects in front of the lens are in acceptable focus, can be calculated mathematically based on the focal length of the lens being used. Staging in depth refers to the placement of actors or objects within the shot: in other words, it is part of the mise-en-scène. Staging in depth can take place with or without deep-focus photography. "Deep focus," or what Toland preferred to call "pan focus," requires keeping all the characters and objects in the frame in clear focus at the same time, regardless of how far they are from the camera.

20. Anonymous review of *Captain Kate* from *Moving Picture World* (29 July 1911), quoted in Keil, *Early American Cinema,* 155.

21. Salt, *Film Style and Technology,* 222–23.

22. James Wong Howe, quoted in Walter Blanchard, "Aces of the Camera VII: James Wong Howe," *American Cinematographer* (July 1941): 346.

23. Victor Milner, quoted in Keating, *Hollywood Lighting,* 231.

24. David Bordwell, *On the History of Film Style* (Cambridge: Harvard University Press, 1997), 223.

25. In order to accomplish the shot, Howe used essentially the same technique Toland adopted in *Citizen Kane.* He shot with a 25mm lens stopped down to f/8, and he used much more light than normal. Alain Silver, ed., *James Wong Howe, The Camera Eye: A Career Interview* (Santa Monica, CA: Pendragon, 2010), 155–56.

26. Robert Carringer only slightly exaggerates in stating that, "with Toland, Wyler, and Ford off to do military service and with Welles washed up after his South American fiasco, the evolution of deep-focus cinematography came to a virtual halt until after the war, when a shift toward realism brought it into the Hollywood mainstream." Carringer, *The Making of* Citizen Kane (Berkeley and Los Angeles: University of California Press, 1995), 85. See also my discussion in chapter 3 of the emergence of deep-focus cinematography in the film noir cycle of the late 1940s.

27. Hal Mohr, "A Lens Mount for Universal Focus Effects," *American Cinematographer* (September 1936): 370–71.

28. According to Barry Salt, the swinging lens mount was "a pointlessly elaborate technique" for achieving results that were not consistently successful, since people or objects in the middle of the frame might still remain out of focus even if the foreground and background were kept in perfect focus. Salt, *Film Style and Technology,* 230.

29. John Howard Lawson, *Film: The Creative Process* (New York: Hill and Wang, 1964), 138.

30. Stanley Cortez, quoted in Wallace, "Gregg Toland," 194.

31. Gregg Toland, "How I Broke the Rules in *Citizen Kane,*" *Popular Photography Magazine* 8 (June 1941): 55; reprinted in Ronald Gottesman, ed., *Focus on* Citizen Kane (Englewood Cliffs, NJ: Prentice-Hall, 1971), 73–77. Toland also discusses his approach to cinematography in two other articles: "Realism for *Citizen Kane,*" *American Cinematographer* (February 1941): 54–55, 80; and "Using Arcs for Lighting Monochrome," *American Cinematographer* (December 1941): 559–60, 588.

32. Carringer, *Making of* Citizen Kane, 83. Throughout his book, Carringer displays a certain distrust of Toland. Although he acknowledges the importance of Toland's contribution to a number of technical innovations that impacted the style of the film, he also accuses him of being "a shameless exhibitionist in the films on which he worked, never missing an opportunity for a flamboyant display of whatever new and sensational visual effect he had come up with" (67). This characterization of Toland seems unfair: while Toland was clearly driven, as Carringer suggests, "by a compulsion to expand the accepted technical boundaries of the medium," there is little evidence of exhibitionism for its own

sake. Rather, Toland was a devoted director of photography who was eager to work with directors who would allow him the freedom to expand the possibilities of the medium as far as the technology of the time would permit.

33. Bordwell, *History of Film Style*, 224.

34. Hilton Als, "The Cameraman," *New Yorker* (June 19, 2006): 48.

35. The f-stop number is calculated in inverse proportion to the size of the aperture, and represents the ratio of pupil diameter to the length of the lens. Thus, if using a 50mm lens at f/4, the pupil diameter would be 12.5mm; if using a 24mm lens at f/8, the diameter would be only 3mm, allowing greater depth of field under similar lighting conditions.

36. Since this intensity of light could not be achieved using the incandescent lighting of the period, Toland used arc lights that were generally reserved for Technicolor filming. Toland, "Using Arcs for Lighting Monochrome."

37. Jan Herman, *A Talent for Trouble: The Life of Hollywood's Most Acclaimed Director, William Wyler* (New York: G.P. Putnam's Sons, 1995), 143.

38. Michael Anderegg, *William Wyler* (Boston: Twayne, 1979), 48.

39. William Wyler, quoted in Ronald L. Davis, "Southern Methodist University Oral History Project: William Wyler" (1979), in Gabriel Miller, ed., *William Wyler Interviews* (Oxford: University Press of Mississippi, 2010), 88.

40. William Wyler, quoted in Gene Phillips, "William Wyler," *Focus on Film* 24 (1976): 7. In fact, the set was a larger and more complex version of the one that had been used for the stage play. This appears to be an example of Goldwyn's misunderstanding of the difference between theater and film, something that Wyler grasped immediately. The intricately constructed set that is highly effective in a stage production can look completely unreal on film.

41. William Wyler, interview with Curtis Hanson (1967), "William Wyler: An Interview," in *Wyler Interviews*, 28.

42. See also Mike Cormack's discussion of the film's cinematography. According to him, the most radical stylistic element in *Dead End* is its use of extreme camera angles, especially low angle shots that emphasize the way in which "the buildings loom over the characters," making the urban environment appear more threatening. Cormack, *Ideology and Cinematography in Hollywood, 1930–39* (New York: St. Martin's, 1994), 135.

43. Douglas Slocombe, "The Work of Gregg Toland," *Sequence* 8 (1950): 71.

44. Patrick McGee, *From* Shane *to* Kill Bill: *Rethinking the Western* (London: Blackwell, 2007), 52.

45. A version of this same shot can be seen as early as *These Three:* in a scene in which Joel McCrae and Merle Oberon are drinking milkshakes in a café, McCrae pushes his glass down the bar toward the camera, as if to create an opportunity for Toland to show off the shot's depth of focus.

46. The titles of several articles on or by Toland referred to "breaking the rules" of Hollywood cinematography. See, for example, "Welles Gets Cameraman to Break Rules," *New York Herald Tribune* (April 27, 1941); and

Toland's own piece, "How I Broke the Rules in *Citizen Kane*," *Popular Photography Magazine* (June 1941).

47. Keating, *Hollywood Lighting*, 237.

48. Walter Blanchard, "Aces of the Camera XIII: Gregg Toland, A.S.C.," *American Cinematographer* (January 1942): 15.

49. André Bazin, "William Wyler, or the Jansenism of Directing," in Bert Cardullo, ed., *Bazin at Work: Major Essays and Reviews from the Forties and Fifties* (New York and London: Routledge, 1997), 16.

50. Slocombe, "Work of Gregg Toland," 74.

51. Gregg Toland, "The Motion Picture Cameraman," *Theatre Arts* 25.9 (September 1941): 648–49.

52. Wyler, quoted in Davis, "SMU Oral History Project: William Wyler."

53. William Wyler, quoted in Axel Madsen, *William Wyler: The Authorized Biography* (New York: Thomas Crowell, 1973), 206.

54. Howard Hawks, quoted in Wallace, "Gregg Toland," 190.

55. Anderegg, *William Wyler*, 107.

56. Undated letter from Gregg Toland to Samuel Goldwyn, in Samuel Goldwyn Papers, Special Collections, Margaret Herrick Library, Academy of Motion Pictures Arts and Sciences.

57. William Wyler, "No Magic Wand" (1947); reprinted in Richard Koszarski, ed., *Hollywood Directors, 1941–1976* (New York: Oxford University Press, 1977), 112.

58. Kozloff, *Best Years*, 46.

59. According to Ralph Hoge, "99 and 9/10th percent" of *The Best Years of Our Lives* was shot with a 40mm lens. Quoted in Wallace, "Gregg Toland," 175.

60. Gregg Toland, quoted in Lester Koenig, "Gregg Toland, Film-Maker," *Screen Writer* 3.7 (1947): 29.

61. Kozloff, *Best Years*, 68. Barry Salt notes that for certain scenes of the film, Toland used an aperture of f/22, even smaller than the minimum aperture he had used in *Citizen Kane*, and shot with extremely high light levels. This allowed him to get significant depth of field even with a 40mm lens. Salt, *Film Style and Technology*, 259.

62. Bazin, "William Wyler," 14–15.

63. Bordwell, *History of Film Style*, 227.

64. Wallace, "Gregg Toland," 168.

65. The film won Oscars for best screenplay, picture, director, actor (Fredric March), supporting actor (Harold Russell), editing, and score.

66. Also strange is the fact that only two films were nominated: it was the only year in the history of the Academy Awards in which so few films were nominated in the category of black-and-white cinematography. Since the decision to nominate so few films cannot be justified by a shortage of well-photographed black-and-white movies, it is plausible to suggest that the low number of films nominated was an attempt to shut Toland out of contention. The winner of the award was Arthur Miller, for *Anna and the King of Siam*.

67. Blanchard, "Aces XIII: Gregg Toland," 15.

CHAPTER 3

1. Janey Place and Lowell Peterson, "Some Visual Motifs," *Film Comment* 10.1 (1974); reprinted in Alain Silver and James Ursini, eds., *Film Noir Reader* (New York: Limelight, 1996), 65.

2. For a dissenting view, see Marc Vernet, "Film Noir on the Edge of Doom," in Joan Copjec, ed., *Shades of Noir* (London: Verso, 1993). Vernet argues that the techniques of "expressionist" lighting used in American film noirs were not new to the cinema of the 1940s, having existed since "at least 1915" both in the United States and Russia. Although techniques used in film noirs were invented much earlier—Barry Salt, for example, has identified the use of low-key lighting as early as 1912—that fact does not in itself contradict the central importance of such techniques to the noir aesthetic or the distinctiveness of that aesthetic within the context of 1950s Hollywood filmmaking.

3. Lea Jacobs, "The B Film and the Problem of Cultural Distinction," *Screen* 33.1 (1992): 3. In my own informal survey of film noir budgets, I find that while many film noirs do fall into this "intermediate" category, there are also a number of film noirs with budgets that are either significantly above or below this range. Films like *The Lady from Shanghai* ($2 million) and *Caught* ($1.5 million), for example, were relatively large-budget A-movie productions, while a film like *Detour* ($30,000) is an extremely low-budget film noir.

4. Shannon Scott Clute and Richard Edwards, *The Maltese Touch of Evil: Film Noir and Potential Criticism* (Hanover, NH: Dartmouth College Press, 2011), 133.

5. Vernet, "Film Noir on the Edge of Doom," 13. This observation is not true of all black-and-white films made during the 1950s, many of which were made in black and white for budgetary rather than aesthetic reasons. However, it does seem plausible that "prestige" black-and-white productions such as those of Alfred Hitchcock, Billy Wilder, Otto Preminger, and Fritz Lang use black and white for primarily stylistic reasons.

6. Robert Sklar, *Movie-Made America: A Cultural History of American Movies* (London: Chappell, 1978); Sheri Chinen Biesen, *Blackout: World War II and the Origins of Film Noir* (Baltimore: The Johns Hopkins University Press, 2005).

7. Patrick Ogle, "Technological and Aesthetic Influences on the Development of Deep-Focus Cinematography in the United States," in Bill Nichols, ed., *Movies and Methods*, Vol. 2 (Berkeley and Los Angeles: University of California Press, 1985); Paul Kerr, "Out of What Past?: Notes on the B Film Noir," in Silver and Ursini, *Film Noir Reader*, 123.

8. Three-point lighting was the default lighting system for cinematographers of the studio era. Patrick Keating summarizes the purpose of the technique as "direct[ing] our attention to the actor's face (which aids storytelling), while also creating an illusion of roundness (which is a kind of realism), and ensuring a pleasing balance of light and dark (which creates a level of pictorial quality)." By the mid-1920s, all Hollywood cinematographers were using

three-point lighting, establishing the technique as a normative feature of studio filmmaking and leading to a greater uniformity of style. Keating, *Hollywood Lighting,* 6, 53.

9. John Bailey, "Film Noir's Sorcerer of Light: John Alton," in John Alton, *Painting with Light* (Berkeley and Los Angeles: University of California Press, 2013), ix.

10. Todd McCarthy, "Introduction: Through a Lens Darkly: The Life and Films of John Alton," in Alton, *Painting with Light,* xxix.

11. During this period, nearly all nominations and awards for best cinematography went to films made by the major studios. Cinematographers at smaller studios such as Columbia and Republic received far fewer nominations than those who worked for the larger studios, and it was virtually impossible for them to win the Oscar. Even within the ranks of the majors, there was a hierarchy: between 1935 and 1950, about two-thirds of the Academy Awards for best black-and-white and color cinematography went to two studios—MGM and Twentieth Century-Fox.

12. By my count, excluding films made for television, Seitz shot a total of 158 feature films. A partial list of the directors with whom he worked includes (in roughly chronological order) Henry King, Rex Ingram, Frank Lloyd, King Vidor, Gregory La Cava, William Beaudine, James Cruze, William Dieterle, Billy Wilder, Preston Sturges, Allan Dwan, Josef von Sternberg, Sam Wood, Clarence Brown, Robert Siodmak, John Farrow, Frank Tuttle, Robert Parrish, Gordon Douglas, Michael Curtiz, and Delmer Daves.

13. Seitz shot six films that are currently on the registry: *The Four Horsemen of the Apocalypse, Sullivan's Travels, The Miracle of Morgan's Creek, Double Indemnity, The Lost Weekend,* and *Sunset Boulevard.* He is closely followed by Chaplin's cinematographer Roland Totheroh, with five films, and Gordon Willis, also with five.

14. James Ursini interviewed Seitz for an extensive oral history in 1975. Excerpts from Ursini, "AFI Oral Interview with John Seitz" are reprinted in Robert Porfirio, Alain Silver, and James Ursini eds., *Film Noir Reader 3: Interviews with Filmmakers of the Classic Period* (New York: Limelight Editions, 2004), 205–12. The full interview can be found in the collection of the American Film Institute in Los Angeles.

15. In *Film Noir Reader 3*, Porforio, Silver, and Ursini list twelve films photographed by Seitz "in the noir style" (213–14).

16. John Seitz, quoted in Liam O'Leary, *Rex Ingram: Master of the Silent Cinema* (Dublin: Academy Press, 1980), 65.

17. Barry Salt, *Film Style and Technology: History and Analysis,* 3rd ed. (London: Starwood, 2009), 210–11. For *The Magician* (1926), Seitz used a slight variant of this approach, with strong bottom lighting and limited top lighting, giving a grotesque appearance to the villain played by Paul Wegener.

18. For *Rogue Cop,* which he shot with director Roy Rowland at MGM, Seitz received an Academy Award nomination for black-and-white cinematography, the sixth of his career. Alain Silver has noted the way in which Rowland

and Seitz use both lighting and mise-en-scène to emphasize the contrast between the crooked ("rogue") cop Christopher Kelvaney (Robert Taylor) and his honest brother, Eddie (Steve Forrest). "Rogue Cop," in Silver, Elizabeth Ward, James Ursini, and Robert Porfirio, eds., *Film Noir: The Encyclopedia,* 4th ed. (New York: Overlook Duckworth, 2010), 253.

19. John L. Seitz (son of John Seitz), interview with the author, July 26, 2013.

20. Dale M. Pollock, "An Unconventional War Film: Death, Disguise, and Deception in *Five Graves to Cairo,*" in Karen McNally, ed., *Billy Wilder, Movie-Maker: Critical Essays on the Films* (Jefferson, NC: McFarland, 2011), 26.

21. Pollock, "Unconventional War Film," 27.

22. Coleman served as assistant director on eleven of Wilder's films; Harrison was editor on seven of his films and supervising editor on several more; Dreier was production designer on six of his films; Rosza composed the scores for *Five Graves to Cairo, Double Indemnity,* and *The Lost Weekend;* and Head designed the costumes for nearly every film Wilder directed between 1942 and 1954.

23. Ed Sikov, *On Sunset Boulevard: The Life and Times of Billy Wilder* (New York: Hyperion, 1998), 192.

24. Pollock, "Unconventional War Film," 37. For one scene, Seitz lashed a camera to the turret of a tank, and used it to follow another tank as it rolled across the desert sand.

25. Cameron Crowe, *Conversations with Wilder* (New York: Knopf, 1999), 96.

26. Hellmuth Karasek, *Billy Wilder: Eine Nahaufnahme* (Tübingen: Hoffmann and Campe, 2006), 250 (my translation).

27. Byron Haskin, quoted in Joe Adamson, "John F. Seitz," *Internet Encyclopedia of Cinematographers,* www.cinematographers.nl/GreatDoPh/seitz.htm.

28. Ursini, "AFI Oral History with John Seitz," American Film Institute, Los Angeles.

29. Sikov, *On Sunset Boulevard,* 187.

30. In the original version of the film, Neff is convicted of murder and executed. Though the scene of Neff's execution was cut before the release of the film, existing stills of the scene suggest that it would have been a visually stunning ending to the film.

31. Biesen, *Blackout,* 109.

32. Billy Wilder, interview with Gene D. Phillips, "Billy Wilder," in Robert Horton, ed., *Billy Wilder Interviews* (Jackson: University of Mississippi Press, 2001), 103.

33. Phillips, "Billy Wilder," 103.

34. Crowe, *Conversations with Wilder,* 53.

35. Sikov, *On Sunset Boulevard,* 206.

36. Billy Wilder, interview with John Allyn, "*Double Indemnity:* A Policy That Paid Off," in Horton, *Billy Wilder Interviews,* 137. For another account of

this technique, see Ella Smith, *Starring Miss Barbara Stanwyck* (New York: Crown, 1973), 177.

37. Keating, *Hollywood Lighting,* 251.

38. Biesen, *Blackout,* 107.

39. Thomas Leitch, *Crime Films* (Cambridge and New York: Cambridge University Press, 2002), 136.

40. Sheri Chinen Biesen, "Billy Wilder," in Alain Silver and James Ursini, eds., *Film Noir: The Directors* (Montclair, NJ: Limelight Editions, 2012), 451.

41. Sikov, *On Sunset Boulevard,* 218–19.

42. Sikov, *On Sunset Boulevard,* 225.

43. According to his son (John L. Seitz, interview with author), Seitz was extremely disappointed at not winning the Oscar for *The Lost Weekend,* since he had felt he was a "shoo-in" to receive the award: "In those days only the cinematographers voted, and all the cameramen at MGM voted en masse for their candidate [Harry Stradling for *The Picture of Dorian Gray*]."

44. Gerd Gemunden, *Foreign Affair: Billy Wilder's American Films* (New York and Oxford: Berghahn Books, 2008), 96.

45. See the discussion of the film's cinematography in Herb Lightman, "Old Master, New Tricks: A Combination That Spelled Success for Photography in *Sunset Boulevard," American Cinematographer* (September 1950), 309, 318–20.

46. The process, introduced by Paramount and DuPont in 1947, was originally seen as a way of reducing lighting costs. Within a few years, the process had spread throughout the industry and become an aesthetic tool for cinematographers wishing to shoot in underexposed conditions. Lisa Dombrowski, "Postwar Hollywood, 1947–1967," in Patrick Keating, ed., *Cinematography* (New Brunswick, NJ: Rutgers University Press, 2014), 66.

47. Despite their very different visual styles, however, both *Double Indemnity* and *Sunset Boulevard* have average shot lengths (ASL) that far exceed those of typical Hollywood films of the period: *Double Indemnity* has an ASL of 17.6 seconds and *Sunset Boulevard* 17.2 seconds. According to Barry Salt, the median ASL for films of the 1940s was nine seconds, though this average increased gradually throughout the decade, with a few films of the late 1940s having ASLs of up to twenty seconds. Wilder's films generally have ASLs that are considerably longer than the norm for Hollywood films, reflecting the director's interest in presenting psychologically complex characters and well-crafted dialogue. In the case of *Sunset Boulevard,* the length of takes is also increased by the amount of camera movement. Salt, *Film Style and Technology,* 266.

48. Sam Staggs, *Close-Up on Sunset Boulevard: Billy Wilder, Norma Desmond, and the Dark Hollywood Dream* (New York: St. Martin's, 2003), 119.

CHAPTER 4

Epigraph: Robert Burks, quoted in Frederick Foster, "Hitch Didn't Want It Arty," *American Cinematographer* (February 1957).

1. For a discussion of Hitchcock's "thoughtful and complex engagement with the aesthetics of color," see Richard Allen, "Hitchcock's Color Designs," in Angela Dalle Vacche and Brian Price, eds., *Color: The Film Reader* (Oxford and New York: Routledge, 2006), 131–32.

2. Donald Spoto, *Spellbound by Beauty: Alfred Hitchcock and His Leading Ladies* (New York: Crown, 2008), 193.

3. The number of different DPs for Hitchcock's American films of the 1940s was at least in part the result of his lack of a regular home studio during these years. Hitchcock made films with four major studios (RKO, Universal, Twentieth Century-Fox, and Warner Bros.) as well as independent producers David Selznick and Walter Wanger.

4. Stephen Rebello, *Alfred Hitchcock and the Making of* Psycho (New York: Dembner Books, 1990), 82.

5. In addition to his dozen films with Hitchcock, Burks was the director of photography on twenty-eight feature films by other directors, most of whom were far less distinguished than Hitchcock. Of Burks's total of forty films as cinematographer, twenty-two are black-and-white films and eighteen are color productions, a relatively typical balance given the years of his career (1944–1967). Among his non-Hitchcock films, the ones that display Burks's cinematography to its greatest advantage are *The Fountainhead* (King Vidor, 1949), *The Spirit of St. Louis* (Billy Wilder, 1957), *The Black Orchid* (Martin Ritt, 1958), and *A Patch of Blue* (Guy Green, 1965). *A Patch of Blue* also received a nomination for best black-and-white cinematography, the only nomination Burks received on a non-Hitchcock film.

6. John Michael Hayes, quoted in Spoto, *Spellbound by Beauty*, 199.

7. Herb Lightman, "Robert Burks, A.S.C., Photographs *The Fountainhead*," *American Cinematographer* (June 1949): 201.

8. In *Blackmail* (1929), for example, Hitchcock used a procedure known as the Shufftan Process to create several shots in the British Museum, which did not have adequate lighting for conventional shooting.

9. Donald Spoto, *The Dark Side of Genius: The Life of Alfred Hitchcock* (New York: Little, Brown, 1983), 326.

10. Warner Bros. veteran special-effects man Hans Koenekamp, who is credited as "special effects director" on the film, also worked with Hitchcock and Burks on the shot.

11. Alfred Hitchcock, quoted in Peter Bogdanovich, *The Cinema of Alfred Hitchcock* (New York: Museum of Modern Art, 1963), 30.

12. Robert Burks, quoted in Hilda Black, "The Photography Is Important to Hitchcock," *American Cinematographer* (December 1952).

13. Frederick Foster, "Hitch Didn't Want it Arty," *American Cinematographer* (February 1957), 85, 113–14.

14. Hitchcock appears on screen at the opening of the film to announce that "this is a true story—every word of it is true."

15. Laurent Bouzereau, dir., *Guilt Trip: Hitchcock and* The Wrong Man (Burbank, CA: Warner Bros., 2004), 20 min. DVD.

16. Paula Marantz Cohen, "Hitchcock's Revised American Vision: *The Wrong Man* and *Vertigo*," in Jonathan Freeman and Richard Millington, eds., *On Hitchcock's America* (Oxford and New York: Oxford University Press, 1999), 156.

17. The members of the future French New Wave were particularly impressed by the film's visual style. Eric Rohmer called it Hitchcock's "most beautiful film" and both Francois Truffaut and Jean-Luc Godard praised it as one of Hitchcock's masterpieces. James W. West, *Hitchcock and France: The Forging of an Auteur* (Westport, CT: Praeger, 2003), 158–60.

18. Bouzereau, *Guilt Trip*.

19. Hitchcock's two previous color films were *Rope* (1948), photographed by Joseph Valentine, and *Under Capricorn* (1949), photographed by British cinematographer Jack Cardiff.

20. Charlotte Chandler, *It's Only a Movie: Alfred Hitchcock, A Personal Biography* (New York: Simon and Schuster, 2005).

21. Grace Kelly, quoted in Spoto, *Spellbound*, 204.

22. Since I have not had the opportunity to view the film in 3-D, I cannot judge the effectiveness of Hitchcock's use of the technology.

23. Steven Jacobs, *The Wrong House: The Architecture of Alfred Hitchcock* (Rotterdam: 010 Publishers, 2007).

24. Scott Curtis, "The Making of *Rear Window*," in John Belton, ed., *Alfred Hitchcock's Rear Window* (Cambridge and New York: Cambridge University Press, 2000), 21.

25. This figure does not include a salary for James Stewart, who worked for a percentage of the gross rather than a salary. Curtis, "Making of *Rear Window*," 47, n.1.

26. For detailed accounts of the cinematography of *Rear Window*, see Arthur E. Gavin, "Rear Window," *American Cinematographer* (February 1954); and David Atkinson, "Hitchcock's Techniques Tell *Rear Window* Story," *American Cinematographer* (January 1990), 34–39.

27. James Stewart quoted in Jonathan Coe, *Jimmy Stewart: A Wonderful Life* (New York: Arcade Publishing, 1994), 140–42.

28. Atkinson, "Hitchcock's Techniques," 37.

29. By way of comparison, the average lighting on interior sets of Hollywood color productions in the mid-1950s was from 350 to 600 foot-candles.

30. Curtis, "Making of *Rear Window*," 54–55.

31. VistaVision is considered a wide-screen format because it was usually displayed with an aspect ratio of 1.85:1, considerably wider than the 1.37:1 "Academy format," though significantly less than other 1950s wide-screen formats such as Cinerama and CinemaScope.

32. Barry Salt notes that it is theoretically possible to maintain depth of focus with VistaVision, but it would require using a 21mm lens. This approach was rarely used by Hollywood filmmakers. Salt, *Film Style and Technology: History and Analysis*, 3rd ed. (London: Starwood, 2009), 276.

33. Patrick McGilligan, *Alfred Hitchcock: A Life in Darkness and Light* (New York: HarperCollins, 2003), 506.

34. McGilligan, *Alfred Hitchcock,* 495–96.

35. Dan Auiler, *Vertigo: The Making of a Classic* (New York: St. Martin's, 1998), 63.

36. Auiler, 99–101. According to Auiler, another complicated crane shot had been planned for the moment in the same scene when Scottie answers the phone and Madeleine is woken up. After getting the shot in nine laborious takes, Hitchcock decided to discard it in favor of a simpler version.

37. According to standard Hollywood procedure, the supervisor of the studio art department, Hal Pereira, was also credited as art director on the film. However, his credit was nominal, as he did not work with Hitchcock on the film's art direction.

38. According to Herbert Coleman, Roberts worked as a second-unit cameraman on all Hitchcock's pictures at Paramount. Ironically, however, he was not given screen credit for his work on *Vertigo.* Hitchcock, in his characteristic desire to take credit for every aspect of his films, claimed that the vertigo effect was one he had been working toward ever since making *Rebecca* nearly two decades earlier. Auiler, Vertigo: *Making of a Classic,* 66.

39. Auiler, Vertigo: *Making of a Classic,* 117.

40. For a detailed account of the production of *The Birds,* see Kyle B. Counts, "The Making of Alfred Hitchcock's *The Birds,*" *Cinefantastique* 10.2 (1980): 15–35.

41. Camille Paglia, *The Birds* (London: British Film Institute, 2008), 15–16.

42. Tony Lee Moral, *The Making of Hitchcock's* The Birds (Harpenden, UK: Karnera Books, 2013), 175–76.

43. Moral, *Hitchcock's* The Birds, 178–79.

44. Hitchcock letter to Bogdanovich, February 14, 1963; cited in Moral, 203.

45. Moral, *Hitchcock's* The Birds, 179.

46. James Morrison notes the film's "feverish color contrasts, its nauseous yellows and bile-greens set against burnished or full-hued auburns and blues." Morrison, "Robert Burks," *Internet Encyclopedia of Cinematographers,* http: cinematographers.nl.

47. According to Robert Boyle, red was meant to suggest disaster and death, while yellow was intended to symbolize the affirmation of life. However, this is an oversimplification of the way in which color actually functions in the film. Yellow appears to be associated not only with hope and affirmation but also with the possibility of social and physical threat. In the opening shot of the film, Marnie is seen from behind, clutching a yellow purse under one arm as she walks away from the camera down the platform of a railway station. The yellow purse contains the money that she has just stolen from Mr. Strutt—and is thus a sign of her criminal character—but it is also the container of money that will allow her to support her mother and to buy her own freedom from dependence on men. When Marnie first arrives in Philadelphia, where she will secure a new job at the Rutland Company, there are two bright yellow taxis (hopefully or ominously) parked outside the train station. Later, Mark Rutland is wearing a yellow bathrobe when he rapes Marnie during their honeymoon.

Tony Lee Moral, *Hitchcock and the Making of* Marnie (Lanham, MD: Scarecrow Press, 2005), 65.

48. Laurent Bouzereau, dir. "The Trouble with *Marnie*" (Universal City, CA: Universal, 2006), 60 min. DVD.

49. Robert Boyle, quoted in Moral, *The Making of* Marnie, 99.

50. Jane Sloan, *Alfred Hitchcock: A Filmography and Bibliography* (Berkeley and Los Angeles: University of California Press, 1993), 10.

51. Herrmann did compose a score for *Torn Curtain,* but Universal Studios pressured Hitchcock to use a more commercial soundtrack. When Herrmann refused to rewrite the music, he was replaced by John Addison.

52. Herbert Coleman, *The Hollywood I Knew: A Memoir, 1916–1988* (Lanham, MD: Scarecrow Press, 2003), 362.

53. Herb Lightman, "Hitchcock Talks about Lights, Camera, Action," *American Cinematographer* (May 1967).

54. Peggy Robertson, production memo, 1965, Alfred Hitchcock Collection, Special Collections, Margaret Herrick Library of the Academy of Motion Picture Arts and Sciences.

55. John Micheal Hayes, quoted in Spoto, *Spellbound,* 199.

56. By the time Hitchcock began photography on his next film, *Topaz,* Burks had died in a fire at his Newport Beach home. Burks and his wife both died of asphyxiation from the fire on May 12, 1968.

CHAPTER 5

Epigraph: Gordon Willis, quoted in Dennis Schaefer and Larry Salvato, eds., *Masters of Light: Conversations with Contemporary Cinematographers* (Berkeley: University of California Press, 1984), 288.

1. The retirements of Hollywood cinematographers during the period included those of Ernest Haller in 1965; Robert Krasker, Ted McCord, and Eugen Shuftan in 1966; Lee Garmes and Floyd Crosby in 1967; Joseph Ruttenberg in 1968; Leon Shamroy and Joseph LaShelle in 1969; Milton Krasner in 1970; Burnett Guffey in 1971; George Folsey, Winton Hoch, and Russell Metty in 1972; William Clothier and Charles Lang in 1973; and James Wong Howe in 1975. Deaths of prominent cinematographers included those of William Mellor in 1963; Leo Tover in 1964; Joseph MacDonald and Robert Burks in 1968; and William Daniels in 1970.

2. There were a few examples of older cinematographers who worked with younger directors to achieve an unconventional style. Robert Surtees, for example, collaborated with Mike Nichols on *The Graduate* (1967) and with Peter Bogdanovich on *The Last Picture Show* (1971).

3. For example, Nestor Almendros collaborated with Robert Benton, Mike Nichols, and Martin Scorsese; Michael Ballhaus established an important long-term collaboration with Scorsese; Sven Nykvist collaborated with Woody Allen, Paul Mazursky, Bob Rafelson, Bob Fosse, and Philip Kaufman; and Vittorio

Storaro established significant collaborations with Francis Ford Coppola and Warren Beatty.

4. David Cook, *Lost Illusions: American Cinema in the Shadow of Watergate and Vietnam, 1970–1979* (New York: Scribner's, 2000), 356.

5. Barry Salt, *Film Style and Analysis: History and Technology,* 3rd edition (London: Starwood, 2009), 308.

6. Conrad Hall, quoted in Schaefer and Salvato, *Masters of Light,* 157.

7. Cook, *Lost Illusions,* 355–56.

8. In the 1970s, 1980s, and 1990s, even faster and less grainy color stocks were produced: these included Kodak 5247, introduced in 1976; Kodak 5294, introduced in 1982; and Kodak Vision 5279, introduced in 1996.

9. For a discussion of the development of new film cameras and lenses in the 1970s, see Cook, *Lost Illusions,* 370–80; and Salt, *Film Style,* 312–14.

10. Richard Misek, *Chromatic Cinema: A History of Screen Colour* (Oxford: Wiley-Blackwell, 2010), 134; and Herb Lightman, "Best Achievement in Cinematography for Butch Cassidy and the Sundance Kid," *American Cinematographer* 51.5 (1970): 474.

11. Vilmos Zsigmond, quoted in Schaefer and Salvato, *Masters of Light,* 335.

12. Vilmos Zsigmond, quoted in Jon Fauer, *Cinematographer Style: The Complete Interviews,* Vol. 1 (Hollywood: ASC, 2008), 329–30. For other accounts of Zsigmond's cinematography in the film, and in particular for his use of the flashing process, see Bob Fisher, "A Conversation with Vilmos Zsigmond, ASC," *International Cinematographer's Guild* (June 2002); and Mitchell Zuckoff, *Robert Altman: The Oral Biography* (New York: Knopf, 2009).

13. David Thompson, ed., *Altman on Altman* (London: Faber and Faber, 2006), 60. Flashing was an important part of Zsigmond's technical arsenal in the 1970s: he was to achieve impressive results on his third film for Altman, *The Long Goodbye,* by using varying levels of flashing in different scenes. For Michael Cimino's *Heaven's Gate,* Zsigmond flashed not only the negative but also the positive print stock onto which the film was transferred. The resulting desaturation was, as Richard Misek has observed, "so extreme that the film sometimes seems to cross an invisible threshold, drifting imperceptibly . . . between color and black-and-white." Misek, *Chromatic Cinema,* 134. Flashing was not used as heavily by other Hollywood cinematographers, although Haskell Wexler flashed the negative of Hal Ashby's *Bound for Glory* (1976) to achieve a look that matched the film's Dust Bowl setting.

14. Originally invented to simulate the effect of fog, fog filters were used by a number of filmmakers of the New Hollywood to reduce contrast and sharpness, while also flaring light sources. In *McCabe,* Zsigmond's use of fog filters contributed to the blurred, flarey look of a number of scenes. Bradley Schauer, "The Auteur Renaissance, 1968–1980," in Patrick Keating, ed., *Cinematography* (New Brunswick, NJ: Rutgers University Press, 2014), 90.

15. Vilmos Zsigmond, quoted in Schaefer and Salvato, *Masters of Light*, 315.

16. John Belton and Lyle Tector, "The Bionic Eye: The Aesthetics of the Zoom," *Film Comment* 16.5 (1980): 13.

17. Cook, *Lost Illusions*, 362.

18. Vilmos Zsigmond, quoted in Zuckoff, *Robert Altman*, 215–16.

19. Robert Self, *Robert Altman's* McCabe and Mrs. Miller: *Reframing the American West* (Lawrence: University Press of Kansas, 2007), 12.

20. Vilmos Zsigmond, quoted in Schaefer and Salvato, *Masters of Light*, 331.

21. Robert Altman, quoted in Gerard Plecki, *Robert Altman* (New York: Twayne, 1985), 38.

22. For an analysis of the film as revisionist Western, see Paul Arthur, "How the West Was Spun: *McCabe and Mrs. Miller* and Genre Revisionism," *Cineaste* 23 (Summer 2003).

23. In addition to his three Academy Awards for best cinematography—for *JFK* (1991), *The Aviator* (2004), and *Hugo* (2011)—Richardson has received a wide range of other awards and nominations, including five additional Academy nominations—for *Platoon, Born on the Fourth of July, Snow Falling on Cedars, Inglourious Basterds,* and *Django Unchained*—as well as awards and nominations from the ASC (ten nominations), the British Academy, and the British Society of Cinematographers.

24. In addition to his eleven films with Stone, Richardson has shot seven with Scorsese, four with Tarantino, and two with Sayles.

25. Robert A. Rosenstone, "Oliver Stone: Hollywood Historian," in Cynthia Lucia, Roy Grundmann, and Art Simon, eds., *Wiley-Blackwell History of American Film*, Vol. 4, *1976 to the Present* (West Sussex: Wiley-Blackwell, 2012), 248.

26. For information about the cinematography in *JFK, Natural Born Killers,* and *Nixon,* see Bob Fisher, "The Whys and Hows of *JFK*," *American Cinematographer* (February 1992); Stephen Pizzello, "*Natural Born Killers* Blasts Screen with Both Barrels," *American Cinematographer* (November 1994); and Ric Gentry, "A Splintered Vision of America," *American Cinematographer* (March 1996). Barry Salt provides a useful discussion of the lighting and other visual techniques of *Natural Born Killers,* which he correctly identifies as the most extreme version of the experimentation carried out by Stone and Richardson. Salt, *Film Style.*

27. Robert Kolker, *A Cinema of Loneliness*, 3rd ed. (Oxford and New York: Oxford University Press, 2000).

28. Oliver Stone, ed., *JFK, The Book of the Film: The Documented Screenplay* (New York: Applause Books, 1992), 199.

29. "Movie Geeks United Interview: Robert Richardson" (April 19, 2012), YouTube video, http://youtu.be/oYVvW2nAOVM. Joe Hutshing and Pietro Scalia are the two credited editors on *JFK*. Corwin, who was credited only as "Additional Editor," received editorial credit on three of Stone's later films: *Natural Born Killers, Nixon,* and *U-Turn.*

30. Pizzello, "*Natural Born Killers*," 38.

31. Fisher, "Whys and Hows of *JFK*," 46. Richardson's cinematography for both *Natural Born Killers* and *Nixon* was of a similar complexity. For *Natural Born Killers*, Richardson used both color and black-and-white 35mm, black-and-white 16mm, Super 8 (Kodachrome and Ektachrome), 8mm video (Hi8) and Betacam, as well as rear-projection photography, animation, and stock footage. For *Nixon*, which was shot primarily in 35mm anamorphic format, Richardson also used a range of different black-and-white film stocks and shot with a panoply of cameras that included standard 35mm and 16mm cameras, 1950s tube cameras, and hand-cranked 35mm and 16mm cameras.

32. Fisher, "Whys and Hows of *JFK*," 45.

33. "Oliver Stone Talks Back," in Stone, *JFK: The Book*, 351–52.

34. Kolker, *Cinema of Loneliness*, 79.

35. Oliver Stone, voiceover commentary on the DVD release of *JFK*.

36. Kolker, *Cinema of Loneliness*, 79. Robert Burgoyne reads the monuments and official spaces of Washington as fundamentally unreadable signs, "as indecipherable and 'riddling' as the glyphs on an ancient tombstone." Burgoyne, "Modernism and the Narrative of Nation in JFK," in Vivian Sobchack, ed., *The Persistence of History: Cinema, Television, and the Modern Event* (New York: Routledge, 1995), 125. This reading seems plausible, especially in light of the scene's dialogue, which suggests that Garrison is beginning to put the pieces of the puzzle together but still lacks the complete picture. "You're close," X tells Garrison. "Closer than you think."

37. Norman Mailer, "Footfalls in the Crypt," in Stone, ed., *JFK: The Book of the Film*, 444.

38. David Bordwell, "Intensified Continuity: Visual Style in Contemporary American Film," *Film Quarterly* 55.3 (2002): 16–28. The visual style of *JFK* exhibits several of the features Bordwell describes, including rapid editing, the use of extreme close-ups, and a free-ranging camera.

39. Steven Spielberg, quoted in Stephen Pizzello, "Five-Star General," *American Cinematographer* (August 1998): 46.

40. Janusz Kaminski, quoted in Christopher Probst, "The Last Great War," *American Cinematographer* (August 1998): 33.

41. Steven Spielberg, interview with Matt Lauer, *Today Show* (23 July 1998).

42. "Saving Private Ryan Is Too Real for Some," *Florida Times-Union* (15 August 1998).

43. Jeanine Basinger and Jeremy Arnold, *The World War II Combat Film: Anatomy of a Genre* (Middletown, CT: Wesleyan University Press, 2003), 254–55.

44. For a discussion of the difference between *Saving Private Ryan* and previous World War II films, see Robert Brent Toplin, "Hollywood's D-Day from the Perspective of the 1960s and 1990s: *The Longest Day* and *Saving Private Ryan*," in Peter Rollins and John O'Connor, eds., *Why We Fought: America's Wars in Film and History* (Lexington: The University Press of Kentucky, 2008), 308.

45. The film was ultimately approved for the more standard R rating.

46. Kolker, *Cinema of Loneliness*, 323.

47. Janusz Kaminski, quoted in Probst, "The Last Great War," 33.

48. Pizzello, "Five-Star General," 48. ENR is a development process named for Rome Technicolor technician Ernesto Novelli. The process leaves more silver in the negative, thus giving the image richer, deeper shadows and desaturated, almost pastel colors.

49. Janusz Kaminski, quoted in Probst, "The Last Great War," 34.

50. Janusz Kaminski, quoted in Probst, "The Last Great War," 34.

51. Salt, *Film Style*, 348.

52. For a detailed description of the technique and its use by various filmmakers, see Stacey Peebles, "Gunning for a New Slow Motion: The 45-Degree Shutter and the Representation of Violence," *Journal of Film and Video* 56.2 (Summer 2004): 45–52.

53. According to Barry Salt, the technique of using uncoated lenses to reproduce a sense of historicism was first adopted in *The Charge of the Light Brigade* (1968), the adding of additional vibration to the camera was pioneered in *The Rock* (1996), and the streaking of highlights for aesthetic effect was used, as noted above, in *Full Metal Jacket* (1987). Salt, *Film Style*, 348. Some of these techniques for achieving a sense of authenticity were used even earlier, in part as a way of making newly shot combat footage match the stock footage that was frequently inserted into battle scenes. James Wong Howe notes that in shooting *Objective Burma* (1945), he and his crew would shake the camera and throw dirt onto the lens in order to give the impression of being in an actual battle. "It adds reality if the battle scenes aren't 'perfect.' . . . You need rough edges, little mistakes, here and there." Alain Silver and James Wong Howe, *James Wong Howe, The Camera Eye: A Career Interview* (Santa Monica, CA: Pendragon, 2010), 62–63.

54. Kaminski's cinematography is more conventional in the nonbattle sequences. In one lushly pastoral scene, for example, the American platoon walks across a green field, passing a flock of white sheep as the John Williams score swells dramatically in the background. In another scene, we see a romantically backlit General George Marshall (Harve Presnell) making the decision to risk the lives of several soldiers and an officer in order to bring Ryan home.

55. Janusz Kaminski, quoted in Probst, "The Last Great War," 36.

56. Stephen Prince, "Graphic Violence in the Cinema: Origins, Aesthetic Design, and Social Effects," in Prince, ed., *Screening Violence* (New Brunswick, NJ: Rutgers University Press, 2000), 29. Standards of realism change over time, and what would have seemed an extremely realistic portrayal of combat in a film made during the 1940s might appear stagey or unrealistic to today's viewers. Notions of filmic realism are relative and contingent rather than absolute: they depend on the technologies available to filmmakers at any given moment, as well as on contemporary attitudes toward what constitutes realism in portrayals of events and situations.

57. Paul Ramaeker, "The New Hollywood, 1981–1999," in Patrick Keating, ed., *Cinematography* (New Brunswick, NJ: Rutgers University Press, 2014),

131. I would agree with Ramaeker that despite the technological and stylistic differences between cinematography of the 1990s and that of the 1970s, the degree of stylization constitutes an important continuity between the two eras.

CHAPTER 6

Epigraph: Lev Manovich, "What is Digital Cinema?" Manovich (1995), http://manovich.net/index.php/projects/what-is-digital-cinema.

1. Since films are increasingly made using a combination of film and digital formats, it is difficult to give an exact percentage of films that fall into each category. However, in my informal survey of the forty top-grossing American films of 2012, approximately half were shot primarily with digital cameras rather than traditional 35mm cameras. In 2013, the portion of films shot digitally was closer to 70 percent.

2. Thomas Schatz, "Seismic Shifts in the American Film Industry," in Cynthia Baron, Roy Grundmann, and Art Simon, eds., *Wiley-Blackwell History of American Film*, Vol. 4, *1976 to the Present* (West Sussex: Wiley-Blackwell, 2012), 43.

3. Kodak filed for Chapter 11 bankruptcy in January 2012 and emerged from bankruptcy in September 2013 as a commercial printing company. Though it no longer sells products to consumers, it continues to sell film to the movie industry.

4. For a thorough discussion of digital special effects that contains some material on digital cinematography, see Stephen Prince, *Digital Visual Effects in Cinema: The Seduction of Reality* (New Brunswick, NJ: Rutgers University Press, 2012). See also Christopher Lucas, "The Modern Entertainment Marketplace, 2000–Present," in Patrick Keating, ed., *Cinematography* (New Brunswick, NJ: Rutgers University Press, 2014).

5. The term *postproduction* is something of a misnomer, since it suggests that editing and visual effects are not part of the production of images. Given the centrality of editing, special effects, and digital processing to the production of visual images in contemporary films, it is no longer possible to separate the production process from the postproduction process as neatly as could be done in earlier periods.

6. Prince, *Digital Visual Effects*, 65ff.

7. Various names for this process have been proposed, including "digital film mastering," "digital color grading," and "selective digital grading," though in recent years the term "digital intermediate" seems to have been widely accepted within the industry. The digital intermediate process can also be applied to digitally shot films, though because the footage is already digital, it does not require a transfer of the image from analog film to digital format.

8. Prince, *Digital Visual Effects*, 70.

9. Aylish Wood, "Pixel Visions: Digital Intermediate and the Micromanipulation of the Image," *Film Criticism* 32.1 (2007): 72.

10. Vilmos Zsigmond, "Darkest Noir," *American Cinematographer* (September 2006): 48–49.

11. For discussions of the making of *The Aviator,* see John Pavlus, "High Life," *American Cinematographer* 86.1 (2005); Michael Goldman, "Scorsese's Color Homage," *Millimeter* (January 2005); and Scott Higgins, *Harnessing the Technicolor Rainbow in the 1930s* (Austin: University of Texas Press, 2007).

12. Richardson's cinematography for *The Aviator* was not intended to be a strict imitation of Technicolor style, and his techniques of lighting and camerawork do not conform to the standards used on films of the 1930s and 1940s. Richardson's lighting, for example, made some attempt to match period techniques, but it did not strictly imitate the lighting of the period. In other areas, such as camera movement, the film's cinematography departs significantly from that of the 1930s or 1940s: Richardson moved the camera far more than would have been possible with bulky Technicolor cameras, and for some shots he used complicated crane moves that would not have been possible with the technologies of the time.

13. The tactics Bordwell identified include more rapid editing; the use of either very short or very long lenses; closer framings of actors' faces in dialogue scenes; and a more free-ranging camera. David Bordwell, "Intensified Continuity: Visual Style in Contemporary American Film," *Film Quarterly* 55.3 (2002): 16–28.

14. I include in this category films that use DI technology to enhance color, as well as films that use the process to desaturate color, create monotone color, or experiment with combinations of black-and-white and color. An example of a fairly unobtrusive use of DI is the visually mainstream film *Seabiscuit* (Gary Ross, 2003), in which DI was used to heighten the color during the horse races in order to create more excitement in those sequences. A far more complex use of the technology can be seen in *Sin City* (Robert Rodriguez, 2005), in which DI is used in a number of ways, including isolating different elements within the frame, adding shadows, separating foregrounds from backgrounds, combining black and white with selective color, and the overall creation of a visual style that approximates that of the original Frank Miller comic books on which the film is based. Wood, "Pixel Visions."

15. John Bailey, "The DI Dilemma, or: Why I Still Love Celluloid," *American Cinematographer* (June 2008).

16. Roger Deakins, "The DI Luddites and Other Musings," *American Cinematographer* (October 2008).

17. The terms *2K* and *4K* refer to the resolution of digital images as measured by the number of horizontal pixels. So, for example, an image that is 4,000 pixels wide and 2,400 pixels tall would be designated as 4K, with an aspect ratio of 1.66:1. In 2004, *Spider-Man 2* became the first feature film to be scanned entirely at 4K. The documentary *Baraka,* originally made by director Ron Fricke in 1992, was scanned at 8K for its DVD and Blu-ray release in 2008.

18. THR staff, "THR's Director Roundtable: Quentin Tarantino Says Digital Projection Is Driving Him toward Retirement: 'It's Over' (Video)," *Hollywood Reporter* (28 November 2012), http://www.hollywoodreporter.com/news/quentin-tarantino-says-digital-projection-394853. Tarantino's most recent

feature film, *Django Unchained* (2012), was shot by Robert Richardson on celluloid.

19. Jeffrey Ressner, "The Traditionalist," interview with Christopher Nolan, *DGA Quarterly* (Spring 2012), http://www.dga.org/Craft/DGAQ/All-Articles/1202-Spring-2012/DGA-Interview-Christopher-Nolan.aspx. Nolan's most recent film, *Interstellar* (2014), was shot on celluloid by cinematographer Hoyte Van Hoytema.

20. Wally Pfister, customer testimonial video, *Kodak: Cinema and Television* (n.d.), http://motion.kodak.com/motion/Products/Customer_Testimonials/Wally_Pfister.

21. *Collateral* was shot in a combination of digital capture and film, with film cameras used for most of the interior scenes and stunt sequences, and digital cameras for most exterior scenes. Jay Holben, "Hell on Wheels," *American Cinematographer* (August 2004). *Miami Vice* was shot primarily in digital format, with only a few scenes shot on film; *Public Enemies* was shot entirely in digital, with film used only for visual effects.

22. In digital data capture, the camera records directly to the drives rather than to tape. The data is then downloaded onto a master drive, where it is stored until it can be edited.

23. *Side by Side,* directed by Christopher Kenneally and produced by Keanu Reeves, contains interviews with directors, cinematographers, actors, and producers. Though the film is slanted toward the "pro-digital" position, it does provide a useful discussion of the issues surrounding the digital turn.

24. Nick Clark, "Martin Scorsese to Abandon Film to Shoot Movies Digitally," *The Independent* (28 June 2012).

25. Michael Goldman, "Boom and Bust," *American Cinematographer* (December 2013): 39–40.

26. Uta Briesewitz, quoted in Prince, *Digital Visual Effects,* 82.

27. This is not to say that the footage shot by cinematographers was never manipulated in predigital films. Karl Struss, for example, complained that in the silent era "often the lab man would develop the negative to his own taste, neutralizing what I'd been trying to do." Struss, quoted in Scott Eyman, ed., *Five American Cinematographers* (Metuchen, NJ: Scarecrow Press, 1987), 21.

28. Edgar Burcksen, "Cinematographer-Editor Collaboration More Crucial Than Ever," *American Cinematographer* (June 2013): 84.

29. Harris Savides, quoted in David Williams, "Cold Case File," *American Cinematographer* (April 2007).

30. "Steven Spielberg and Martin Scorsese: The Joy of Celluloid," *Guardian* online edition (10 October 2011), www.theguardian.com/artanddesign/2011/oct/10/steven-spielberg-martin-scorsese-celluloid.

31. George Lucas, quoted in Brian McKernan, *Digital Cinema: The Revolution in Cinematography, Postproduction, and Distribution* (New York: McGraw-Hill, 2005), 31.

32. Since systems of digital storage change over time, there is no secure way of storing digital information over the long term. Given legitimate concerns

about the long-term preservation of digital data, producers have continued to archive their digital products on celluloid as a more secure backup to digital storage. Kodak has developed a film stock specifically intended for preserving digital content. Ironically, studios' need to preserve their digital productions on a more stable medium, rather than the production of new content, may sustain the production and availability of celluloid film.

33. The breakdown of the long-standing aesthetic divide between film and television is attributable both to the increasing digitization of filmic media and to the improvement in production values of televised media. When films are shot digitally, it becomes a matter of indifference—other than the size of the screen—whether their images are shown in a movie theater, on the television, or on a laptop computer. Further, as the quality of the televised image improves—with larger and higher-resolution screens—it can no longer be assumed that the visual quality of television is inherently inferior to that of movies. "As the TV image approaches the film image in [both] resolution and scale," notes Carroll, "it can sport mise-en-scène as elaborate as any movie [and provide] expressive visual qualities audiences are meant to notice and appreciate." Noel Carroll, *Engaging the Moving Image* (New Haven: Yale University Press, 2003), 272. In the last decade, the production values of television programs have continued to improve, to the extent that they are even closer to the visual quality of film. Like films, television series are shot in various formats: digitally (*House of Cards*), on 35mm film with digital intermediate (*Breaking Bad*), or on 16mm film (*The Walking Dead*). The quality of television cinematography has been recognized by the ASC, which now gives awards for television programs as well as feature films. The ASC currently gives separate awards for half-hour series, hour-long series, and television films or miniseries.

34. Christopher Lucas, quoted in Keating, *Cinematography*, 153.

35. Christopher Lucas, quoted in Keating, *Cinematography*, 135.

36. "Spielberg and Scorsese: Joy of Celluloid," *Guardian* online edition.

37. The American Society of Cinematographers is currently considering whether to institute a separate award category for "hybrid" films—films that use a combination of live-action and computer-generated footage.

38. The visual effects supervisor Tim Webber estimated that 80 percent of the film was created by CG effects rather than live action cinematography. Wikipedia entry for *Gravity*.

39. Burcksen, "Cinematographer-Editor Collaboration," 82, 85.

Works Cited

Abel, Richard, and Rick Altman, eds. *The Sounds of Early Cinema.* Bloomington: Indiana University Press, 2001.

Adamson, Joe. "John F. Seitz." *Internet Encyclopedia of Cinematographers* (www.cinematographers.nl/GreatDoPh/seitz.htm).

Allen, Richard. "Hitchcock's Color Designs." In *Color: The Film Reader,* edited by Angela Dalle Vacche and Brian Price. Oxford and New York: Routledge, 2006.

Allyn, John. "*Double Indemnity:* A Policy that Paid Off." In *Billy Wilder Interviews,* edited by Robert Horton. Jackson: University of Mississippi Press, 2001.

Als, Hilton. "The Cameraman." *New Yorker* (June 19, 2006).

Alton, John. *Painting with Light,* 1949. Rev. ed. Berkeley and Los Angeles: University of California Press, 2013.

Anderegg, Michael. *William Wyler.* Boston: Twayne, 1979.

Arnold, John. "Art in Cinematography." *American Cinematographer* 13.4 (1932).

Arthur, Paul. "How the West Was Spun: *McCabe and Mrs. Miller* and Genre Revisionism." *Cineaste* 23 (Summer 2003).

Atkinson, David. "Hitchcock's Techniques Tell *Rear Window* Story." *American Cinematographer* 71.1 (1990).

Auiler, Dan. Vertigo: *The Making of a Classic.* New York: St. Martin's, 1998.

Bailey, John. "The DI Dilemma, or: Why I Still Love Celluloid." *American Cinematographer* 89.6 (2008).

———. "Film Noir's Sorcerer of Light: John Alton." In John Alton, *Painting with Light.* Berkeley and Los Angeles: University of California Press, 2013.

Ballinger, Alex. *New Cinematographers.* New York: HarperCollins, 2004.

Balshofer, Fred, and Arthur Miller. *One Reel a Week.* Berkeley: University of California Press, 1967.

Barry, Iris, and Eileen Bowser. *D.W. Griffith.* New York: Museum of Modern Art/Doubleday, 1965.

Basinger, Jeanine, and Jeremy Arnold. *The World War II Combat Film: Anatomy of a Genre.* Middletown, CT: Wesleyan University Press, 2003.

Bazin, André. "William Wyler, or the Jansenism of Directing." In *Bazin at Work: Major Essays and Reviews from the Forties and Fifties,* edited by Bert Cardullo. New York and London: Routledge, 1997.

Beck, Tony, and Tony Granada, eds. *Lowering the Boom: Critical Studies in Film Sound.* Urbana: University of Illinois Press, 2008.

Belton, John, and Lyle Tector. "The Bionic Eye: The Aesthetics of the Zoom." *Film Comment* 16.5 (1980).

Biesen, Sheri Chinen. "Billy Wilder." In *Film Noir: The Directors,* edited by Alain Silver and James Ursini. Montclair, N J: Limelight Editions, 2012.

———. *Blackout: World War II and the Origins of Film Noir.* Baltimore: Johns Hopkins University Press, 2005.

Bitzer, G.W. *Billy Bitzer: His Story.* New York: Farrar, Straus, and Giroux, 1973.

———. "D.W. Griffith." In David W. Griffith Papers, 1897–1934, Manuscript Division, Library of Congress.

———. "*Intolerance:* The Sun Play of the Ages." *International Photographer* (October 1934).

Black, Hilda. "The Photography Is Important to Hitchcock." *American Cinematographer* 33.12 (1952).

Blanchard, Walter. "Aces of the Camera VII: James Wong Howe." *American Cinematographer* 22.7 (1941).

———."Aces of the Camera XIII: Gregg Toland, A.S.C." *American Cinematographer* 23.1 (1942).

Bogdanovich, Peter. *The Cinema of Alfred Hitchcock.* New York: Museum of Modern Art, 1963.

Bordwell, David. "Intensified Continuity: Visual Style in Contemporary American Film." *Film Quarterly* 55.3 (2002): 16–28.

———. *On the History of Film Style.* Cambridge: Harvard University Press, 1997.

Bordwell, David, Janet Staiger, and Kristin Thompson. *The Classical Hollywood Cinema: Film Style and Mode of Production to 1960.* New York: Columbia University Press, 1985.

Bowser, Eileen. *The Transformation of Cinema, 1907–1915.* New York: Scribner's, 1990.

Brown, Karl. *Adventures with D.W. Griffith.* London: Secker and Warburg, 1973.

Burch, Noel. *Life to Those Shadows.* Trans. Ben Brewster. Berkeley and Los Angeles: University of California Press, 1990.

Burckson, Edgar. "Cinematographer-Editor Collaboration More Crucial Than Ever." *American Cinematographer* 94.6 (2013).

Burgoyne, Robert. "Modernism and the Narrative of Nation in *JFK.*" In *The Persistence of History: Cinema, Television, and the Modern Event,* edited by Vivian Sobchack. New York: Routledge, 1995.

Cagle, Chris. "Classical Hollywood, 1928–1946." In *Cinematography,* edited by Patrick Keating. New Brunswick, NJ: Rutgers University Press, 2014.

Caldwell, John T. *Production Culture: Industrial Reflexivity and Critical Practice in Films and Television.* Durham: Duke University Press, 2008.

"Captain Kate." Review. *Moving Picture World* 9.3 (1911).

Carringer, Robert. *The Making of Citizen Kane.* Berkeley and Los Angeles: University of California Press, 1995.

Carroll, Noel. *Engaging the Moving Image.* New Haven: Yale University Press, 2003.

Chandler, Charlotte. *It's Only a Movie: Alfred Hitchcock, A Personal Biography.* New York: Simon and Schuster, 2005.

Christensen, Jerome. *America's Corporate Art: The Studio Authorship of Hollywood Motion Pictures.* Stanford, CA: Stanford University Press, 2012.

Clark, Nick. "Martin Scorsese to Abandon Film to Shoot Movies Digitally." *Independent* (June 28, 2012).

Clarke, Charles. *Highlights and Shadows: The Memoirs of a Hollywood Cameraman,* edited by Anthony Slide. Metuchen, NJ: Scarecrow Press, 1989.

Clute, Shannon Scott, and Richard Edwards. *The Maltese Touch of Evil: Film Noir and Potential Criticism.* Hanover, NH: Dartmouth College Press, 2011.

Coe, Jonathan. *Jimmy Stewart: A Wonderful Life.* New York: Arcade, 1994.

Cohen, Paula Marantz. "Hitchcock's Revised American Vision: *The Wrong Man* and *Vertigo,"* In *On Hitchcock's America,* edited by Jonathan Freeman and Richard Millington. Oxford and New York: Oxford University Press, 1999.

Coleman, Herbert. *The Hollywood I Knew: A Memoir, 1916–1988.* Lanham, MD: Scarecrow Press, 2003.

Cook, David. *A History of Narrative Film,* 4th ed. New York: Norton, 2004.

———. *Lost Illusions: American Cinema in the Shadow of Watergate and Vietnam, 1970–1979.* New York: Scribner's, 2000.

Cooper, Miriam. *Dark Lady of the Silents: My Life in Early Hollywood.* Indianapolis: Bobbs-Merrill, 1973.

Cormack, Mike. *Ideology and Cinematography in Hollywood, 1930–39.* New York: St. Martin's, 1994.

Counts, Kyle. "The Making of Alfred Hitchcock's *The Birds." Cinefantastique* 10.2 (1980): 15–35.

Crafton, Donald. *The Talkies: American Cinema's Transition to Sound, 1926–1931.* Berkeley: University of California Press, 1999.

Crowe, Cameron. *Conversations with Wilder.* New York: Knopf, 1999.

Curtis, Scott. "The Making of *Rear Window."* In *Alfred Hitchcock's* Rear Window, edited by John Belton. Cambridge and New York: Cambridge University Press, 2000.

Davis, Ronald L. "Southern Methodist University Oral History Project: William Wyler." In *William Wyler Interviews,* edited by Gabriel Miller. Oxford: University Press of Mississippi, 2010.

Deakins, Roger. "The DI Luddites and Other Musings." *American Cinematographer* 89.10 (2008).

Dombrowski, Lisa. "Postwar Hollywood, 1947–1967." In *Cinematography,* edited by Patrick Keating. New Brunswick, NJ: Rutgers University Press, 2014.

Drew, William M. *D. W. Griffith's* Intolerance: *Its Genesis and Vision.* Jefferson, NC: McFarland, 1986.

Dyer, Richard. "Introduction to Film Studies." In *Oxford Guide to Film Studies,* edited by John Hill and Pamela Church Gibson. Oxford and New York: Oxford University Press, 1998.

Ettedgui, Peter. *Cinematography.* Woburn, MA: Butterworth-Heinemann, 1998.

Eyman, Scott. *Five American Cinematographers.* Metuchen, NJ: Scarecrow Press, 1987.

Fairservice, Don. *Film Editing: History, Theory, and Practice.* Manchester, UK: Manchester University Press, 2001.

Fauer, Jon. *Cinematographer Style: The Complete Interviews,* Vol. 1. Hollywood: ASC Press, 2008.

Fisher, Bob. "A Conversation with Vilmos Zsigmond, ASC." *International Cinematographer's Guild* (June 2002).

———. "The Whys and Hows of *JFK.*" *American Cinematographer* 73.2 (1992).

Foster, Frederick. "Hitch Didn't Want It Arty." *American Cinematographer* 38.2 (1957).

Fulton, A. R. *Motion Pictures: The Development of an Art from Silent Films to the Age of Television.* Norman: University of Oklahoma Press, 1960.

Gavin, Arthur. "Rear Window." *American Cinematographer* 35.2 (1954).

Gemunden, Gerd. *Foreign Affair: Billy Wilder's American Films.* New York and Oxford: Berghahn Books, 2008.

Gentry, Ric. "A Splintered Vision of America." *American Cinematographer* 77.3 (1996).

Gish, Lillian. *The Movies, Mr. Griffith, and Me.* New York: Prentice Hall, 1969.

Glennon, Bert. "Cinematography and the Talkies." *American Cinematographer* 11.2 (1930).

Goldman, Michael. "Boom and Bust." *American Cinematographer* 94.12 (2013).

———. "Scorsese's Color Homage." *Millimeter* (January 2005).

Gunning, Tom. "The Country Doctor." In *The Griffith Project,* Vol. 2, *Films Produced in January–June 1909,* edited by Paolo Cherchi Usai. London: British Film Institute, 1999.

——— "True Heart Susie." In *The Griffith Project,* Vol. 10, *Films Produced in 1919–46,* edited by Paolo Cherchi Usai. London: British Film Institute, 2006.

——— "The White Rose." In *The Griffith Project,* Vol. 10, *Films Produced in 1919–46,* edited by Paolo Cherchi Usai. London: British Film Institute, 2006.

Hansen, Miriam. *Babel and Babylon: Spectatorship in American Silent Film.* Cambridge, MA: Harvard University Press, 1989.

Henabery, Joseph. *Before, In, and After Hollywood: The Autobiography of Joseph Henabery,* edited by Anthony Slide. Lanham, MD: Scarecrow Press, 1997.

Henderson, Robert. *D.W. Griffith: His Life and Work.* New York: Oxford University Press, 1972.
Herman, Jan. *A Talent for Trouble: The Life of Hollywood's Most Acclaimed Director, William Wyler.* New York: G.P. Putnam's Sons, 1995.
Higgins, Scott. *Harnessing the Technicolor Rainbow in the 1930s.* Austin: University of Texas Press, 2007.
Higham, Charles. *Hollywood Cameramen.* London: Thames and Hudson, 1973.
Holben, Jay. "Hell on Wheels." *American Cinematographer* 85.8 (2004).
Horak, Jan-Christopher. "Southern Landscapes of the Mind's Eye: Griffith's *The White Rose.*" In *Image on the Art and Evolution of the Film: Photographs and Articles from the Magazine of the International Museum of Photography,* edited by Marshall Deutelbaum. New York: Dover, 1979.
Hulfish, David S. "Art in Moving Pictures." *Nickelodeon* 1.5 (1909).
Jacobs, Lea. "The B Film and the Problem of Cultural Distinction." *Screen* 33.1 (1992).
Jacobs, Lewis. *The Rise of the American Film: A Critical History.* New York: Teachers College Press, 1967. First published 1939 by Harcourt, Brace.
Jacobs, Stephen. *The Wrong House: The Architecture of Alfred Hitchcock.* Rotterdam: 010 Publishers, 2007.
Jesionowski, Joyce. *Thinking in Pictures: Dramatic Structure in D.W. Griffith's Biograph Films.* Berkeley: University of California Press, 1989.
"John Leezer," *American Cinematographer* 3.2 (1922).
Johnson, Julian. "The Shadow Stage." *Photoplay Magazine* 11.1 (1916).
———. "The Shadow Stage." *Photoplay Magazine* 16.3 (1919).
Karasek, Hellmuth. *Billy Wilder: Eine Nahaufnahme.* Tübingen: Hoffmann and Campe, 2006.
Keating, Patrick, ed. *Cinematography.* New Brunswick, NJ: Rutgers University Press, 2014.
———. *Hollywood Lighting: From the Silent Era to Film Noir.* New York: Columbia University Press, 2010.
Keil, Charlie. *Early American Cinema in Transition: Story, Style, and Filmmaking, 1907–1913.* Madison: University of Wisconsin Press, 2001.
———. "Intolerance." In *The Griffith Project,* Vol. 9. *Films Produced in 1916–18,* edited by Paolo Cherchi Usai. London: British Film Institute, 2004.
———. "Transition through Tension: Stylistic Diversity in the Late Griffith Biographs." *Cinema Journal* 28.3 (1989).
Kerr, Paul. "Out of What Past?: Notes on the B Film Noir." In *Film Noir Reader,* edited by Alain Silver and James Ursini. New York: Limelight, 1996.
Koenig, Lester. "Gregg Toland, Film-Maker." *Screen Writer* 3.7 (1947).
Kolker, Robert. *A Cinema of Loneliness.* 3rd ed. Oxford and New York: Oxford University Press, 2000.
Koszarski, Richard. "The Cinematographer." In *New York to Hollywood: The Photography of Karl Struss,* edited by Barbara McCandless, Bonnie Yochelson, and Richard Koszarski. Fort Worth and Albuquerque: Amon Carter Museum/ University of New Mexico Press, 1995.

Kozloff, Sarah. *The Best Years of Our Lives.* London: BFI/Palgrave Macmillan, 2011.

Lastra, James. *Sound Technology and the American Cinema: Perception, Representation, Modernity.* New York: Columbia University Press, 2000.

Lawson, John Howard. *Film: The Creative Process.* New York: Hill and Wang, 1964.

Leitch, Thomas. *Crime Films.* Cambridge and New York: Cambridge University Press, 2002.

Lightman, Herb. "Best Achievement in Cinematography for *Butch Cassidy and the Sundance Kid." American Cinematographer* 51.5 (1970).

———. "The Film Artistry of D.W. Griffith and Billy Bitzer," *American Cinematographer* 50.1 (1969).

———. "Hitchcock Talks about Lights, Camera, Action." *American Cinematographer* 48.5 (1967).

———. "Old Master, New Tricks: A Combination That Spelled Success for Photography in *Sunset Boulevard," American Cinematographer* 31.9 (1950).

———. "Robert Burks, A.S.C., Photographs *The Fountainhead." American Cinematographer* 30.6 (1949).

LoBrutto, Vincent. *Principal Photography: Interviews with Feature Film Cinematographers.* Westport, CT: Praeger, 1999.

Lucas, Christopher. "The Modern Entertainment Marketplace, 2000–Present." In *Cinematography,* edited by Patrick Keating. New Brunswick, NJ: Rutgers University Press, 2014.

Madsen, Axel. *William Wyler: The Authorized Biography.* New York: Thomas Crowell, 1973.

Mailer, Norman. "Footfalls in the Crypt." In JFK, *The Book of the Film: The Documented Screenplay,* edited by Oliver Stone. New York: Applause Books, 1992.

Maltin, Leonard. *The Art of the Cinematographer.* Rev. ed. Mineola, NY: Dover, 2012.

Manovich, Lev. "What is Digital Cinema?" Manovich. www.manovich.net/TEXT/digital-cinema-htm.

McCarthy, Todd. "Through a Lens Darkly: The Life and Films of John Alton." In John Alton, *Painting with Light.* Rev. ed. Berkeley and Los Angeles: University of California Press, 2013.

McGee, Patrick. *From* Shane *to* Kill Bill: *Rethinking the Western.* London: Blackwell, 2007.

McGilligan, Patrick. *Alfred Hitchcock: A Life in Darkness and Light.* New York: HarperCollins, 2003.

McKernan, Brian. *Digital Cinema: The Revolution in Cinematography, Postproduction, and Distribution.* New York: McGraw-Hill, 2005.

Merritt, Russell. "D.W. Griffith's *Intolerance:* Reconstructing an Unattainable Text," *Film History* 4.4 (1990).

———. "The Making of *Hearts of the World.*" *Quarterly Review of Film Studies* 6.1 (1981).

———. "The Musketeers of Pig Alley." In *The Griffith Project,* Vol. 6, *Films Produced in 1912,* edited by Paolo Cherchi Usai. London: British Film Institute, 2002.

———. "On First Looking into Griffith's Babylon." *Wide Angle* 5.1 (1979).

Misek, Richard. *Chromatic Cinema: A History of Screen Colour.* Oxford: Wiley-Blackwell, 2010.

Mitchell, George. "*America:* 1924's Forgotten Classic." *American Cinematographer* 71.10 (1990).

———. "Billy Bitzer: Pioneer and Innovator." *American Cinematographer* 45.12 (1964).

Mohr, Hal. "A Lens Mount for Universal Focus Effects." *American Cinematographer* 17.9 (1936).

Moral, Tony Lee. *Hitchcock and the Making of* Marnie. Lanham, MD: Scarecrow Press, 2005.

———. *The Making of Hitchcock's* The Birds. Harpenden, UK: Karnera Books, 2013.

Musser, Charles. "The Early Cinema of Edwin S. Porter." In *Wiley-Blackwell History of American Film,* Vol. I, *Origins to 1928,* edited by Cynthia Lucia, Roy Grundmann, and Art Simon. Oxford: Wiley-Blackwell, 2012.

———. *The Emergence of Cinema: The American Screen to 1907.* New York: Scribner's, 1990.

———. "Pre-Classical Modes of American Cinema: Its Changing Modes of Production." In *Silent Film,* edited by Richard Abel. New Brunswick, NJ: Rutgers University Press, 1996.

Nolan, Christopher. Interview. *DGA Quarterly* (Spring 2012).

O'Brien, Charles. *Cinema's Conversion to Sound: Technology and Film Style in France and the U.S.* Bloomington: University of Indiana Press, 2005.

Ogle, Patrick. "Technological and Aesthetic Influences on the Development of Deep-Focus Cinematography in the United States." In *Movies and Methods,* Vol. 2, edited by Bill Nichols. Berkeley and Los Angeles: University of California Press, 1985.

O'Leary, Liam. *Rex Ingram: Master of the Silent Cinema.* Dublin: Academy Press, 1980.

Paglia, Camille. *The Birds.* London: British Film Institute, 2008.

Pavlus, John. "High Life." *American Cinematographer* 86.1 (2005).

Peebles, Stacey. "Gunning for a New Slow Motion: The 45-Degree Shutter and the Representation of Violence." *Journal of Film and Video* 56.2 (2004).

Phillips, Gene. Interview with Billy Wilder. *Billy Wilder Interviews,* edited by Robert Horton. Jackson: University of Mississippi Press, 2001.

———. "William Wyler." *Focus on Film* 24 (1976).

Pizello, Stephen. "Five-Star General." *American Cinematographer* 79.8 (1998).

———. "*Natural Born Killers* Blasts Screen with Both Barrels." *American Cinematographer* 75.11 (1994).
Place, Janey, and Lowell Peterson. "Some Visual Motifs." In *Film Noir Reader*, edited by Alain Silver and James Ursini. New York: Limelight, 1996.
Plecki, Gerard. *Robert Altman*. New York: Twayne, 1985.
Pollock, Dale M. "An Unconventional War Film: Death, Disguise, and Deception in *Five Graves to Cairo*." In *Billy Wilder, Movie-Maker: Critical Essays on the Films*. Jefferson, NC: McFarland, 2011.
Pratt, George C. *Spellbound in Darkness: A History of the Silent Film*. Greenwich, CT: New York Graphic Society, 1973.
Prince, Stephen. *Digital Visual Effects in Cinema: The Seduction of Reality*. New Brunswick, NJ: Rutgers University Press, 2012.
———. "Graphic Violence in the Cinema: Origins, Aesthetic Design, and Social Effects." In *Screening Violence*, edited by Stephen Prince. New Brunswick, NJ: Rutgers University Press, 2000.
Probst, Christopher. "The Last Great War." *American Cinematographer* 79.8 (1998).
"The Qualitative Picture." *Moving Picture World* 6.25 (1910).
Rainsberger, Todd. *James Wong Howe: Cinematographer*. New York: A.S. Barnes, 1982.
Ramaeker, Paul. "Notes on the Split-Field Diopter." *Film History* 19 (2007).
———. "The New Hollywood, 1981–1999." In *Cinematography*, edited by Patrick Keating. New Brunswick, NJ: Rutgers University Press, 2014.
Rebello, Stephen. *Alfred Hitchcock and the Making of* Psycho. New York: Dembner Books, 1990.
Robertson, Peggy. Production memo, 1965, Alfred Hitchcock Collection, Special Collections, Margaret Herrick Library of the Academy of Motion Pictures Arts and Sciences.
Robinson, David. *From Peep Show to Palace: The Birth of American Film*. New York: Columbia University Press, 1996.
Rosenstone, Robert A. "Oliver Stone: Hollywood Historian." In *Wiley-Blackwell History of American Film*, Vol. 4, *1976 to the Present*, edited by Cynthia Lucia, Roy Grundmann, and Art Simon. West Sussex: Wiley-Blackwell, 2012.
Salt, Barry. *Film Style and Technology: History and Analysis*. 3rd ed. London: Starwood, 2009.
Sarris, Andrew. *The Primal Screen: Essays on Film and Related Subjects*. New York: Simon and Schuster, 1973,
"*Saving Private Ryan* Is Too Real for Some." *Florida Times-Union* (August 15, 1998).
Schaefer, Dennis and Larry Salvato. *Masters of Light: Conversations with Contemporary Cinematographers*. Rev. ed. Berkeley and Los Angeles: University of California Press, 2013.
Schatz, Thomas. *The Genius of the System: Hollywood Filmmaking in the Studio Era*. New York: Pantheon, 1988.

———. "Seismic Shifts in the American Film Industry." In *Wiley- Blackwell History of American Film,* Vol. 4, *1976 to the Present,* edited by Cynthia Baron, Roy Grundmann, and Art Simon. West Sussex: Wiley-Blackwell, 2012.

Schauer, Bradley. "The Auteur Renaissance, 1968–1980." In *Cinematography,* edited by Patrick Keating. New Brunswick, NJ: Rutgers University Press, 2014.

Schickel, Richard. *D.W. Griffith: An American Life.* New York: Simon and Schuster, 1984.

Seitz, John F. Interview. In *Film Noir Reader 3: Interviews with Filmmakers of the Classic Period,* edited by Robert Porfirio, Alain Silver, and James Ursini. New York: Limelight Editions, 2004.

Seldes, Gilbert. *The Seven Lively Arts.* New York: A.S. Barnes, 1962.

Self, Robert. *Robert Altman's* McCabe and Mrs. Miller: *Reframing the American West.* Lawrence: University Press of Kansas, 2007.

Sellors, C. Paul. *Film Authorship: Auteurs and Other Myths.* London: Wallflower, 2010.

Sikov, Ed. *On Sunset Boulevard: The Life and Times of Billy Wilder.* New York: Hyperion, 1998.

Silver, Alain. "Rogue Cop." In *Film Noir: The Encyclopedia,* edited by Alain Silver, Elizabeth Ward, James Ursini, and Robert Porfirio. 4th ed. New York: Overlook Duckworth, 2010.

Silver, Alain and James Wong Howe. *James Wong Howe the Camera Eye: A Career Interview.* Santa Monica, CA: Pendragon Press, 2010.

Simmon, Scott. *The Films of D.W. Griffith.* New York: Cambridge University Press, 1993.

Sklar, Robert. *Movie-Made America.* New York: Random House, 1974.

Slide, Anthony. *The Big V: A History of the Vitagraph Company.* Metuchen, NJ: Scarecrow Press, 1987.

Sloan, Jane. *Alfred Hitchcock: A Filmography and Bibliography.* Berkeley and Los Angeles: University of California Press, 1993.

Slocombe, Douglas. "The Work of Gregg Toland." *Sequence* 8 (1950).

Smith, Ella. *Starring Miss Barbara Stanwyck.* New York: Crown, 1973.

Spoto, Donald. *The Dark Side of Genius: The Life of Alfred Hitchcock.* New York: Little, Brown, 1983.

———. *Spellbound by Beauty: Alfred Hitchcock and His Leading Ladies.* New York: Crown, 2008.

Staggs, Sam. *Close-up on* Sunset Boulevard: *Billy Wilder, Norma Desmond, and the Dark Hollywood Dream.* New York: St. Martin's, 2003.

Stern, Seymour. "11 East 14th Street." *Films in Review* 3.8 (1952).

"Steven Spielberg and Martin Scorsese: The Joy of Celluloid." *Guardian* online ed. (October 10, 2011).

Stokes, Melvyn. *D.W. Griffith's* The Birth of a Nation: *A History of the Most Controversial Motion Picture of All Time.* Oxford and New York: Oxford University Press, 2007.

Stone, Oliver, ed. JFK, *The Book of the Film: The Documented Screenplay.* New York: Applause Books, 1992.

Struss, Karl. "Dramatic Cinematography." *Transactions of the Society of Motion Picture Engineers* 34 (1928).

———. "Photographic Modernism and the Cinematographer." *American Cinematographer* 15.11 (1934).

Thompson, David. ed. *Altman on Altman.* London: Faber and Faber, 2006.

Thompson, Kristin. "Dream Street." In *The Griffith Project,* Vol. 10, *Films Produced in 1919–46,* edited by Paolo Cherchi Usai. London: British Film Institute, 2006.

"Through the Editor's Finder," *American Cinematographer* 23.2 (1942).

Toland, Gregg. "How I Broke the Rules in *Citizen Kane.*" In *Focus on Citizen Kane,* edited by Ronald Gottesman. Englewood Cliffs, NJ: Prentice-Hall, 1971.

———. Letter to Samuel Goldwyn (undated), Samuel Goldwyn Papers, Special Collections, Margaret Herrick Library of the Academy of Motion Pictures Arts and Sciences.

———. "The Motion Picture Cameraman." *International Photographer* (February 1941).

———. "The Motion Picture Cameraman." *Theatre Arts* 25.9 (September 1941).

———. "Realism for *Citizen Kane.*" *American Cinematographer* 22.2 (1941).

———. "Using Arcs for Lighting Monochrome." *American Cinematographer* 22.12 (1941).

Toplin, Robert Brent. "Hollywood's D-Day from the Perspective of the 1960s and 1990s: *The Longest Day* and *Saving Private Ryan.*" In *Why We Fought: America's Wars in Film and History,* edited by Peter Rollins and John O'Connor. Lexington: University Press of Kentucky, 2008.

Ursini, James. "AFI Oral History with John Seitz." Unpublished transcript, American Film Institute.

Vernet, Marc. "Film Noir on the Edge of Doom." In *Shades of Noir,* edited by Joan Copjec. London: Verso, 1993.

Walker, Joseph, and Juanita Walker. *The Light on Her Face.* Los Angeles: ASC Press, 1993.

Wallace, Roger. *Gregg Toland: His Contributions to Cinema.* PhD diss., University of Michigan, 1976.

"Welles Gets Cameraman to Break Rules." *New York Herald Tribune* (April 27, 1941).

West, James W. *Hitchcock and France: The Forging of an Auteur.* Westport, CT: Praeger, 2003.

Williams, David. "Cold Case File." *American Cinematographer* 88.4 (2007).

Wollen, Peter. "The Auteur Theory." In *Auteurs and Authorship: A Film Reader,* edited by Barry Keith Grant. Malden, MA: Wiley-Blackwell, 2008.

Wood, Aylish. "Pixel Visions: Digital Intermediate and the Micromanipulation of the Image." *Film Criticism* 32.1 (2007).
Woollcott, Alexander. "Second Thoughts on First Nights." *The New York Times* (September 10, 1916).
Wyler, William. "No Magic Wand." In *Hollywood Directors, 1941–1976*, edited by Richard Koszarski. New York: Oxford University Press, 1977.
Zsigmond, Vilmos. "Darkest Noir," *American Cinematographer* 87.9 (2006).
Zuckoff, Mitchell. *Robert Altman: The Oral Biography.* New York: Knopf, 2009.

Index

Abyss, The, 165
Act of Violence, 88
Adventures of Dollie, The, 22
Adventures of Huckleberry Finn, 94
Age of Innocence, 165
Aitken, Harry, 23–24, 36
Allen, Lewis, 94
Allen, Woody, 2
Alonzo, John, 11, 140
Altman, Robert, 11, 16, 143, 144–58; visual approach of, 145–46
Alton, John, 10, 88, 90–91, 99, 177
America, 53
American Cinematographer, 9, 61, 65, 73, 120
American Film Manufacturing Company, 92
American in Paris, An, 90
American Madness, 62
American Mutoscope Company. *See* Biograph Company
American Society of Cinematographers (ASC), 8–9, 212nn33,37
Among the Living, 94–95
Anderegg, Michael, 66, 76–77
Anderson, G.M., 6
Andrews, Dana, 79
Antonioni, Michelangelo, 137
Arkle, Steve, 168
Arnold, John, 9–10
Arsenic and Old Lace, 117
Arzner, Dorothy, 58
Ashby, Hal, 11, 144
Asner, Ed, 151
August, Joseph, 11, 182n27
auteurism (director as auteur), 1–5, 21–22, 179n2
authorship. *See* auteurism
Avatar, 176
Avenging Conscience, The, 37
average shot length (ASL), in *Best Years of Our Lives*, 84; in *Double Indemnity*, 200n47; in *JFK*, 152; in *Sunset Boulevard*, 200n47
Aviator, The, 168–70, 210n12

Bacon, Kevin, 153
Bailey, John, 90, 170
Baldwin, Alec, 169
Ball of Fire, 70, 76
Barnes, George, 58, 115
Barrie, Wendy, 68
Barthelmess, Richard, 49, 51
Basevi, James, 72
Basinger, Jeanine, 157
Battle of the Sexes, The, 36–37
Baxter, Anne, 96, 119
Bazin, Andre, 64, 73, 78, 83–84
Beatty, Warren, 144, 147
Beaudine, William, 93
Beebe, Dion, 172
Bel Geddes, Barbara, 130
Belton, John, 146

Bergman, Ingmar, 137
Bergman, Ingrid, 104
Best Years of Our Lives, The, 56, 58, 65–66, 78–84, 82*fig.*, 83*fig.*, 196nn59,61; attempt at realism in, 79–81; deep focus in, 81–84; visual style of, 79–82
Beyond the Forest, 117
Biesen, Sheri Chinen, 87, 99–100, 103–5
Big Clock, The, 92
Big Sleep, The, 117
Biograph Company, 8, 19, 21–24, 27–30, 32, 35–36, 183n2, 185n21, 186n27
Birds, The, 15, 115, 125, 131–33, 133*fig.*, 134, 139; special effects in, 131–32
Birth of a Nation, The, 24, 32, 37–45, 41*fig.*, 42*fig.*, 48, 187nn51,56; lighting in, 38–40, 187nn48,49,50
Bitzer G.W. ("Billy"), 7, 12, 19–54, 55, 116, 149, 168, 177, 183nn2,10, 184nn12,13,15,16,17, 185nn18,21,26, 188n60, 190n78, 191n91, 192n97; decline of career, 52–54; techniques developed by, 25–28
Bitzer, Louis, 45
Blackhat, 172
Black Hawk Down, 158, 160
Blade Runner, 3
Blanchard, Walter, 85
Blanchett, Cate, 169
Blue Gardenia, The, 88
Bogart, Humphrey, 68
Bogdanovich, Peter, 133, 135–36, 144
Boleslawski, Richard, 58
Booth, Elmer, 33
Bordwell, David, 4, 8, 55, 63, 84, 155, 169–70, 210n13
Boyle, Robert, 15, 115, 134–137
Brackett, Charles, 96, 105, 108
Brady, Matthew, 39
Brennan, Walter, 70
Briesewitz, Uta, 172–73
Brodine, Norbert, 88
Broken Blossoms, 49–51, 185n18, 191n86; "soft style" in, 50–51
Brontë, Emily, 68
Brown, Karl, 24–25, 28, 38, 40, 41, 43, 45–47, 49, 52, 184n17
Bruner, James, 144
Bumstead, Henry, 115, 128, 130, 138
Burks, Robert, 15, 111, 115–39, 149, 201n5; replacement of on *Torn Curtain,* 137–39; special effects background, 117, 133, 139
Burr, Raymond, 124
Butch Cassidy and the Sundance Kid, 143
Butler, Bill, 11, 140

Cabanne, Christy, 36
Cabiria, 43
Cain, James M., 99–100
Call Northside 777, 89
cameras: 3-D, 121; Arriflex, 142, 144; Biograph, 29; digital, 171, 173–74, 211n22; Éclair, 142; Kinetograph, 29; Panaflex, 142, 150; Pathé, 38, 45, 53; Steadicam, 142, 159; Super-8, 150; Technicolor, 210n12
Cameron, James, 176
Candy, John, 153
Capra, Frank, 60, 62, 149, 153
Captain Corey, U.S.A., 94
Captain Kate, 61
Cardiff, Jack, 115
Carmichael, Hoagy, 82
Carnal Knowledge, 144
Carrere, Edward, 117
Carringer, Robert, 64
Carroll, Noel, 175
Caserini, Mario, 42
Casler, Herman, 29
Cat People, 90
Chandler, Raymond, 99
Chaplin, Charlie, 92
Chapman, Michael, 11, 140
Children's Hour, The (play), 65
Christie, Julie, 144
CinemaScope, 87
cinematographer: creative control by, 8–11, 23–24, 56, 162, 170, 172–73, 175; film noir and, 89–90; function

of, 1–2, 5–7, 166–67, 175; technology and, 5, 12, 16–17, 87–88, 141–43, 166, 176; transition to sound and, 59–60
Citizen Kane, 2, 14, 55–58, 61–62, 64–65, 70, 72–73, 76, 85, 110, 113–14
Class of '61, 155
Clifton, Elmer, 39
Clooney, George, 167
Coe, Wayne, 155
Coen, Ethan, 167, 169
Coen, Joel, 167, 169
Cohen, Paula Marantz, 120
Coleman, C.C., 97
Coleman, Herbert, 138
collaboration: of director and cinematographer, 1–2, 5–6, 11–17, 20–22, 55–56, 90–91, 93, 116–17, 143, 149, 167, 173, 175–77, 181n17; in New Hollywood, 11; in silent era, 7–8, 12, 183n3
Collinge, Patricia, 78
color: desaturation of, 141–43, 145–46, 159, 166–67, 205n13; in digital intermediate process, 166–69, 210n14; in Hitchcock films, 121, 201n1; in New Hollywood, 141–43, 145–46, 159; in postwar era, 15, 87
Columbia Pictures, 10, 65, 123, 198n11
Connery, Sean, 134
Cook, David, 19, 141–142, 147
Cooper, Gary, 71
Cooper, Miriam, 39
Cooper, Wilkie, 115
Coppola, Francis Ford, 11, 143
Corman, Roger, 141, 155
Corner in Wheat, A, 31–32, 32*fig.*
Cortez, Stanley, 63–64
Corwin, Hank, 150
Costner, Kevin, 150, 153
Country Doctor, The, 26, 31
Coutard, Raoul, 141
Crisp, Donald, 36, 39, 49
Cronenweth, Jeff, 172
Cronenweth, Jordan, 3, 11, 140
Crosby, Bing, 104
Crossfire, 149
Crowe, Cameron, 97
Cuarón, Alfonso, 176
Cummings, Robert, 63
Curtis, Scott, 122

Daniels, William, 13, 88
Dark Corner, The, 89
Dark Prince, The, 160
Daves, Delmer, 117
Davies, Marion, 93
Davis, Bette, 3, 77
Dawley, J. Searle, 6
Dead End, 67–68; camera angles in, 195n42; lighting in, 67; set of, 67–68
Deadly Affair, The, 143
Deakins, Roger, 167, 169–170
Decae, Henri, 141
deep-focus cinematography, 3, 14, 61–65, 69–84, 110, 193n19, 195n45
DeMille, Cecil B., 7, 44, 112
Dempster, Carol, 52
DeSylva, Buddy, 94
Devil and Daniel Webster, The, 63
Dial M for Murder, 121–22; 3-D filming of, 121, use of visual space in, 121–22
DiCaprio, Leonardo, 169
Dickson, W.K.L., 29
Dieterle, William, 63
digital image capture, 170–74
digital intermediate process, 165–70, 171, 209n7, 210n14
Di Palma, Carlo, 141
directors: function of, 1, 166–67, relationships with cinematographers, 1–3, 5–7
Diskant, George, 88
Disney, Walt, 131
Disney Studio, 131
Di Venanzo, Gianni, 141
Divine Lady, The, 93
Dixon, Thomas: *The Clansman: An Historical Romance of the Klu Klux Klan*, 37
Double Indemnity, 91, 92, 95, 99–104, 101*fig.*, 102*fig.*, 104*fig.*, 105, 110,

Double Indemnity (continued) 200n47; as film noir, 99–100; lighting in, 100–1, 103; visual style of, 99–101, 103
Dream Street, 51, 53
Dreier, Hans, 94, 97, 103
Drunkard's Reformation, The, 25
Dryburgh, Stuart, 172
Dubin, Mitch, 159
Duryea, Dan, 76
Dye, Dale, 156, 158
Dyer, Richard, 4

East Lynne, 93
Eastmancolor, 15
Edison, Thomas, 29
Edison Studio, 8, 20, 22, 28
Eisenstein, Sergei, 37, 63, 76
Elliott, Laura, 117
Enforcer, The, 117
Ericksen, Leon, 148
Escape, The, 36–37
Essanay Company, 8, 20, 27, 92

Fallen Sparrow, The, 90
Farrow, John, 94–95
Fenton, Leslie, 94
Ferguson, Perry, 80
Fildew, William, 45
film noir, 86–91, 99–100, 104–5, 182nn27,33, 197nn2,3
Fine Arts Studio, 38–39
Fiore, Mauro, 176
Fischbeck, Harry, 10, 53
Five Graves to Cairo, 91, 95–99, 100; visual style of, 96–99
flashing, 16, 143, 145–46, 205n13
Fleming, George S., 6, 20
Fly-By-Night, 94
Folsey, George, 10
Fonda, Henry, 120–121
Fonda, Peter, 144
Ford, Hugh, 6
Ford, John, 56, 70, 72, 79, 148, 182n27
Foreign Correspondent, 115
Forrest Gump, 165
Fountainhead, The, 117
Four Horsemen of the Apocalypse, The, 93, 111–12
Fraker, William, 11, 140
French Connection, The, 144
Friedkin, William, 11, 144
Full Metal Jacket, 159
Fulton, A.R., 44
Fulton, John, 129

Gabel, Martin, 135
Gage, Fred, 98
Garden of Allah, The, 93
Garmes, Lee, 9, 10, 13, 115
Garnett, Tay, 94
Gaslight, 104
Gemunden, Gerd, 109
Gibbons, Cedric, 100
Girl and Her Trust, A, 26
Girl Who Stayed at Home, The, 49
Girl with the Dragon Tattoo, The, 172
Gish, Dorothy, 36
Gish, Lillian, 33, 36, 39, 49–50, 51, 52
Gladiator, 160
Glass Key, The, 94
Glass Menagerie, The, 117
Glennon, Bert, 60, 72
Godard, Jean-Luc, 137
Godfather, The, 143
Going My Way, 104
Goldwyn, Samuel, 3, 57, 66–68, 71, 77, 79–80, 84, 195n40
Goldwyn Studio, 10, 57–58, 68
Gone Girl, 172
Gone with the Wind, 10
Goosson, Stephen, 3, 73
Granger, Farley, 118
Grant, Cary, 127
Grapes of Wrath, The, 56, 70
Gravity, 176
Greatest Question, The, 49, 190n80
Greatest Thing in Life, The, 49
Great Gatsby, The, 94
Great Love, The, 49
Green, Hilton, 135
Griffith, D.W., 5, 7, 12, 19–54, 55, 61, 149, 183nn2,6,10, 184nn15,16,17,

185nn21,24,26, 186n27, 188nn59,60,62, 189n75; innovations of, 27–28; visual style of, 28
Grim Prairie Tales, 155
Guffey, Burnett, 11, 89
Gun Crazy, 88
Gunning, Tom, 31

Hall, Conrad, 11, 140–141, 143
Haller, Ernest, 10, 117
Hamilton, Gilbert P., 20
Harlan, Russell, 88
Harold and Maude, 144
Harrison, Doane, 97
Harron, Robert, 36, 52
Haskin, Byron, 98
Hathaway, Henry, 89
Hawks, Howard, 56, 58, 70, 76, 148
Hayes, John Michael, 116–17, 139
Head, Edith, 15, 97, 122
Hearts of the World, 49, 190n78
Hecht, Ben, 68
Heckroth, Hein, 137
Hedren, Tippi, 132–34
Heisler, Stuart, 94
Hellman, Lillian, 3, 65, 74
Hellstrom, Gunnar, 144
Herman, Jan, 65–66
Herrmann, Bernard, 15, 137
Hill, George Roy, 143
Hitchcock, Alfred, 6–7, 15, 68, 111, 115–39, 149, 156, 201nn1,3; as collaborative filmmaker, 115–16, 136; visual approach of, 115–16
Hively, Jack, 94
Hoffman, Bud, 132–33, 137
Hoge, Ralph, 84
Holden, William, 109
Home, Sweet Home, 37
Hopkins, Miriam, 66
Horak, Jan-Christopher, 53
House of Darkness, The, 34–35, 36*fig.*
Howard, William K., 62
Howe, James Wong, 2, 9–11, 13, 62, 63, 88, 117, 208n53
Hulfish, David S., 6–7
Huston, John, 63

I Confess, 119; visual style of, 119
Impossible Convicts, The, 22
Industrial Light and Magic (ILM), 165
Ingram, Rex, 7, 92–93
Ingster, Boris, 63, 90
Intermezzo, 10, 70
Intolerance, 25, 32, 42–49, 43*fig.*, 48*fig.*, 187n58, 188nn59,60,62,69, 189nn70,72,75; camera movement in, 44–47; visual style of, 42–45
Iwerks, Ub, 131

Jacobs, Lewis, 45
Jacobs, Steven, 122
Jenkins, George, 80
JFK, 16–17, 143, 148–55, 154*fig.*, 161; editing style of, 150; lighting in, 152–53; visual style of, 143, 149–53
Johnson, James MacMillan, 115, 122
Johnson, Julian, 48, 50–51
Jones, Tommy Lee, 153
Judith of Bethulia, 25, 35–36, 45
Jurassic Park, 165

Kalem Company, 8, 27
Kaminski, Janusz, 17, 143, 155–61, 208n54
Kantor, MacKinley: *Glory for Me*,79
Karasek, Helmuth, 98
Kazan, Elia, 88, 90
Keating, Patrick, 5, 8–9, 12–13, 59–60, 73, 103, 182n29
Keaton, Buster, 112
Keighley, William, 90
Keil, Charlie, 6, 23, 32–33, 35, 44, 61–62, 183n2
Kelly, Grace, 121, 122, 126, 127
Kennedy, J.J., 35
Kentucky Feud, A, 29
Kid from Spain, The, 63
King, Henry, 92–93
King's Row, 63, 117
Klute, 144
Knock on Any Door, 89
Koenig, Lester, 80–81
Kolker, Robert, 149, 153–154, 158
Kovacs, Laszlo, 11, 140–141, 144

Krasner, Milton, 90
Krim, Arthur, 90
Kubrick, Stanley, 159

La Bohème, 51
Ladd, Alan, 94–95
Lady of the Pavements, 54
Lake, Veronica, 94–95
Landis, James, 144
Lanfield, Sidney, 94
Lang, Charles B., 10
Lang, Fritz, 88–89
LaShelle, Joseph, 89, 104
Last Days of Pompeii, The, 42
Last Picture Show, The, 144
Laszlo, Andrew, 140, 143
Laura, 89, 104
Lawson, John Howard, 63
Lee, Lawrence, 20
Leisen, Mitchell, 94
Lemmon, Jack, 151, 153
Les Misérables, 58
Lewin, Albert, 94
Lewis, Joseph, 88–90
Lifeboat, 115
Life of Pi, The, 176
lighting: in early sound era, 59; in film noir, 88–89; three-point, 89, 197n8
Lightman, Herb, 138
Lincoln, Elmo, 47
Lindley, John, 167
Little Foxes, The, 3, 66, 70, 72–78, 75*fig.*, 77*fig.*, 78*fig.*, 110; deep focus in, 73–76, visual style of, 73–74, 78
Lloyd, Frank, 93
Logan, Joshua, 2
Lonedale Operator, The, 26
Long, Walter, 39
Long Voyage Home, The, 56, 70
Lorre, Peter, 100
Lost Weekend, The, 91, 95–96, 104–9, 106*fig.*, 107*fig.*, 108*fig.*, 110; extreme close-up in, 108–9; as film noir, 104–5; lighting in, 106–7; visual style of, 104–7
Loy, Myrna, 82
Lubetski, Emmanuel, 176
Lubin Company, 27
Lubitsch, Ernst, 95
Lucas, Christopher, 175
Lucas, George, 165, 174
Lumet, Sidney, 143

M, 100
MacArthur, Charles, 68
MacDonald, Joseph, 88–89
MacMurray, Fred, 99
MacWilliams, Glen, 115
Madame X, 94
Mailer, Norman, 154
Major and the Minor, The, 95
Malick, Terrence, 158
Maltese Falcon, The, 63
Maltin, Leonard, 58
Mamoulian, Rouben, 56, 58
Mann, Anthony, 88, 90–91
Mann, Daniel, 2
Mann, Michael, 172
Manovich, Lev, 163–164
Man Who Knew Too Much, 127
Marie Galante, 93
Marion, Frank, 20
Marnie, 15, 115, 133–37, 135*fig.*, 137*fig.*; camera movement in, 134–36; use of color in, 134–35, 203n47; visual style of, 134–36
Marsh, Fredric, 79
Marsh, Mae, 36, 39
Marshall, Herbert, 3, 77
Marvin, Arthur, 23, 30, 184n15
Marvin, Henry, 35
*M*A*S*H*, 146
Mate, Rudolph, 115
Mayo, Virginia, 81
Mazursky, Paul, 11
McCabe and Mrs. Miller, 16, 143–48, 146*fig.*, 161; use of flashing in, 145–48, 205n13, visual style of, 143, 145–48, use of zooms in, 146–47
McCarey, Leo, 104
McCarthy, Todd, 90
McCrae, Joel, 66, 68
McCutcheon, Wallace, 6, 20, 30

McGee, Patrick, 72
McGilligan, Patrick, 127
Merritt, Russell, 34
Metty, Russell, 149
MGM Studio, 8, 10, 65, 93–94, 98, 100, 123, 198n11
Milland, Ray, 105, 107
Miller, Arthur, 51, 56, 94, 192n5
Miller, Mae, 51
Millet, Jean-Francois, 31
Milner, Victor, 10, 63
Milsome, Douglas, 159
Miranda, Claudio, 176
Mitchell, George, 53
Mohr, Hal, 60, 63
Moon and Sixpence, The, 94
Moore, Owen, 26
Mother and the Law, The, 43
Moving Picture World, 7, 23
Mr. and Mrs. Smith, 115
Murnau, F.W., 13
Musketeers of Pig Alley, The, 32–35, 34*fig.*
Musser, Charles, 5, 20–21, 183n3
Musuraca, Nicholas, 88, 90, 99
Mutual Film Company, 23, 36
My Name Is Julia Ross, 89

Nakamura, Stephen, 168
Naked City, The, 88
Name of the Game is Kill, The, 144
Nana, 58
National Film Registry, 92
Natural Born Killers, 149, 150, 152, 207n31
New York Dramatic Mirror, 27
New York Times, 47
Nichols, Mike, 11, 144
Nickelodeon, 6
Niven, David, 68
Nixon, 207n31
Nolan, Christopher, 171
North by Northwest, 15, 115, 127
Norton, Steven, 92
Notorious, 115, 135
Notz, Thierry, 155
Novak, Kim, 128
Nugent, Elliott, 94
Nyquist, Sven, 141

Oberon, Merle, 66, 68
O Brother, Where Art Thou?, 167
Ogle, Patrick, 57
Oldman, Gary, 152
Olivier, Laurence, 68
On with the Dance, 51
Orphans of the Storm, 52
Out of the Past, 90
Owen, Seena, 46

Pabst, G.W., 95
Paget, Alfred, 46
Pakula, Alan, 11, 144
Panic in the Streets, 88, 90
Paradine Case, The, 115
Paramount Studio, 8, 10, 90, 92, 94–95, 110, 116, 122–123, 126, 128–129
Pastrone, Giovanni, 42–43
Patriot, The, 160
Patsy, The, 93
Paull, Lawrence, 3
Peckinpah, Sam, 144
Pesci, Joe, 153
Peterson, Lowell, 86
Pfister, Wally, 171
Photoplay, 47
Pickford, Mary, 26
Pines, Josh, 168
Place, Janey, 86
Pleasantville, 167
Poe, Edgar Allan, 37
Polito, Sol, 117
Pollock, Dale, 96–97
Porter, Edwin S., 5–6, 20–21, 25, 185n21
Postman Always Rings Twice, The, 100
Preminger, Otto, 89, 104
Prieto, Rodrigo, 172
Prince, Stephen, 161, 166
Psycho, 115
Public Enemies, 174

Qué Viva Mexico!, 63

Rafelson, Bob, 11
Ramaeker, Paul, 4, 162
Rapper, Irving, 117
Ratoff, Gregory, 70
Ray, Nicholas, 88–89
Rear Window, 15, 68, 115, 120, 122–26, 123*fig.*, 126*fig.*, 135, 139; camerawork in, 125-26; lighting of, 123–25; set of, 122–23
Rebecca, 115
Rebello, Stephen, 116
Reid, Carl Benton, 76
Richardson, Robert, 16–17, 143, 148–55, 162, 168–70, 207n31; collaborations with directors, 148–49
RKO Studio, 65, 90, 201n3
Road to Glory, The, 58
Roberts, Irmin, 129, 203n38
Robertson, Peggy, 138
Robinson, Edward G., 100
Rodriguez, Robert, 166
Roizman, Owen, 11, 140
Romance of Happy Valley, A, 49
Rope, 115
Roseanna McCoy, 57
Rosenstone, Robert, 149
Rosher, Charles, 13
Ross, Gary, 167
Rossen, Robert, 88
Rosza, Miklos, 97
Rowland, Roy, 95
Russell, Harold, 79
Ruttenberg, Joseph, 88

Sadist, The, 144
Saigon, 94
Salt, Barry, 4–5, 141, 160
Salvador, 149, 151–52
Sarris, Andrew, 56
Sartov, Hendrik, 49–50, 52–53, 191nn81,82
Savides, Harris, 172–74
Saving Private Ryan, 17, 143, 155–61, 157*fig.*; techniques used in, 143, 158–61; visual style of, 158–61
Sayles, John, 149
Scarlet Days, 49
Scarlet Letter, The, 51
Schatz, Thomas, 2, 163
Schickel, Richard, 22, 51
Schindler's List, 155
Schoonmaker, Thelma, 172
Schurr, William, 125
Scorsese, Martin, 11, 149, 168–70, 172, 176
Scott, Ridley, 3, 158
Seitz, George, 94
Seitz, John F., 7, 13, 14–15, 88, 91–114, 116, 198nn17,18, 200n43; collaborations with directors, 92–95; and film noir, 92, 95; technique of, 92, 95–96, 98, 101–2
Seitz, John L. (son), 95
Seldes, Gilbert, 37
Selig Company, 8, 27, 185n21
Sellors, C. Paul, 1
Selznick, David O., 10–11
Sergeant Madden, 94
Seven Ages, The, 27
Seymour, Clarine, 52
Shadow of a Doubt, 115
Shipman, Bert, 63
Shore Acres, 92–93
Side by Side, 172
Side Street, 88
Siegel, Don, 89
Sikov, Ed, 108
Sintzenich, Hal, 53
Siodmak, Richard, 90, 94
Sirk, Douglas, 149
Six Hours to Live, 93
Sklar, Robert, 45, 87
Sloan, Jane, 137
Slocombe, Douglas, 68, 73
Social Network, The, 172
South, Leonard, 125
Spacek, Sissy, 153
Sparkuhl, Theodor, 95
Spellbound, 115
Spielberg, Steven, 11, 17, 143, 155–61, 171; visual approach of, 155–56
Spinotti, Dante, 172
Spiral Staircase, The, 90

Spoto, Donald, 115, 118
Stagecoach, 72
Stage Fright, 115
Staiger, Janet, 4
Stanwyck, Barbara, 99, 104
Star Trek II: The Wrath of Khan, 165
Sten, Anna, 58
Stern, Seymour, 21
Stevens, George, 159
Stewart, Heather, 174
Stewart, James, 122–24, 126, 128
St. John, Al, 58
Stone, Oliver, 16–17, 143, 148–55
Storaro, Vittorio, 141, 162
Stradling, Harry, 10, 115
Stranger on the Third Floor, The, 90
Strangers on a Train, 115, 117–19, 118*fig.*; special effects in, 117–19
Straw Dogs, 144
Street of Chance, 94–95
Street with No Name, 90
Struss, Karl, 10, 13, 54
Sturges, Preston, 92, 94
Summer Children, 144
Sunrise, 13
Sunset Boulevard, 91–92, 95–96, 99, 109–14, 111*fig.*, 112*fig.*, 113*fig.*, 200n47; camera movement in, 110–11, lighting in, 111–12, swimming-pool shot, 113–14, visual style of, 109–111
Surtees, Robert, 11, 88
Sutherland, Donald, 153–54
Swanson, Gloria, 109, 111–12
Sylbert, Paul, 120–121

Talk Radio, 152
Tamiroff, Akim, 96
Tarantino, Quentin, 149, 171
Task Force, 117
Taylor, Rod, 132
Technicolor, 15, 168–69, 177, 195n36, 210n12
Tector, Lyle, 146
Temple, Shirley, 94
Terry, Alice, 111, 112
Terry, Philip, 105
Tetzlaff, Ted, 115
These Three, 65–67, 195n45; visual style of, 65–67
They Live By Night, 88
Thieves Highway, 88
Thin Red Line, The, 158
This Gun for Hire, 92, 94–95
Thompson, Kristin, 4, 51
Thorpe, Richard, 94
Three Kings, 160
Thunder Afloat, 94
T-Men, 88, 90, 91
To Catch a Thief, 120, 126–27
Toland, Gregg, 2–3, 9–10, 14, 55–85, 110, 114, 116, 177, 192nn2,5, 193nn13,19, 194n32; development of deep-focus technique, 55–57, 58, 61–65; as stylistic innovator, 57, 61, 70, 85
Tom, Tom, the Piper's Son, 29
Tomasini, George, 15, 122, 137
Tone, Franchot, 96
Torn Curtain, 116, 137, 138–39
Tough Kid's Waterloo, 29
Tourneur, Jacques, 90
Transatlantic, 62
Trifling Women, 93
Trouble with Harry, The, 127
True Heart Susie, 49, 190n80
Trumbull, Douglas, 3
Turner, Lana, 100
Tuttle, John, 94–95
Twentieth Century-Fox Studio, 8, 65, 89–90, 93–94, 198n11, 201n3

Unchanging Sea, The, 31
Under Capricorn, 115
Union Pacific, 63
United Artists Studio, 65
Universal Studio, 132, 201n3
Ursini, James, 98

Valentine, Joseph, 115
Valentino, Rudolph, 93, 98, 112
Vernet, Marc, 87
Vertigo, 15, 111, 115, 125, 127–31, 129fig., 134–135, 139; camera

Vertigo (continued)
movement in, 128–29; use of color in, 129–30; visual style of, 128–30
Vidor, King, 56, 58, 93, 117
VistaVision, 15, 87, 126–27, 202n32
visual style: and digital cinematography, 166–67; in Hollywood studio system, 10, 12–14, 181n22; in New Hollywood, 16–17, 140–43; in silent era, 6–7
Vitagraph Company, 27, 28, 185nn21,25
Von Sternberg, Joseph, 3, 94
Von Stroheim, Erich, 96, 109

Walker, Joseph, 10, 60, 62, 149
Walker, Robert, 118
Wallace, Richard, 90
Wallace, Roger, 58
Walsh, Raoul, 39–40
Walthall, Henry, 36, 40
Warner Brothers Studio, 10, 116–117, 119, 121–122, 192n2, 201n3
Warren, John, 138
Watchers 2, 155
Way Down East, 51–52, 185n18
Wedding Night, The, 58
Welles, Orson, 2, 55–56, 62, 70, 76, 114
Well-Groomed Bride, The, 94
Westerner, The, 70–72; deep focus in, 72, visual style of, 72
Wexler, Haskell, 11, 140–141
Whipsaw, 10
White Rose, The, 53
Whitlock, Albert, 131–132
Wilder, Billy, 14–15, 92–114, 116; visual approach of, 97
Wild Harvest, The, 94
Willis, Gordon, 2, 11, 140, 143, 162
Wollen, Peter, 2–3, 179n4
Wood, Aylish, 166
Wood, Sam, 63, 94
Woods, Frank, 36, 38
Woolcott, Alexander, 47
Wortman, Huck, 46, 187n51
Wright, Teresa, 78, 81
Wrong Man, The, 15, 119–21, 156; innovative shots in, 120–21; visual style of, 120–21
Wuthering Heights, 56, 68–70, 69*fig.*, 70*fig.*, 71*fig.*; deep focus in, 69; lighting in, 68–69; visual style of, 68–70
Wyatt, Jane, 105
Wyckoff, Alvin, 7
Wyeth, Andrew, 145
Wyler, William 3, 14, 55–85, 116, 192n2

Young, Freddie, 143
You're a Big Boy Now, 143

Zanuck, Darryl, 58
Zapruder, Abraham, 17, 151
Zinneman, Fred, 88
Zodiac, 172, 174
Zsigmond, Vilmos, 11, 16, 140–141, 143–58, 162, 166; technique of, 147–48, 205n13